Still Fucking Alive

This book is for sinners, not saints

Still Fucking Alive:

The true story of transforming from a victim and survivor into a fighter

---

Marissa Hardy

"He that descends is the same also that ascends up far above the heavens"
Ephesians 4:9

Disclaimer:

This book contains personal experiences and reflections from the author's life, including sensitive topics such as mental health struggles, rape, drug use and attempted suicide. The intention of sharing these experiences is to provide insight, raise awareness, and offer a sense of connection to readers who might have faced similar challenges. It is important to note that the content is based on the author's own unique experiences and should not be considered professional advice. All names have been changed in order to protect the identities of others.

It is strongly encouraged for readers who are struggling with their own mental health to seek help from qualified mental health professionals, counselors, or relevant support services. The content in this book should not be used as a substitute for professional guidance, diagnosis, or treatment. If you or someone you know is in crisis or experiencing thoughts of self-harm or suicide, please reach out to a mental health helpline or a medical professional immediately.

The author disclaims, without limitation, any and all liability that may arise from your use of this book. By reading this book, you acknowledge that you have read and understood this disclaimer, and you agree to approach the content with sensitivity and awareness of its potentially triggering nature.

Carmelo,

You gave me the space and confidence to write my story. You taught me how to swim the rapids. Without you, I wouldn't have an ending. Thank you for loving all of me.

"Life's duality is going in the dark, where we become lost, just enough. Where it's quiet, just enough. Only to shine our own light and find ourselves walking back home and seeing we are just enough."

-Marissa Hardy

Contents

Part One: The Voice

Part Two: The Heart

Part Three: The Mind

Part Four: The Fallen

Part Five: The Risen

Preface

I felt called to write this book and share my experience for the purpose of changing the narrative that those who are far, near and in-between people like me are not alone in this world. There is a much greater force behind what looks back at us in the mirror and through sharing my darkest, vulnerable moments, I hope to shed a light on sensitive topics like addiction, sexual assault and suicide. I began writing my story December of 2021 when I was 23 years old, although this story began writing itself over a decade ago. I am now 26 years old and have put my reputation, heart and future on the line by sharing this story. Even if I just help one person to find their voice or inspire one lost soul to find themselves again, then it's worth it for me. As a reader, I hope that you not only enjoy this story but transform your inner knowledge to an inner knowing of the fall and the rise between the voice, heart and mind. The versus throughout the book are words I wish knew then; they do not reflect my character in those moments as they do now.

Introduction

To say I came from humble beginnings would be a lie. To say my parents weren't good people and didn't try would be a lie. To say I saw outside of my inhabitations would be a lie. To say that I wasn't the problem, that I indulged in toxic habits and created a false identity would be a hard truth I'd come face to face with.

When the mask revealed what could no longer be held in secret. My first reaction wasn't to help myself in a normal, methodical ordinary way. My first reaction was a feeling I had known would come to the surface for a long, long time. It's part of the reason I wore a mask all those years during my late teens and early twenties.

I chose suicide. Although that night it felt as if suicide had chosen me. I knew my time had come. "tonight, is the night" I said to myself in a way which had struck me to my core with such force and inspiration my destiny became inevitable.

I had no emotion when I made the decision, I had no outside thoughts. It was as if I had stepped into a colorless void seduced in the obsession of death to a point of no return. That tunnel with the light at the end of it folks talk about, well, in my experience was the light on the other side. I had been living a life of sin and darkness for so long and I had finally reached the end of it; I could see the light.

I had romanticized and envisioned what my suicide would look like throughout the entire eight years of my addiction, at times even praying the men who had taken advantage and abused me would do it on my behalf.

I knew I wanted to feel my breaths become shallow. I knew I wanted to feel so completely numb that it brought me to a state of euphoria. I knew that the moment I would shut my eyes it would be my last, and how peaceful that would be.

What I didn't know is what has led me to write this book. For the higher power who gave me a second chance and my reason in life has a message for the ones far, near and in-between people like me.

My name is Marissa Hardy, and this is the story, stories and personal experiences I've had before, during and after my awakening into the conscious cognitive shift. You could call this a self-help book, adventure story or testimony. What you will find while reading is up to you, you may resonate with my writings, you may find it purely entertaining, or you may find it to be not aligned with you at all. And each opinion is okay because at the end of it all, I did this for myself and the message which resides beyond these pages. My existence on earth has been nothing short of feeling misunderstood, layered in complexity and unique in self-discovery, the true self of my being.

Each of us are a divine stitch in the fabric of time, speeding up, slowing down, reversing and fast forwarding. The gift of being truly present with ourselves is a lost virtue; a controlled and manipulated fear-based avoidance of the inner child and imprinted trauma. With that comes the entities of ego, shame, regret, and guilt which I believe holds humanity hostage against the purity of our freewill. I've read many books, engaged with many teachers and have sat with myself in solitary yet none of it compares to the lessons and enlightenment I received through the flux of soul swinging experiences I've had between the within and without, above and below, light and dark, higher and lower dimensional frequencies and realities. As you read through, you will notice a change in rhythm; I owe that to the layers of inner progression and healing of my soulful spirit. I am not alone; for I know my higher power, inner child, higher self and guardian angel are with me. For a long time, I believed I was going mental, and with each voluntary and involuntary experience the truth of the happening became.

This is our story.

Part One:

The Voice

Chapter 1

The Mind is so Kind

"The mind governed by the flesh is
death, but the mind governed by
the spirit is life and peace."
Romans 8:6

I always felt I was special because my skin tone resembled the perfect baked loaf of banana bread. Mom and dad perfected a recipe so sweet and delicate they opened a bakery, in Carmichael, California called Hardy Breads. My parents were honest people making an honest living as bakers. I didn't quite understand what that meant growing up, all I knew were the early mornings, batter licking and banana peeling I did. Life was simple, we had a routine which was set by the order of bread, baking and delivering to coffee shops, theatres, delis and restaurants in and outside of Sacramento.

Hardy Breads brought life into our family as enriched as the flour we used. My family came together as one, each day because of the bakery. My three sisters and I had our assigned jobs whether that be cracking ten dozen eggs, peeling twenty fourteen pounds of bananas, or labeling different flavors of bread. Each of us took pride in our duties, although, some days we would moan and groan about going to the bakery. Now that I am twenty-six, I wish I would've held onto those days a little longer.

No matter how hard the day had been, the reward of being wrapped in the industrial ovens heat carrying the aroma of banana bread batter so sweet you could almost taste it in the air became an essence of what it meant to be a Hardy. The sounds of the oven creaking as it rotated one hundred plus batches would echo in the background of whatever day time soap opera we watched together as a family; some days if we got lucky, we'd catch Bob Barker on The Price is Right.

If they were no errands to run, (like going to general produce or the UPS store to ship orders) while the bread baked, dad would turn up our bulky old school radio and we'd listen to local stations playing early 2000s hits. My sisters and I would perform as if the space between bread racks served as a stage off Hollywood boulevard. We had assignments on who was the lead, co-lead and back up performers. Joan who is the oldest was usually the lead, Harper who is the second oldest was co-lead, Marie who is the youngest performed back-up with me. And that's just how it was. Not only did we sing and dance with one another, we would recreate our favorite plays and imagine different scenarios of pretend games; our favorite game we called "House". House involved us girls building carboard box homes and pretending to be anything from moms to dogs. Our imaginations together created a world outside of our own.

It was as if my parents had created our own slice of heaven; one which we all found so much comfort in. When I think of the perfect love, it smells, sounds, tastes and feels something like the days at the bakery. I loved going on bread deliveries, it was always before the sun had risen so it was cool and quiet out. Falling asleep in the back of the car while mom or dad delivered was one of my favorite things to do. Well, that and occasionally getting treats from café owners; poppyseed muffins were always my first choice.

My first memory in life happened while delivering banana bread with my mother, I was four years old at the time. Mom was listening to Armstrong and Getty morning radio show and they were discussing the suffering which had come from 9/11 and the now war in the middle east. I could see the worry on moms face through the rear-view mirror and without warning I say to mom in hope of an answer, "This is God's world, not their world, don't they understand that?"

From a young age I've had an inner knowing of God's love and for the first memorable time I had the experience of witnessing human suffering. Not only my mother, but the nations collective suffering through the broadcasting of two men on AM radio.

Mom had no answer for me, I think she herself was surprised I was even listening let alone speaking with confidence about something like this. The naivety and curiosity of the suffering human is a seed which cultivated deeply into my subconscious from that day forward. I remember feeling a deep sense of yearning for God's grace. But this moment was fleeting, as any moment is for a young child.

I went on about enjoying my early childhood years. Mom coached me in soccer before I went on to play for an Olympic development program and higher competitive leagues. Dad performed alongside me in the nutcracker ballet and coached me in track and field. Life was relatively perfect. I had passions which fueled me as a youngin' and I took pride in pursuing and maintaining them, sports and my family were my identity and where I found stability. I was the type of kid who hung up every sports medal, trophy and ribbon on her bedroom wall. I was not only gifted in sports, I also regularly received academic awards which I too, so proudly hung on my bedroom wall. The only thing my foundation knew to be true was my family dynamic, the bakery, school and sports. I felt from a young age that the world was mine and never had I thought about what could deter me from the path of success. My dreams of going to college on a full ride athletic scholarship to UNC or USC ran through my head often by the time I was in the 6th grade. I envisioned myself going to medical school and becoming a doctor; I distinctly remember one Christmas asking my parents for a first aid kit and to this day that is still one of my favorite gifts from them. My parents were proud of me; they loved going to my games, mom and dad shared the spotlight as my number one fans. The first time I saw my father cry was the day I was accepted into the first technological middle school in California, I remember taking on the interview process as if I had already gotten in.

To say I was the favorite growing up amongst my sisters is a truth we all knew to some degree, and I say that with grace because it was short lived. What fueled me to do my best was the love and support of my parents, I only cared about making them proud and in turn they made me proud.

Mom and Dad's hard work paid off, they bought a beautiful home which faced acres of meadows, hundreds of trees and river which ran through. Our new home had eight bedrooms, seven bathrooms, a library, piano room, a guest house which my great grandmother would be living in and a beautiful courtyard. My first time seeing the house I remember mom and dad playing tag throughout the giant home they bought; my sisters and I smiling and laughing along with them. Life couldn't have been any better than it was in this moment.

Our new home hosted friends, family and neighbors for summer bar-b-ques, Thanksgiving, Christmas, and Easter. It was more than just a giant house it was a home for anyone near and dear to us and on multiple occasions, kids who needed a place to stay. I'm not sure how my parents did it all, but they did. My favorite part of my childhood home was my great grandmother (who we called GG), was with us. My father loved his grandmother and unknowingly her presence kept the temperament in our home respectful and peaceful.

Finding out GG had terminal cancer a few months after moving into our new home was the beginning of years of suffering for our family. It was as if things had been so good for so long that my family didn't know how to handle the devastation of watching the matriarch of my father's lineage slowly die. The night GG passed every member of our family was at our home; this wasn't like the other gatherings were everyone had their best face on, instead it was heartbreaks, cries and disbelief that the day had come. Unfortunately for my father he was most effected by her passing, for my GG was a mother to him. The home dad and mom bought was for her. GG was a hope and light in his life, now gone.

Dad was never really the same after this, like I said, GG seemed to have kept the temperament in our home respectful and peaceful. Dad worked nights on duty as a deputy sheriff for Sacramento county than began early mornings at the bakery; his weekend drinking switched from Coors to a Seagrams gin. I remember the day when Harper and I opened the fridge in the garage to sneak a beer to share with each other in the meadows across the street and to our surprise, there were no Coors left. Yet, in the distance the stainless-steel cocktail shaker was rattling with the sound of mixing dad's new drink.

His patience wore thin with us girls and mom. My sisters and I knew that when dad came home it was time to either go into our bedrooms or go find solace in the meadows. My sisters and I found comfort in doing things together like working out in our home gym, watching movies with each other, playing with our barbies or listening to music. Dad became more aggressive, an aggression and instability we didn't recognize but soon became accustomed and adjusted to. Looking back, I understand he was stressed, tired, grieving and in the beginning stages of alcoholism; I cannot imagine what that weight must've felt like along with having four young daughters to care for. Due to the drinking we began to

5

see him change as heavily as his hand which poured his gin. It was very difficult to lose the dad I once adored. It was a slow and gradual change. I remember him as always maintaining his fitness, kind and sweet, knew what to say or how to make us laugh but this all changed. Our family began to crumble piece by piece, or rather it'd be more appropriate to say person by person.

My sisters and I began walking around on eggshells, trying not to upset him or get in any type of trouble. We learned to be quiet and not voice our emotions or opinions because of his unpredictable reactions. Although four girls against one man naturally created a lot of push back resulting in traumatizing drunken fights and random outbursts of anger towards one or all of us. Especially mom, it's hard to bear what she felt and faced silently. It's taken me years of therapy, sacred plant ceremonies and 60 days of rehab to finally let go of the verbal and physical abuse my sisters and I witnessed and received. It's took me realizing and letting go of the identity that I am not a victim. Although at this time in life the identity of victimhood was just beginning.

The perfect life I knew, the stability I had grounded myself into was now shaken up and flipped upside down. Dads drinking and anger wasn't the only thing we dealt with in the same year as my GG's passing; mom discovered dad had been cheating on her. I'll never forget the morning us girls found out. Moms' eyes had changed, she looked like she had been treated with electric shock therapy; nothing but a long-lost gaze in her eyes. Her smile that once lifted the spirits in any room was now gone, she looked utterly defeated.

But, we still had business to do at the bakery and as a family we all piled into the suburban. The ride was awkward and uncomfortable. I think us girls were in disbelief that our family tie had been broken; I could see the ways my sisters were trying to understand and grasp what had happened, it didn't make any sense; our family was perfect, right? As much denial as we had all been in about my father's changes, it become real (at least for me) when I saw the change in my mother.

My sisters, mother, father and I were now those suffering humans I had once thought about eight years ago. I now understood what it meant to lose sight of God.

The saying the "mind is so kind" I recently learned in therapy. I don't remember much of this time in my life because of the uprooting and trauma which bestowed; I do however remember the feelings I felt. The mind of a suffering human can go into survival mode, which includes many things but, the one thing it does which is astounding to me, is the way it protects us from bad experiences by allowing us to forget or disassociate from them.

That suburban ride is the last thing I remember from that year until the third storm had hit our family. Now, which seemed to have been karma or God himself screaming for my father to slow down and open his eyes; dad fell terribly ill.

It was the beginning of fall and dad was out in the backyard, when suddenly he dropped to the concrete floor. Marie and I were close by to witness this. We rushed over as he was struggling to get up when he looked up to us and said, "Call mom."

Immediately my mother came home and brought my father to the hospital. I think about the ways she stuck by his side and how hard it must have been to go through the emotions of all she was feeling and still be strong for my sisters and I. Dad was diagnosed with a staph infection called MRSA. I remember thinking, "if he dies, we can be happy again."

This is very hard for me to admit, but I was so

heartbroken that my once hero turned villain and not once did my sisters and I ever get a genuine apology. Sure, he said "I'm so sorry" but his actions never showed. Thankfully for him, my mother stood by his bedside through the illness, doctors' appointments and surgery. The infection had gotten so bad the doctors considered removing his infected leg. Mom wouldn't stand for that, so she took him to another hospital with better doctors where they took good care of dad.

After his surgery, us girls were brought in to visit with him. I had an anger inside of me when I walked in the hospital room and saw him still breathing while my mother tended to his bedside. Without a care, I sat on his hospital bed as lousy as could be and his leg moved in an uncomfortable way; he tensed up with pain. Mom shouted, "be careful, Marissa!"

I couldn't have cared less; my heartbreak, suffering and betrayal of this man ran through my veins. And seeing mom put her feelings aside for him lit a fire which turned me from heartbroken to angry.

It wasn't long until mom seemed to have forgotten about dads' affairs and he was back in our home recovering from surgery. This was all so confusing and troubling for me. I began to resent my mother for taking care of my father, even expressing on multiple occasions how I no longer respected her for taking him back. I no longer cared to make my parents proud or what moral guidelines they tried to instill; it was as if their word held no weight with me anymore.

The middle of the storm continued into the following years as the bakery began to fail because of the 2008 recession and suddenly money became tight; this resulted in Hardy Breads closing. It wasn't until 2011 my parents' world had come crashing down just as perfectly as it had come up. It wasn't until years after my father had recovered from his infection that our families home went into bankruptcy and we had no other choice but to downsize; although downsizing just meant going from an eight bedroom with luxuries to five bedrooms and a dark cloud surrounding our family. I guess moving into this new home mom and dad were trying to work things out. I'm not sure why my mother held on for so long but, it would soon come to an end.

The years from 2006-2014 are so vague for me. It's hard to remember what life was aside from a suffering and obvious instability within myself. The new home we moved into my sophomore year of high school felt so different than our last home. Mom and dad weren't playing tag, my sisters and I weren't laughing and smiling; Joan and Harper were both off at college now, it was now just Marie and I. Marie and I always felt we had different parents than Harper and Joan. The mom and dad the two oldest sisters knew were long gone. Unknowingly to my 13-year-old self, this home would be the place where the first acts of sexual abuse, physical abuse and my inability to say yes and no began.

Chapter 2

Yes and No

"Therefore, put on the full armor of
God, so that when the day of evil
comes, you may be able to stand
your ground."
Ephesians 6:13

The days are numb because I need them to be, to make it through. A numbness so dazing and opaque I cannot bring myself to add color and life. At night, the foggy daze disappears. The emotion of colors mix like watercolor on canvas. I'm alone and the only voice I hear is the one I've been silencing all day. She's mad, frustrated and helpless. She wants my attention and presence so badly. It's never mattered what violence or danger it takes to get her (me) there. She/her/it/me? Makes me want to vomit to feel some type of relief. A relief only a girl filled with heartbreak knows. I am so fragile but the idea of destroying myself... those thoughts release the pressure in my head. To let them play out, I see me. We're tired, we can hardly think straight.

January 4th, 2022 I am supposed to see a psychiatrist. My boyfriend, Carmelo, keeps repeating to me while I'm going down this rabbit hole, "picture this going well."

His voice is like a rescue rope; hoping I'll grab on and pull myself out of this dark hole. I haven't thought for myself in so long, I don't know what a happy ending is, well that and the last time I was seen by a mental health professional, she sent me to the psych-ward. Whether if I have failed myself or others, I don't know if "things going well" is possible for me anymore. I am a mess inside and out; the sun is rising, and my appointment is in three hours.

I slick my curly hair back into a bun, with my baby hairs laid on my forehead, face washed and moisturized, pills taken, socks on. The same morning routine I've had since I went to rehab. I don't have the energy to hide my swollen face or the bags under my eyes anymore. If I wasn't so tired, maybe I'd have the energy to conceal the obvious sickness that lays on my face. But I am tired of covering up the truth of who I am when the light dims and dark shadows occupy all four corners of the room. Although I'm nervous for my appointment I'm still ready two hours early. What should a manic-depressive ex addict do to consume this idle time without going off the rails? I play "Bella's Lullaby" on a two-hour loop hoping it'll bring me some stillness and peace. Between the symphonies I'm able to find space to breathe for a moment. The music slowly rocks me to sleep, and I find myself in a dream. The feeling of dreaming is as if my body is floating in a salt pool, all senses turned off except the sixth one. Although, right before things truly start to feel peaceful, I wake up.

I'll never fully grasp how my mind can be the hardest place some times and the softest place others. It's now thirty minutes until my appointment. My grey sweats match the cloudy grey skies, and the cold weather makes my nose drip. Ten months sober and a wet nasal passage continues to trigger a craving. I tell myself, "clean yourself, get in the car and drive." Something my dad would say to me. It's funny how his voice is the only other voice I can hear besides my own.

My 1992 Honda starts ugly, but she gets me from point A to point B. It's early yet my boyfriend made a point to call. I explain to Carmelo how I am functioning but not doing well; he says something like, "well if they try to take you back to the ward, I'll show em' crazy." Great, a true Romeo and Juliet story I think to myself as we get off the phone.

Walking into the ill lit facility is eerie and bleak. Looking around, there's fellow mentally ill patients who look different than myself, but the energy inside of us is all the same. Not one moment of eye contact is made between another patient and me.

The smudged faced woman at the counter hands me a clipboard with questions I'm supposed to rate one through five. The questions asked gives the doctor a baseline of where the patient is mentally. But these questions are like salt on a wound, there's no denying the truth that's on paper looking back at you. Or how a simple question like "Does alcoholism run in your family?" bring up bad memories and feelings. But I genuinely want help, so I'm doing my best answering these questions. Marking down a one on the chart means "never" and five being "yes/all the time" and everything else is just a lesser yes or no.

I ended up with a perfect score, but most physicians would say I'm off the charts. Which, as predicted Dr. Jones did. He looked over my answers with a raised eyebrow, asked me some follow up questions and then left the room. Immediately my body went into survival mode, this reminded me of my last experience at one of these appointments. To be honest with a physician, also known as a mandated reporter, is like playing roulette. There's a 50/50 chance they'll get you the help you need or report your state of being to the psych-ward or local police.

Unfortunately, my first experience with a mental health professional went south. She ended up sending me to the psych-ward because I was a danger to myself. Luckily, I was only checked in for five hours on a Thursday afternoon in Los Angeles. That experience discouraged me at the time but, the psych doctor who evaluated my mental status inside of the ward that day saved me. The demeanor of this doctor's attitude when I told him I was forty days sober gave me permission to be kind to myself. That day I realized this was my first-time feeling emotions without substances in almost six years. I left the ward that day with my head held high, but also a little more scared to speak my truth. Fast forward to the present moment of me waiting in Dr. Jones' office, I text Carmelo immediately and write, "he left after reading my chart I hope he doesn't come back with bad news."

Panicking and scared, I begin to question myself. "I deserve whatever happens, right?"

After about three minutes the doctor walks back in and diagnoses me with bipolar 2 disorder. I don't remember anything he said after that. Dr. Jones sounded like a Muppet in the background of my inner dialogue.

Miracles and clarity come packaged and delivered in the most random and peculiar ways. Although I received this diagnosis, this was a beautiful moment for me. After all these years of asking myself, "what's wrong with me?" I finally had an answer.

Bipolar is just a label that allowed me to really get an understanding for the highs and lows I experience. The diagnosis gave me permission to be kind to myself, to forgive myself and take accountability for myself. Life truly provides the answers. I was the problem but when I became the student, the equation began to solve itself. After years of insecurity and self-medicating so I could feel "normal", I almost instantly became grateful for myself and this journey. Learning about myself sober had been such a challenge the last 10 months but now I felt I was able to simplify it all.

Dr. Jones told me he was going to prescribe me risperidone, an antipsychotic which treats schizophrenia, bipolar disorder, and irritability caused by autism. Granted, I was taking 20mg of Lexapro and 12.5mg of buspirone already. Getting on these medications in rehab were right for me at the time but deep down I knew I didn't need them to get by anymore, let alone another drug. I was almost 10 months sober off street drugs and alcohol, but still taking prescription drugs. It was an act of courage when I found myself sitting up straight, wiping my tears and looking Dr. Jones straight in the eye when I said, "No."

This diagnosis brought me to a place where I wanted to try first. I had purpose in my healing now. Since getting sober, I had only ever been medicated on prescription drugs. I wanted to try to help myself or at least get to know myself without the street drugs or prescription ones. Adding an additional prescription which had greater hormonal and psychiatric altering properties was not what I felt was best for me.

I explained this to the doctor, he chuckled before saying, "so you don't want to take the easy way out, huh?" His demeanor was out of profession in a positive way, which showed me he understood me as a person, not a patient.

"I'm not rejecting the diagnosis and if I really need the meds, I'll reach out." I say with confidence.

A long pause held space between the doctor and I. "Also, my anti-depressant and anxiety medication did their job, I want to ween off those too." He looked a little disappointed but carried on with my request, explaining the proper way to do it for the next month. I couldn't believe that things were going well for me. I kept repeating to myself, "the quick and easy fixes have no permeance on my soul."

This was the day I relearned the value of yes and no. At the time, I was twenty-four years old and the last 8 years I had been struggling with knowing what is right, what is wrong, and the boundaries held with the words yes and no. January 4th, 2022 was a day that not only healed me but showed me the butterfly effect in the words yes and no.

My first experience with sexual assault at the age of 16 was the start of a dwindling ability to say yes and no or even know the difference between the two; solely because as sexual assault turned into sexual abuse over my teen years, I wasn't given the option to say yes or no. In my experience with sexual abuse and assault it not only greatly affected my body but had longing effects on my mental health. Sexual abuse exposed me to an overwhelming sense of unworthiness, trauma and inability to know the boundaries within the words yes and no.

Chapter 3

The Root of It

"For, whoever would love life and
see good days must keep their
tongue from evil and their lips from
deceitful speech."
Proverbs 6:18

I was sixteen years old the first time, he was
seventeen. At this time in life, I still had my innocence about
the world and the people who occupy it. This was the
beginning of what would change my rose-colored glasses to
broken glass. My parents were gone, and Kareem who lived
in the apartments outside of my neighborhood had stopped by
for a glass of water on his walk home from school. It was
early September but the weather in Roseville, California was
still too hot for anyone to be walking outside. As naïve as I
was, I didn't have a hidden agenda, but this "friend" of mine
did. I thought no problem, a quick visit because my parents
would be home sometime soon, and boys were not allowed in
the house under any circumstances.

When Kareem arrived, I greeted him with a big Hardy
smile and hospitality, that was something I had learned from a
young age; to always be kind, generous and friendly. And I
most certainly was this type of kid, even as much as strangers
telling me I have an old soul or remind them of sunshine. I
always had a kind, generous and friendly approach but what I

hadn't learned was boundaries. Boundaries wasn't a thing for me growing up. I had three sisters who I shared just about everything with. My father went from a classic American man, who happened to also be my best friend, first love and hero to an alcoholic abusive father within a matter of a year; subconsciously I learned a lot from seeing the switch in character and values in him. And my mother, who was the most perfect mold of a human, ended up putting up with my dad for years; subconsciously I learned a lack of boundaries and subpar communication. But I didn't know this about myself at the time. I was unaware of all the nature and nurture adaptations and habits I had developed within myself.

Kareem entered my house on September 11th, 2013, it was a Wednesday afternoon with a high of 100 degrees. When he reached my air-conditioned home, he looked most grateful and relieved. I was happy to host my friend. He was tall, dark and sweaty. My father being a SWAT detective at the time was cautious of us having boys over, particularly boys who fit a description. I can imagine with the line of work my father did, his paranoia of having a potential "gang member" or a family member of one (as he would say to us) in the house was a fear of his. But I knew my friend and from what I knew all he did was sell small bags of weed to kids at school. I didn't think any more or any less of it. I showed Kareem the kitchen where he could rest and take off his school bag. We chatted lightly as I poured him a glass of ice-cold water. Although his energy changed, I thought maybe he was exhausted or maybe was feeling relieved from the heat when he got silent. But that wasn't the case.

Kareem stood about 6 inches taller than me, while I stood at 5 feet 8 inches. He rose out of his chair and stood over me in a way that was alarming. I had no interest in kissing this guy or even really hugging him because of his sweat. I don't know if it was my friendly, kind heart or the lack of boundaries which oozed out of me like a sore, but he became handsy while looking down on me. Calling his

17

uninvited touch tickling. It seemed harmless, I was for sure uncomfortable, but I laughed it off and softly said "stop."

He didn't listen. His tickling became wrestling, and this is when he gained dominance over me. The laughing stopped, and the terror in my voice, not knowing what to say, began to make small cries out of struggle. I said stop, I said chill out, I said no. I remember even saying "please stop."

That always stuck with me. I had politely asked this boy to stop violating me, he most certainly wasn't being polite or even asking for my permission. My fight or flight activated in me; I knew if I didn't fight back there would be no turning back. Visions of what he might to do me flashed through my mind as he wrestled me into my room and onto my bed. With my back on my bed and he on top of me I knew I had one more chance before things got worse. With everything in me, I kicked him off. The force of my strong athletic legs hit the middle of his body, right below his chest. I leg pressed him into the standing armoire. The piece of furniture made a noise so odd it was as if God had stepped into the room. A moment of silence so thick the room become tense. I think in this moment, he realized what he had done and so did I. Looking at him I said, "I asked you to stop."

Kareem replied, "yo, I was playing" in a defensive humor.

His answer made me feel sick. Is he really denying the truth of how his aggression made me feel? I lied and told him my parents would be home any minute and he needed to leave. I could still smell his sweat lingering in the room, I could see his lip stain on the water glass, and I could still hear the sound of his silence when I asked him again and again to stop.

After Kareem left, I phoned a close friend, Brandon. Brandon and I had known each other since the 6th grade, he

18

was friends with Kareem as well. My intention was to make sense of the situation. Something like this had never happened to me before and I didn't know what to do or how to feel. I felt that a third-party friend could reassure me in some way and help me resolve this situation. I was always a problem solver and conflict-resolution-type-of-kid. But, Brandon, in one way or another exposed my experience I had shared with him to others; including Kareem. Hours later, a game of telephone started about what had happened. The story became twisted at the hands and mouths of others. It was not only heard across three high schools, but all of social media. I was still processing what had happened during this time; I showered, washed my bedding and repositioned my armoire back to its original standing place.

My parents were now home, and I didn't know how to share this with them. I knew I'd be in a hell of a lot of trouble for having a boy over and was to scared of the consequences. So, I hid out in my room, when suddenly notifications from social media began flooding my cell phone. Kareem exposed the whole situation and completely twisted up the story. He dogged me out to hundreds of high schoolers, many chimed in. Completely belittling and bullying me, it was a modern-day public execution of my character and being. I attempted to write back but more notifications came to me. I didn't even know where to start or what to say, I was completely ashamed and embarrassed. The disappointment hundreds of high schoolers faced because of my resilience to rebuttal Kareems now personal attacks on social media.

Many people who I thought were my friends turned on me and took a side. I was gaslighted about my experience and overall bullied; not by one group or a couple of mean girls, but high schoolers across the county. I'll never forget one girl, Becca, posted, "your life is so miserable, find something better to make up."

The amount of likes she got from it, let alone the

positive reactions Kareem got from the complete slander and violation of me; I was done for. I felt completely alone and violated. Everyone had something nasty to say about me and not once did anyone even consider if what he was saying was true. I thought to myself if I had seen this happening to another girl, I would've checked in on her, but everyone including people who I thought were my best friends were cowards.

I absolutely dreaded going to school the next day. The looks and stares, the gossip and chatter behind my back was so loud, I still couldn't process the initial incident of assault. I made the mistake of telling the wrong person when I needed help, now everyone was looking at me with judgement. The reality of being shred to pieces on the internet is extremely humiliating and embarrassing. I couldn't control my nervous system by any means. The school cop had to get involved the situation had gotten so bad. Teachers looked the other way and some even joined in with the kids, making fun of the situation and calling me a liar. The first 16 hours everyone knew, except for my parents. I still had to tell them what happened. My biggest fear was telling them I had a boy in the house, the punishment was something I didn't want to face. Although, I couldn't keep this secret, things were getting worse by the minute and I was drowning.

At this time in life, my parents were going through a rough patch in their marriage. Dad was drinking heavily, and my mother was mentally and emotionally absent, needless to say, they both weren't in their right mind. But I knew I needed to tell them about what was going on. That was until, my dad got a call from the schools' principle. I was headed to my club soccer practice while my dad was at home reading what was said online and going through my text messages from his work laptop. I don't know what that experience was like for him in the moment, but I felt it later that night.

Soccer had always been a safe space for me, I was

looking forward to seeing my teammates and getting my mind off everything that was happening around me. As I was walking onto the field for practice, I overheard the team talking about some girl who lied about sexual assault and how it was the talk of their high school. I said in an upbeat matter, hoping to gain some control over the situation, "that was me."

I didn't realize how exploited the situation had become until my safe space was now tainted with my trauma. "Fuck, this is bad" I thought to myself. Yet no one, including coaches or parents who overheard, asked me if I was okay. I don't recall ever asking myself if I was okay.

Practice was a blur, when this time had always been where I had focused most. It was hard for me to understand why everyone was talking about sexual assault so lightly or how I became prey to many. Soccer was my first sport, my first passion, the place I could escape, perform and excel was now, along with school, a place I felt unsafe and insecure. On my ride home from practice, I felt lost and a great sense of shame. I wanted my parents' guidance and support after this snowball of suffering I had found myself in. This was not the case unfortunately. My mother was severely depressed and distant while my father was heavy with the hard liquor this night. Which resulted in my experience of a disconnected mother and a quick-to-anger father. I never knew what personalities I would come to face walking in the door.

Nothing could've prepared me for this night. I seldomly walked through my front door, beaten up after the most emotionally and socially draining day of my life when I saw my dad down the hall, in the living room. The protection I was seeking was now too, violated. My mother and father sat me down to discuss the incident. It was very difficult to feel comfortable enough to speak about the sexual assault not only because of the harassment and embarrassment which followed but it wasn't easy to speak my truth or even at all to my parents. I had just been publicly humiliated and defeated

21

for speaking my truth, my hopes weren't high for myself even in the presence of my mother and father.

The conversation went quickly from the sexual assault to the simple fact I had a "gang member" over at the house. Which wasn't necessarily even true. My father didn't show me any grace or empathy for what I had gone through, it was as if he thought I deserved what happened to me for breaking his rule. My confidence began to descend into a dark hole that shed no light. My mother was focused on getting the facts straight but was timid to show empathy because of my father's reaction. She excused herself upstairs to shower in the middle of the conversation, leaving me alone with my father. She had been at the grip of my fathers' drunken anger and knew how to shut off like a robot and retreat like a deer whenever he was getting ready to go off.

I sat next to my father as he questioned me. As if I was being interrogated, he kept coming up with his own conclusions while I responded with answers which I thought my father wanted to hear or what I thought would get me out of the trouble I was in. My mind had gone into full on survival mode. I was shaking with fear and filled with embarrassment. My father brought up my social media accounts in-between his sips of gin and Kool-Aid. I attempted to explain the assault that happened the afternoon before and what trauma followed. Instead, my father read every post from Kareem and peers out loud. His breath reeked of sweet Kool-Aid and harsh silver gin; his words were of the sharpest tongue I had received throughout this whole ordeal.

Kareem hadn't stopped belittling me since the moment he started bullying me on social media. Kareem made more comments about me inside and out, once even comparing my skin color and texture to a candy crunch bar, you know the one with the lumps on top? My deepest and surface leveled insecurities were now internet material for others to shame me about and laugh at. This was the first time I had thought I was better off dead; I was absolutely humiliated and hopeless. As I was thinking this, my father, the man who boasted about always protecting my sisters and I, turned to face me. With red over his eyes and the energy of disgust and anger oozing out of him, he then said to me, "you're a fucking idiot. A slut."

This moment truly broke what was left of my heart. I had become the villain to my hero. He then grabbed both of my hands with his left and slapped me across the face with his right. My left cheek took the impact, but the right side of my jaw popped. The impact was so hard and burned so badly, I peed myself.

The place I should've been able to seek guidance and protection from was now the most dangerous. This moment in life, changed me forever. I learned how my "yes" and "no" didn't matter, I believed every merciless word said about me, I saw my father turn his back on me when I needed him, but most of all it taught me that my voice didn't matter. And I believed this for years, to the point where I became unaware of how I kept attracting the same energy or situations, which were to only get worse from here on out. Sometimes I wonder if my father or any other adult stepped up to handle this situation, would I even be writing this book?

After my father slapped me, he continued to yell in my face a slew of things, calling me names and barely giving me the chance to breath in-between his words. I can't remember most of his words and slurs, but I remember exactly how they made me feel; worthless. He took my phone which wasn't a big deal to me, but then my father told me I was done playing soccer. The one thing I had in my life that gave me hope and inspiration… gone. It felt like everything I had known in my life was being stripped away from me at the hands of the one who provided it to me.

I ran to my mom like a small child with a sore face

and soiled shorts. Urine ran down my leg with each step up the stairs. For some reason, I was scared to call for help, I moved in silence. I didn't want my father to know I was going to my mom, I thought he might chase me into their bedroom. I opened my parents' bedroom door where my mother was. I think she, herself, was seeking peace. That was until I interrupted her. I could only mutter the words, "I peed myself."

Mom saw the mark on my face, she was frightened and shocked. Growing up, in so many ways, I was considered my father's favorite daughter; I was his little buddy as he would say. My mother knew this, and when she saw the results of my father physically and verbally abusing me, it was the last straw for her. She instructed me to pack a small bag with needed items quickly while my father was downstairs.

Our plan was to stay in a hotel for the night, but it ended up being three nights. The night my mother, Marie and I left, was the beginning of the end for my parents' relationship. My mother saw what my father did to me which was completely out of the norm for his abusive pattern. The moment my mother saw what her husband did to my face was a wakeup call. It gave her a reason bigger than herself to get out, it catapulted our new life. There was no denying or excusing his abuse now. Marie, my younger sister, was twelve years old and had no idea what was going on except that we were leaving. My two older sisters, Harper and Joan were in college, out of state. Luckily for the two of them, they weren't around for what was the worst part of my father's addiction and my mother's emotional absence. I really missed them, but they had worked hard to get out of the mess which was our home and create a new life of their own.

And now, my mother, Marie and I were on a journey to do the same. Granted we didn't have a plan or an idea of where and what this meant but it was a journey of faith and

24

resilience. The sudden change of this left me confused and hurt, as I'm sure it did Marie. As we made our way out the door my father continued to verbally abuse us. The relief which came over my mother and I as we drove to the Comfort Inn Hotel was like a cool light breeze on a dry summer day. I don't remember going to a hotel this night, my mother, when I asked her about this night shared our experience of seeking safety. As the saying goes in chapter one, "the mind is so kind." I would continue to forget huge parts of my life.

We slept at the Comfort Inn. Marie and I still had school the next day and mom had work. So, as if everything was normal, we set out together for our day.

My whole foundation for the last sixteen years of my life that I had known was ripped out from beneath me. Family, friends, soccer, my reputation was now gone. The emotion of it all took over. I sat in my first period unable to focus or participate because of the mental suffering. I was unable to hold it in anymore and began to have a panic attack greater than I had ever experienced even to the present day. My teacher called for the school yard duty to assist me to the nurses' office where I shared my last 36 hours. I couldn't hold it in anymore. My body was trembling, and tears uncontrollably fell from my face, I couldn't breathe at one point. After releasing all of this she got me to tell her exactly what happened. I told her about the sexual assault, the bullying, my father's abuse and sleeping in a hotel. Again, I wanted comfort, someone to listen to me and guide me. The school nurse, with no real thought in my opinion, called both of my parents. I was terrified of my father at this point. "Why do people keep putting me in danger?" I thought to myself, not realizing this was protocol for the school.

Luckily my mother came to pick me up before my dad could get to me. I felt so guilty my mother had left work to come rescue me, again. Everything was a daze at this point. I was filled with shame, as I walked with my head down to the front of the school's office where my mother was standing. She embraced me and immediately called my pediatrician, Dr. Snyder. My mother didn't know what to do so this was our best option. Unfortunately, my long-time pediatrician was no longer with Kaiser Hospital, but she gave us a referral to be seen by a nurse practitioner that day, which was the first good thing that happened to us during this time.

Being seen by a professional made me feel safe. She was sincere and kind, she had the knowledge of what to do and how to do it. I told her my story while holding my mother's hand the whole time. A part of me wished the physician would hear our story and take us home with her. The physician examined my jaw which was sore from my father's slap. To this day, the right side of my jaw clicks when I chew. My jaw didn't break or have any injuries according to her evaluation, but the impact did something to me physically which has been a reminder of that awful moment every meal, every day. What I failed to realize about sharing this experience with a physician, was that she was going to make a report about the physical abuse. It hadn't even crossed my mind that my father was going to get in any kind of trouble. But, after seeing the deep concern on the physicians face, the severity of the incident became really, real for me. I became scared to go home, my mother was scared to go home, and Marie was scared to go home. Things had gotten so out of hand and into the hands of others the only thing to do was to not go home.

My mother, Marie and I went back to the Comfort Inn in Rocklin, California. It was inexpensive and a safe area for the three of us to go. That night we showered, ate and slept as best we could. My mother was busy looking for an apartment for us to move into. Child Protection Services (CPS) was now involved which was never my intention, but I received blame for. It really sucks being held responsible for someone else's actions in this way. I had never heard of CPS or even knew what that meant for my family and me. The result of speaking to two separate health providers meant there were two separate reports made within the same day. This was an urgent matter and with CPS involved they gave my mother and father an ultimatum. Either my mother leaves, my father leaves, or CPS takes Marie and me. So, my mother decided to leave and get an apartment. It was now September 13th, 2013 which was my maternal grandmothers' birthday. My mother says, that the spirit of her mom helped her find an available apartment near our school so quickly. Life really made a turn in an unpredictable direction within a matter of days for our family.

It was very difficult for me to not put the blame of my parents' separation on myself, which I did for years. Eight years later as I write this, I remember how heavy this string of events weighed on me at the time. How I was blamed by my father for ruining our family, how I even blamed my mother for ruining our family because she left. I had no idea what CPS had told her until I started writing this book. I remember thinking at times my father would never forgive me for the betrayal I did to him, I remember feeling the resentment from Marie because what she saw and understood at this age was that I was the reason for mom and dad's split; when in fact I was just the straw that broke the camel's back. It's taken many years for me to truly release this from my subconscious and it wasn't until I sat down to write this book that the lasting roots of this trauma uplifted and released from me. All of it.

The apartment my mother acquired was on the west side of Roseville. It was on the second story, with a view of the pool and had two bedrooms. As much as I was surprised, she had gotten it, I think my mother was too. There were angels working for us and through other people to make it happen. We barely had any furniture, but we had a safe and peaceful place we could call home. Marie and I shared the second bedroom while my mother had her own room. The first night we didn't sleep in our new home because we hadn't acquired any furniture yet. We went to a family friends house; her name is Natasha. She had two younger boys that lived with her, the oldest being four years younger than me. Natasha invited us over for a home cooked meal and a cozy place to relax. It was the first time in days I felt like I had a sense of myself. I had known Natasha for as long as I could remember, seeing her face was a reminder of the good days. Her vision of me had not changed and I could feel that internally. Natasha also made my mother feel at ease, which gave me some comfort. Her young boys were so innocent and goofy, they made me smile for the first time in days. This moment felt good for the soul. I was still distraught over our now situation and my personal traumatization, but here I found some hope.

Natasha's eleven-year-old son offered his bed to me that night so I wouldn't have to sleep on the couch. His selfless gesture brought tears to my eyes. This act of kindness has always stuck with me. He didn't know what I had gone through, what I was perceived to be or what trauma had started it all. He did it out of the kindness of his heart. An essence of care and thoughtfulness I had needed from my dad came in the form of selflessness from a young boy. I said, "thank you, are you sure?"

He replied, "yeah, I'm going to sleep with my mom tonight." And proceeded to walk out with a stuffed bear that was on his bed.

"Goodnight." he says.

"Goodnight." I reply.

The room smelled like farts and had a musty stench, but I slept well. It didn't matter what blessings came to me or how they were packaged, it just felt good to have them come. My mother, Marie and I left Natasha's house the next day with a bit of happiness in our hearts. We knew we had to go back the house and move our things into the apartment. I don't remember the move all too well, because of the verbal and emotional abuse I was still facing with my father.

Natasha's 11-year-old son had told his dad I had slept in his room, which was taken out of context by this man who told my father. It is completely absurd, but my father turned this into his own fabricated story. He went on to tell my older sisters, uncles and aunts that I had attempted to sleep and "fool around" with an 11-year-old boy. I remember hearing this lie and being completely shocked, disgusted and confused. A moment that was surrounded in innocence and kindness was now manipulated and painted with extreme false accusations. How could my father, who knew I was recently sexually assaulted, accuse me of doing this to a young boy? Like I said, my father was an alcoholic with major anger issues. In his mind, I was the reason for my mother leaving, intentionally went after him with CPS and I was the whore he made me out to be. But I was none of these things, yet it still cut me deep.

I had gone from victim to villain. The lies, manipulation and bullying I suffered because of my father psychologically changed me. My mother did her best to comfort me, she stood by my side this whole time. All of this hurt her as much as it did to me. Within a week, we were written off by my father and put on the top of his shit list. Maybe it was the fact he didn't want to own up to all the years of abuse, his drinking problem or the fact he stopped being a dad, but I was made out to everyone in my family to be his reason for it all. I couldn't talk to anyone about what was happening. As far as soccer went, I stopped going to practice because my father had pulled me out. The team I was once a captain of thought I quit. I no longer had a cell phone and had no way of talking to my older sisters. It was just me and my mother; Marie was going back and forth between my parents' homes. She was very young and had been through enough, and aside from that every time she came back from my fathers, she had an obscure and manipulated view of me. I felt she lost respect for me and believed the things he told her. I can't blame her; she was so young, but subconsciously it effected our relationship for years. Joan and Harper never called to check in on me, they too, had been brainwashed by my father. I had really lost everything except for my mother.

September 2013 is the start of when my depression and suicidal ideation began. The only thing that had stopped me from hurting myself or offing myself was the thought that my mother, the person who stood by me and protected me, would be the one to find me. There were many nights I sat in my room, in the dark, alone, thinking of ways to do it. I thought that if I were to go through with any of the plans I had made, my mother would never be able to move on from my father. These thoughts were the only thing that kept me hanging on. My mother became my external source of happiness and peace. Her strength and resilience during this transition is what inspired me to hold on.

Growing closer to my mother was a miracle, I had never felt close to her growing up. I was always a daddy's girl and only felted connected to him; I was as dark as him whereas my sisters were all light skinned. The simple reality was that mom was white, and I didn't feel I could relate to her because we looked different. But what came to be, was that my mother and I are a lot alike. It wasn't until I was sixteen years old, in a quiet home with her, where I consciously felt her motherly presence. She protected me, she provided for me, she made me strong. My mother gave me strength while she was fighting for her own. That in itself is power.

Mom worked every day managing a deli about an hour away. She worked tirelessly and most days I was home alone for about four hours after school. School still wasn't easy, I kept to myself and did what I could, which wasn't much. I thought I started to heal on my own. But at the time I didn't even know what the word heal meant outside of healing from a physical injury. I sought out alcohol. It was what I grew up with and what I heard other kids did for fun, and I wanted to have fun. I began drinking at the age of sixteen thanks to the local liquor store guy viewing me as a 21-year-old adult woman because of my height and womanly attributes. Whether it was a Four Loko or a fifth of Smirnoff, I had a drink every day before and after school so I could relax my nerves. It was the only thing I had access to which allowed the thoughts in my head to stop. I did this for months, every day after school, walk home and help myself to my stash before my mother returned. My Junior year of high school is really a drunken, messy blur.

The only time I had heard from my father was through the grapevine. One day in particular I was torn up about how my father had treated me, so I called my uncle. I wanted a fatherly spirit to tell me that my dad was wrong, and I didn't deserve this treatment. Mom and I were driving on highway 80 headed back from dinner at Natasha's to our apartment when I used my mother's cell phone to dial my uncle. He answered the phone in an unwelcomed, serious tone. I cried to him about the treatment I received from my father and begged him to talk some sense into him. He listened to me and when I was finished there was a long pause, he said, "Marissa I know about the abortion."

He continued to speak, but I wasn't listening. Tears rolled down my face, my heart broke into little pieces all over again. I just said okay and hung up the phone after about a minute. The last month I had been lied on and defeated again and again by peers, my attacker and my father. I had no more fight in me. I never corrected my uncle; I never called my father out on it. What was the point. I was socially shaped into something I never was by things I never did. And yet, no one asked if I was okay.

My last hope for some type of conflict resolution was gone, my father had manipulated anyone I could talk to and I was made out to be a complete fuck up. This night, I slept in my mother's bedroom with her. I truly started to believe all the things said about me, I was losing my mind. Gaslighting is real. It happened to me when I didn't even know what the word meant.

This lasting torment of my father went on, but I chose to embrace my new home with my mother and focus what energy I had there. She was a single mom now; I still needed a father and subconsciously I yearned for the presence of one. This lack of awareness led me into the hands of Jack.

Chapter 4

Yes and No pt.2

"All you need is a simple 'Yes' or 'No'; anything beyond this comes from the evil one"
Matthew 5:37

Jack was 37 years old at the time when he came into my life through a social website for users to post and discuss anything and everything. I used the forum to seek advice and a place to vent. Jack commented on all my posts, offering guidance, advice and most of the time validating my feelings. We interacted here and there as internet pals for a few months. Our connection to me felt like good friends. He knew quite a bit about me, and I knew quite a bit about him. One afternoon I had posted about bus fare. I was tired of walking home from school every day and had never used public transportation; seeking knowledge from the online community turned into a surprising offer from Jack.

He direct messaged me, which was never the standard between us unless it was a meme. "A message from Jack? Interesting." I thought to myself.

He wrote "I think you are a special lady Marissa, and I'd like to mentor you. Maybe I could start by picking you up from school?"

A part of me was flattered. It had been months of extreme verbal abuse and manipulation; this was the first time a male had anything kind to say about me and to me. However, I do remember seeing this message and thinking of all the warnings my father told us about men on the internet. But my father turned out to be the one who really hurt me, so why would I listen to him?

Jack and I had been messaging for months at this point, the March weather was beginning to bring spring showers and I felt there was nothing to be scared about. What else did I have to lose? I still hesitated to respond. Something inside of me needed time to think about his offer.

My mother recently gotten me a phone for Christmas. I only used it to talk to her and Marie. I don't remember receiving a phone call from my father or my older sisters. There was no one for me to talk to anymore outside of my mother. I became isolated and abandoned in my own world. There was no room for resentment at this time, the pain and manipulation of it all created mental blocks for me. There is a lot I don't remember from the age of 15-17. A whole two years of my life felt like a fever dream. The absence of the mind is a dangerous place. It created an energy of victimhood and helplessness which attracted predators like Jack; although I didn't realize this at the time.

I gave my cell number to Jack a week after he had made his offer, which is when we went from internet friends to texting friends. I still hadn't taken him up on his offer. We texted for about a week, every morning and every night. Until one Friday night when I was high off an edible and one more shot away from being drunk, he called me. Seeing his name, hell, anyone's name light up my phone brought me excitement. We were messaging over text and he called right in the middle of me replying. "Was it to see if I was really high?" I thought to myself. Maybe it was the simple fact that I

34

was heavily under the influence and this wolf who wore sheep's clothing saw an opportunity.

Our first conversation was intimidating. The maturity is his voice and vocabulary he used really brought light to our age difference. He knew I was 16, I knew he was 37 with a wife and three kids. I trusted what I thought was sincere mentorship and friendship, but it was his way of grooming me. We talked for about an hour, he explained how he and his wife had gotten into some type of fight and he left for a drive. I vividly remember asking him, "Why did you call me instead of a friend?"

He replied, "Well, we are friends, right?"

See, I lost my friends and it felt good to have someone consider me a friend or, at least someone they looked forward to talk to. So, I agreed, "Yeah, we are. Does that mean your offer still stands?"

Jack replied, "Of course, it does, but since I'm out right now how about we meet before I pick you up from school? That way you're not having to look hard for me." Jack said with a mischievous undertone.

I agreed. It made sense to me and I didn't want peers from school seeing me flag down an older man who wasn't my dad. They already had enough to talk about. I gave Jack the name of my apartment complex and he said he'd be there in forty-five minutes. Jack lived in West Sacramento, and Roseville where I lived, was a long drive but he insisted on it.

He arrived about an hour later due to traffic. I thought that excuse was weird considering it was now 11pm on a Friday night. When I saw his text message that he was at the gate, I made sure to shut my mother's bedroom door, as I snuck out the front door. It was dark and a little chilly out. I dressed in sweats, a bralette topped with a t-shirt and a hoodie. He texted me, "I'm parked in the back, in a grey tundra."

I saw his lights and headed that way. It was kind of scary walking towards a car and the headlights shining into my eyes. But, as a suicidal person, taking part in risky actions is part of the subconscious way I played with suicidal ideation. I believed I had no fear, but really, I was so desperate in so many ways and in my mind if I ended up dead, at least I didn't do it to myself. This is the mind of a severely sick person, which I was, and I had no idea who I was starting to become.

I made it to the passenger side of the car, where I saw his profile as he unlocked the door. I got into the car and it was my first-time seeing forum user the "Killing Joker". He was a tall, well-built white man, with big bulging blue eyes and an even bigger nose. We made eye contact for a moment and I said, "It's finally good to meet you."

He replied, "you sure don't look 16, I pictured you different. I'm a little nervous now."

His statement making me feel as if I had control. I had my bottle of Smirnoff with me and offered him a sip. He declined, but I still took a swig. For me, it was an offering to break the ice but in Jacks mind he saw a weak target. As the bottle left my lips, he got closer. He put his hand on my sweats and asked if it was okay. Like I said, I didn't care about my life let alone any morals or standards I previously had so I said "It's fine" with a partial smile. A part of me felt cared for or at least it felt good to think I was being cared for. My confidence and fearlessness began to grow as our conversation and my drinking in his parked car continued.

There was a trauma bond created between Jack and I that night. He shared more with me about his wife and three young kids, one girl and two boys. He expressed the marriage problems he had and how she didn't understand him, but I, a 16-year-old girl with a drinking problem, did. He really made me feel special and important that night.

As I'm writing, it's very difficult to be transparent and honest about this. I have never talked to anyone about Jack the way I am talking to you, the reader. His way of grooming me started before I even felt any type of connection to him. He had been planting seeds in my head for months. I had no idea. I truly felt like he was a mentor and someone I could trust. Jack had only given me good practical advice; I didn't feel like there was a hidden agenda. But still, I was just a baby, barely 16 years old with a now drinking problem and unhealed trauma from my recent past. He continued to share sob stories with me that made me feel like I wasn't the only one going through it, that he and I were no different. This is how predators' prey. They make you feel like you have a friend, you can trust them, you're special and that they are no different than you.

I know this now because Jack turned into something I could've never imagined happening to me. We ended up hanging out until 1am, I was barely coherent. I was ready to go back up to my mothers' apartment and say goodbye when he stared at me. It was uncomfortable at first because I didn't know what to expect, but then he came over the center console and grabbed my face with his hands while his knee pinned my arm down. And that's when he kissed me. I attempted to pull back, but his grip on the back of my head kept me from moving.

Again, I had no say in a yes or no. Maybe the way I perceived myself gave him that permission. I thought, why the hell not? I really have nothing to lose. I eventually kissed back. The moment I did, Jack put his hand up my shirt and grabbed held of my bralette. I was not afraid of his touch, but I didn't want it. I asked him, "What're you doing?"

He replied, "Doesn't this feel right?"

Jack always responded to my questions with a question. Every time, this made me question myself instead of him. Another strategy predators and manipulators do to control their prey. So here I was submitting to the role he had prepared me for subconsciously all these months. He grabbed held of my breast while his other hand released from the back of my head as he started to take hold of my upper thighs. I wasn't ready for sex. I didn't want to have sex with him. But the last time I tried to use my voice it had been rejected, twisted, manipulated and ran through the mud.

I didn't feel I had the option to use my voice. Jack continued to feel me up over my clothes. He began to praise me and apologize for what others had done. This is another example of how predators take control of their prey. I nervously laughed and said, "This is moving fast, and I'm really tired."

He pulled back with a questionable look and said, "Yeah it's definitely passed your bedtime."

How he went from treating me like I was a woman, to now responding to me as if I was a child disgusted me. This form of manipulation was used by him to plant seeds in my mind. It made me want to prove I wasn't a child, and I could handle myself. The truth is he knew what he was doing.

The domino effect of the last six months had really taken a control of me. This time in my 16-year-old life, shaped who I'd became for the next 8 and a half years. As I'm writing this chapter it is as if the remaining pieces of mind control and abuse from Jack are leaving my body. The visions that cross my mind as I am writing every word of this are visions of times in my life, I wish I knew better. It has taken a lot of therapy, toxic relationships, a few sacred plant sessions, 60 days of rehab, three failed suicide attempts, two stays in the psychiatric ward, prescription medicine, mushrooms, LSD and ultimately facing what I had become in result of the actions of men who destroyed me at a young age; to understand what happened to me, how it happened, what dynamics were present, how I fell into a victimhood complex, and the way my addiction numbed me from my reality.

And here I am today, January 4th, 2022, almost 9 years later, finally entering a place where I am able to forgive myself, forgive others and accept who I am. The miracle that came delivered and packaged in Dr. Jones' office wasn't just about prescription medicine, it was as deep as 16-year-old Marissa. Finally, being able to stand up for herself and do what was right and best for her. It was a moment, I was able to finally say "yes and no" without any manipulation, judgement or abuse, and just be heard.

Chapter 5

Honeysuckle

Be alert and of sober mind. Your
enemy the devil prowls around
roaming like a roaring lion looking
for someone to devour.
1 Peter 5:8

     Throughout this time spent in Jack's truck I hadn't felt a sense of threat, although the feeling of being wanted by someone was ever present and overflowing. It very well could've been the liquor coursing through my body. I knew I felt something change inside of me. Whether his intention lacked boundaries and transparency the notion of it felt like love. Now, I was not interested in beginning a relationship with this married man who I'd just met, but once we had said our goodbyes and I crept back into my mother's apartment, Jack was now interested in that. To my beknowing this wasn't right, but a part of it felt right; it wasn't expected, but it sure felt like destiny. My overriding purpose to fill a void and separate myself from my darkness compounded my conscious choices.

     Growing up, my life had always been lived for and controlled by someone else. This newfound connection with Jack was now my own farsighted delusion which I mistook for a dream come true. In my mind, he was someone I was going to use to get what I deserved and wanted, a father. Jack was someone who would help me fulfill the empty goals, desires and happiness which was fleeting and fading inside of me. My essence, motives and thinking were now a toxic whirlpool I situated myself into comfortably. Contrary to Jacks actions and ideas about me, it was now fuel for my ideas and actions towards myself. The simple duties my father once did, and my mother no longer had time for, was now Jacks responsibilities.

Through the weekend, Jack clung to his time spent with me while reluctantly being at home with his wife and three young children. He began to throw his heart at me through text message, email and calls, which were all saturated with manipulated techniques summoning his love for me in hopes I would respond the same. My state of mind was not there let alone was I even mature enough to understand and comprehend the burden his words carried. I, myself was all over the place in thought and feeling.

I felt he was a sorry loser in so many ways for looking for something in me I could never give him, I felt we were no different because I too, was doing the same. I thought he was a complete weirdo for coming onto me, while also thinking, "Didn't I position myself to allow this?"

The manipulation Jack had primed and prepped me for had me questioning myself in ways where I felt the only right answer was to answer to him, not myself, not a higher power, but to him.

I had become completely numb to sexual assault because of my most recent and first experience with it. I knew that it was normalized in such a way that to judge the act of it or speak up about it meant I was just admitting to my own predetermined whore ways. At least that's what I came to believe. Along with the truth I succumbed to face, that I wasn't valued more than a rock which lays on the bottom of a riverbed, ultimately worthless to others. But Jack believed in his dark twisted mind, I had value. Value which only stretched to the benefit of his inappropriate desires, he had to convince himself it was true love wrapped in a forbidden fantasy. He made it clear to keep things a secret and how the wrongness of it all made it feel more intensely right. He played into my struggles and trauma which made him now my knight in shining armor.

Again, my immaturity and vulnerable mind had accepted that this was okay and true. The month of March brought spring showers which I was not fond of due to the long walks home from school. The day was March 26th, 2014, when Jack offered once again to pick me up from school. It was a Wednesday, about a week after our first encounter. He insisted his desires to be at the center of my life mattered more to him than anything else. I finally agreed to him picking me up from school. Our arrangement was for him to park his truck behind the wetlands, past the public library, a short, yet secluded distance from my high school gates. This way no one took notice of him or I.

The day held a high of 62 degrees accompanied by wind and rain. Although the rain had stopped by the time 2:35pm came around and the final school bell rang, the weather felt razor close to just fine. But Jack was positioned and ready for my arrival, I couldn't back out now.

I made my way through the once dirt trail, now muddied from the weather. The rain which fell earlier in the day lifted the scent of wet drooping pussy willows to my nose. The pungent familiar aroma followed me to a bridge which was my crossing between one world and soon to be another hidden life.

I noticed a blooming honeysuckle plant and stopped to pick the maturing flowers which were now my sweet treat. The innocence and purity of picking a honeysuckle on a spring day is a moment I believe my subconscious allowed me to remember during this walk. The air was quiet, my surroundings were distinctive and for a moment I captured my essence. But, I mistook my essence for a lightness towards my fate waiting for me on the other side of this bridge.

I continued my walk savoring the sweetness of the honeysuckle and passing by children who played freely amongst their parents. My eyes stared on as I wished to be them. To be as innocent and pure like flowers blooming on trees or a child who is completely carefree, was long gone for me. These thoughts and feelings filled me from my toes to the last layer of skin on my head. How I missed my father, my sisters and the girl I was before.

The longing stare onto others and sweet honeysuckle simultaneously became bitter as my path aligned with Jack's truck. I wasn't happy to see him, nor did I have a sliver of gratitude. The breaths of wonder faded, and my reality of burden and suffering came into light the closer my body was in distance of this predatorial person. My own will to make a better decision for myself was withered and muddled. Reaching for the doors handle to step into his space was as if I had signed an agreement which stated, "I am in agreeance to your visions of me and consent to your desires."

In some respects, this was true to a degree if I were conscious of the unspoken agreement. But I wasn't. This was still just a ride home from school to me. Jack carried an awkward smile on his face, almost as if it was forced. He said, "Hi cheeks, how was school?"

He choked on his words as they came out of his mouth as if he had been practicing in the mirror and almost forgot his line. Again, making me feel as if I had control which most certainly was his intention.

I replied, "The weather ended up being nice, thank you for picking me up. But I'm ready to go home now." Jack was not fond of this answer nor did he appreciate my brut attitude. A part of me felt violated that my chubby baby cheeks which rested on my face was now his new nickname for me. The feature of mine which was just about the only physical sign of youth on my body was his favorite. Now that I am twenty-five years of age and having to write about this in detail, it is sickening to think my childish looks is what he was drawn to the most.

Jacks' facial expression disagreed with my response as if he came out of character. He expressed how good it was to see me, how much he had missed me since the last time we saw each other and that it was only right we spend the late afternoon, early evening together. His victimizing and romancing ways toiled with my ability to disagree or come up with my own thoughts. A symptom of being intertwined with a narcissist is the desire to please. Inherently, I did anything to keep the narcissist at bay even at the expense of my own peace and happiness. Jack was for sure a narcissist. I figured I had nothing else to do and what was my time worth anyways? The acting, the persuading, the mind control was all a part of a sick one-sided game. It showed me that I was now his external source of happiness, entertainment and love. But what did I show him? I exposed the lack of thoughtfulness I had for myself in wake of his desires, wants, and demands.

Jack had this way of stroking my ego which I took as genuine appreciation and consideration. He knew I was desperate for love, acceptance and attention; It wouldn't be until I became spiritually enlightened later in life that I would realize this. This was his way of hooking his claws deeper into me. I had become attached so quickly, not because of him, but because of what I was missing. You know the old saying, to a starving soul something bitter can become sweet.

Nothing had seemed right or wrong for so long. After what happened with my father and the sexual assault I experienced from Kareem, I no longer knew what was right or

44

wrong anymore.

Jack suggested we go somewhere with more privacy, strictly so people wouldn't see us. Before he turned the key to start the engine, he paused for a moment looking onward and then back to me; as if a voice had been whispering to him and directing his next methodical move. Jack wasn't just a predator, he thought out every step as if he was playing chess. Continuously consoling the voice in his head, whether that be how to govern my thinking or what streets had fewer cameras, he was always calculated and intentional with his schemes. The heaviness he disguised as passion filled the space between. He looked into my eyes not blinking once. I observed him as he desperately tried to connect with me. Nothing honorable or beautiful held true in his eyes. It was merely a pit of dreary darkness and deviance. He leaned towards me and without a word, grabbed my face just as he did the first time, paused to examine my features and kissed me. It was just as forced and unwanted as the first time. He pulled back and returned to his seated position. His lingering body language was as if he held the most precious stone in his hands the way he gawked at me desperately trying to convince me to engage with his physical touch further.

The energy coming from me must have felt unamused because Jack turned the key in the ignition while asking me, "What radio station do you like?"

I responded, "103.5 or 101.1 is what I listen to most of the time."

He chuckled as if my response gave away a piece of information he had been looking for. He tuned the radio and said, "Now that we've got our music set, let's take a drive."

I started to understand his game at this point. Jack would ask me a question pertaining to whatever he had in mind to allow him to feel as if I was consenting. And when I

45

would answer, he would tell me what we were going to do. The things he should've asked me, he didn't; and unrelated things that wouldn't change his plans, he did ask for my opinion or permission.

Via a slight tilt of my head, I stared out the windshield capturing one last glance of the place I had just picked honeysuckles and watched children play, but my vision became distant as Jack backed his truck out. Jack was still a stranger. A stranger who I had been entwined with so fast, nothing about it made sense, but I allowed it. The love he gave which made my skin crawl was a love I became accustomed too; one which felt like the nature of man. The abusive actions from my father and my attacker showed me another side of man which took hold of my beliefs. Beneath the hair which rose from my skin and far past the depth of nerves and reflexes; inside of my soul were forgotten and rotten threads of the girl I once was. The care and fight I had in me to ask where we were going was no longer there. Again, I felt if he were to kill me, at least I wouldn't have to do it myself. The empty wishes of death upon myself directed my fearlessness and unthoughtful choices.

I began to ruminate on the lost and forgotten threads of who I was. Out loud I spoke of the leader I used to be, the straight "A" student and lively sister I once was. Stories of my past life comforted and distracted me from my current reality with Jack. Jack listened obnoxiously as he attempted to join in. But I ignored him and kept speaking as if he wasn't there. The words fell out of my mouth like water droplets from a facet. I shared stories of what small portion life was like before dad started drinking and became abusive. I talked about the times my sisters and I would play imaginary games at our family's bakery in-between batches of baked bread. I remembered the glow my mother had before my father had cheated on her.

These were now distant memories. Jack was only

familiar with the traumatized girl I became before I met him. He interjected with lofty words to portray his care for me. He wanted to become those memories and fill the void inside of me. Subconsciously I clung onto Jack because of this, and it was his gateway to taking full advantage of me. Which is so textbook of him and naïve of me, but it's how things began to unfold and how I walked right into the mouth of the beast.

Our drive continued out of Sacramento and towards Davis, California. I'll never forget the moment the hydraulics of his truck began to bounce due to the causeways uneven ground, my breasts moved in synchronicity with the motion of the truck. This caught his eye and he made comments only a dirty old man would make. Again, gawking at me as if he had never seen breasts before; the immaturity of his simple ape like brain was as primal and present as ever. I stayed quiet and continued to look onward.

We passed the UC Davis college campus where I wondered what life could be. Was this life with Jack leading me to a path of greatness or destruction? It was now about an hour since we had set out on this journey together and my body was craving my after-school drink. These thoughts, conversations and sights made my nerves run mad. It was around this time we decided to stop and pick up a fifth of Amsterdam. Not so much for him, but for me. My addiction was his way in, he knew that and preyed on it. So, we went into Fairfield, Jack pulled off to a liquor store while I sat in the truck with my seat leaned back trying not to be seen by anyone. The one person who hadn't seen me, my mother was now calling me. It was now, about 4:30 when my mother called, "where are you sweetheart?" she says in a desperate voice. It was as if her intuition told her, I was in trouble.

Solemnly I replied, "With friends right now, momma, I'll be home in a few hours."

My mother was surprised to hear I was with friends

because I had been a hermit for so many months. Our phone call ended as Jack was getting back into the truck. With a mischievous grin and excitement, he handed me the fifth and said, "Drink up kid."

The vodka was an absolute given for my own personal escape within this moment. The only thing I had control over was how much I could consume while we continued our drive. Jack did not proceed to the freeway, instead he went further down a bare country road where we pulled into the Fairfield Inn Suites. I looked up from my dwindling bottle and asked him what the plan was. Jack replied, "You're going to stay in the car while I get a room, okay?"

Unsure of my fate and what this meant for my life in the moment, I leaned into the store-bought liquor a little more. My safety net was the ability to not remember whatever was going to happen next. Jack seemed as if he was on a mission and nothing could to stop him. He knew my mother called looking for me, he knew I was drinking this time away and he knew most of all he wanted to have sex with me which I wasn't ready for.

I watched him as he came out of the hotel lobby with a purposeful stride; sporting a grey hoodie, black sunglasses and a hat to cover his appearance; incognito was his MO. I thought maybe this really is the day I end up on the FBI missing watch list. But as my blood alcohol level rose, so did my "fuck it" attitude. Jack was no threat, right? He heard me out, listened to my story and showed care; a piece of me believed he had my best interest at heart and maybe I was just closed off because of my trauma. All the same, I intensely became exposed to a dangerous situation.

Jack motioned for me to get out of the car with one hand. I unzipped my school bag securing the fifth of vodka and what little control I had with me. Stepping out of his truck, I followed blindly to the back of the hotel, through the back door and up two flights of stairs. Not one word was said between Jack and I until he reached the hotel room. Before opening the room with his key, he says "Are you ready?"

I replied, "Ready for what?"

As if my words unlocked the door, he rushed me in with a swift movement so jarring, it became my answer. I knew for certain what his plans were now and surrendered to the happening of it. The door shutting behind Jack was more movement than I had made standing on the other side.

He exclaimed, "Isn't this nice! I got this room for us; we can relax here."

Perhaps he didn't have an agenda with me I thought to myself all too soon. Nothing particularly fancy or attractive adorned the hotel room. It seemed to be the place for long road truckers to stop, or by chance it was for married men to bring their side pieces. Albeit the essence of the room was stale, insubstantial and took no parts of feeling like home. Which Jack tried so heavily to do. The room was set up like a granny flat, a small kitchen with a breakfast nook attached, shared the space with a tv room and couch tucked by the window. The bedroom had its own entrance with a bathroom. The smell of cleanliness left by the maids were the only thing close to some type of purity. I sat on the couch with my school bag against my back propping me up right, with my legs crossed waiting for his next command.

Jack was scoping out the room like a hawk, I knew I was his prey and the anticipation of when he was going to strike weighed on me heavily, I was scared to speak or move. In stillness, I watched him as he moved throughout the hotel room. What was he looking for? What was he waiting for? He entered the bedroom, and I was left alone on the couch for a minute. I heard noises which signaled for me the act of him undressing himself and then I heard the sound of metal which was the echoing of his wedding ring being dropped on the nightstand. Jacks' energy filled the room and touched me before he entered into the space I was in. The strong cynical energy of a man preparing to commit sin rushed from the inside of him and out. There I sat like a sitting duck as he walked out of the bedroom naked.

Jack stood at 6 feet 4 inches and 240 pounds, his man-hood hung effortlessly as did his stature. He stood in front of me as if I was a painter from the 1800s creating a canvas piece of anatomy. Again, no words from me. I had never been in a position where a man had presented himself this way to me, what was I to say or do? This grown man was expecting me to please him. Jack waltzed over to me in four long steps, once basking in the sun that peeked through the blinds. He reacted as if the sun had given him powers; his ego became inflated as he took a deep breath in and any proper judgement exhaled out. I watched him, not once taking my eyes from him. I'm not sure if I was in shock, scared or just plainly in a "what the fuck" state of mind, but I hadn't moved, hadn't breathed and most certainly hadn't said a word.

"Cheeks, I want you to know I am in love with you and want to show you that." Jack said as he sat down next to me. "Why don't you take off your backpack? I want you to get as comfortable as I am."

He continued as he reached for the straps on my shoulders, pulling them down slowly, attempting to create some type of romance between he and I. My eyes watched him as he took my backpack off, with terror in mine and excitement in his; I became sick to my stomach. The mixture of the warm vodka I had chugged, and his grotesque advances brought acidic vile to the back of my throat.

"I need to throw up. I'm sick." I said while clearing my throat.

50

Jack did not acknowledge my words, but I still proceeded to excuse myself to the bathroom. Trying my best to not look afraid, I walked purposefully through the bedroom and into the bathroom.

I locked the door behind me and took a moment to breath. Looking into the mirror I examined myself as if it were the last time I'd be able to see myself in this light again. Immediately, I vomited all over the sink and myself. The thought of my innocence and essence on the verge of being taken from me made me puke. The thought of a naked man waiting for me outside of the door frightened me. I yelled, "I puked on the sink, I need to clean it up, give me a minute."

Jack responded in a low irritable tone, "Take your time."

The liquor started to make me dizzy while I cleaned my mess up from the sink. About two minutes had passed when Jack knocked on the door, "Cheeks do you need help?"

"No, I am fine, I just need to clean myself up"

Jack replied, "Well, I am here when you're ready, you know that right?"

"How can I trust you?" I drunkenly slur.

"You can keep my ring hostage, how about that?"

His response was so unexpected and left me confused. I thought to myself how does my trust for him and the wedding ring he took off to be with me signify any type of trust between us?

"I'm going to rinse off in the shower, I have thrown up all over myself." I say.

Without hesitation Jack said, "I can help you!" I completely ignored him, any time he was offering help or aid it was for his own perverted desires.

"I'll be out soon." I say with hardly any confidence. I started the shower and allowed the bathroom to fill with steam. I wanted to sweat out every ounce of alcohol or maybe with good luck I'd pass out on the bathroom floor. I undressed myself in silence although in my head I was reminding myself how to do it.

"Okay Marissa unzip your pants, pull them down, step one foot out, get your balance, step another foot out." I had to talk myself through every movement not only because of my drunkenness, but because it soothed me through the action of preparing my body for my soon to be rapist. Essentially this is what I was doing; yes, there was throw up on me which needed to be cleaned, but deep down I knew this man was going to rape me. Yes, rape. I didn't want it. I knew there was no escape at this point. I showered myself slowly, the hotel soap left a film on top my skin. I washed my hair as if it were to be the last time I'd feel the years of innocence in each strand.

Stepping out of the shower was a fever dream, without any time in between drying myself and reaching for my clothes, Jack knocked on the door again. "Don't bother putting on your clothes unless you want them ripped off."

I replied, "Jack, please, I'm not ready for this."

He replied in a very demanding tone, "You will be. I told you to trust me, I picked you up from school, so you didn't have to walk, I've cared for you when no one else would and now you won't love me?!" he said aggressively.

I was speechless, I would have much rather walked home than have to pay my way for a car ride with sex. I began to cry; Jack heard my cries through the door. He then said, "Cheeks, who has been there for you all this time?" I took one last look at my body before wrapping myself in a towel and opened the door.

There he stood, naked and so did I. In tears, shaking and saddened that I somehow was now in this position of debt to this man, I mumbled the words, "Please don't hurt me."

Jack lifted my chin, and forcibly kissed me. My tears and fears fueled a passion inside of Jack. He ripped my towel off and said, "There is nothing I could do to hurt you more than your father did."

Jack picked me up over his shoulder as I cried out so desperately and deeply for someone to hear me. I remember crying and screaming for help so loudly my voice cracked. The higher my voice went the more his penis became erect. He threw me on my stomach and shoved my face into the bed. I could barely breath. With everything in me I pushed my chest up from the bed and the only glimpse I saw was his wedding ring on the nightstand. He shoved me back down and whispered in my ear, "If you don't relax, I'll have to make you relax. Do you understand cheeks?"

A small cry came out of my mouth followed by me saying, "Yes, I understand."

In full submission now, I was too scared of what the alternative might be. As much as I had fantasized about death, now that it was a possibility, I didn't want it at the hands of Jack. He placed his left forearm on the middle of my back pressing my stomach down, and his right-hand inching in-between my thighs. I could feel his hard stiff penis pressing into my vaginal lips. And with all two hundred and forty pounds his ten inch long and two- and half-inch wide penis forcibly entered my vagina. Ripping my vagina open and filling me up to what felt like my stomach, Jack began to rape

53

me. I screamed and cried the whole time begging him to stop. He did stop only once to slap me in the face so hard it took my breath away.

He continued and sweated and moaned and groaned all over me as I continued to cry and plead for him to stop. What felt like an hour might've only been twenty minutes when there was a knock at the door. "Hello this is the front desk" a woman said from the outside of the hotel room.

Jack covered my mouth instantly and said, "If you scream, I will kill you." He slowly removed his hand from my mouth not breaking eye contact once. I began to sob and covered my own mouth as he put shorts on and headed to the door.

He answered, "Hey, what is this about?"

The woman replied, "We got a noise complaint about a woman screaming, we just wanted to check and make sure everything was okay?"

He said, "Oh it's our anniversary, I'll make sure she keeps it down. So sorry about the complaint." The woman didn't question him at all. I had wondered if she noticed my school bag on the couch or the tension coming from Jack. But maybe she herself was scared of him. Now that I am twenty-five years of age, I realize that if I would've used my voice to say anything whether that be "help" or "I'm only sixteen" I would've been saved.

Jack shut the door and made his way back to the bedroom. He laid his naked body on top of mine and said, "See how I protected you, I told you I'd show you how much I love you."

I felt completely sickened by him and scared. I said, "Can we please stop, this hurts."

54

He laughed and said "No, I need to finish and take care of you. But this time if you don't stay quiet, I'll have to make you quiet, do you understand?"

I didn't say a word. And Jack continued to rape me. I tried to imagine myself anywhere else but where I was and what was happening. Nothing could distract me though. The pain was so bad I felt as if my legs were numb and my throat was being choked, I could barely breath, I couldn't move. I didn't dare open my eyes solely because I knew I didn't want to have any visual memories.

Jack raped me for four hours that day. I was completely disassociated by the time the first hour had passed, I hadn't moved, I hadn't said a word, I was just lying there on my stomach enduring the physical and psychological pain praying to God for it to stop. God didn't answer this day or so I thought. This was the day any last bits of hope, innocence, self-respect or self-worth I had, died. As much as I didn't believe Gods presence wasn't around me, my cry for help was heard and came knocking on the door, looking back I didn't realize the option I had for help for the reason that I was paralyzed in fear and had no knowing of what my voice could do.

Chapter 6

Honeysuckle pt. 2

For I am the Lord your God who
takes hold of your right hand and
says to you, do not fear; I will help
you.
Isaiah 41:13

Half-conscious my mind slowly returned to my body
while recovering from the disassociation and physical
exploitation of my being. The process was absolutely
desensitizing surrounded in darkness. All five senses were
turned off completely as well as the sixth sense; my intuition
or inner voice as some might call it. I was nothing more than a
mere shell of a human in this moment. Though, the only
memory I have after my fall from grace turned out to be the
tears which shed uncontrollably as I curled into a fetal
position alone, with the lights off in my bedroom. I held my
stomach as my uterus pulsed, contracting back to its natural
shape. The pain was a lingering echo of the inability to use
my voice yet again. The learned behavior and shamefulness I
felt for speaking up for myself was now an immediate first
reaction. My soul ceased to return home into my body; while
the devil which occupied Jack found comfort in me now. The
possession of my spirit became penetrated with anger, guilt,

shame and a darkness so wicked I hadn't given myself the chance to fully grieve or recover.

The phenomenon of sexual abuse which became true for me, is that the victim subconsciously desires to gain control of the situation. Whether this is caused by denial of the truth or attempting to rewrite the story of abuse; 85% of sexually abused people go back to their abuser in some way. In my case, Jack had been an emotional support for me which in turn resulted in my experience of Stockholm syndrome. Stockholm syndrome is a coping mechanism which conditions the abused person to feel positive emotion towards their abuser. At the time, I had no knowledge of any syndromes or phenomenon's which occurred during abuse. My desire to speak to Jack again was fueled by the lack of control buried in my subconscious and a syndrome I developed to cope with my reality.

Unable to sleep the night which followed the sexual abuse, due to the psychological trauma and physical pain I laid awake until the sun rose. It was now Thursday morning and I still had to make it through the school day. My mother was getting ready for work, listening to her Christian music while applying rouge. The way she rose with the sun every morning was comparable to a ritual; the music and her routine were consistent and soft. There was no way I was going to speak about what I had endured. In my mind she didn't deserve the personal drama which followed me continuously. I felt in my heart this would break hers. To disrupt her day or possibly life again would've been so selfish, I thought. I had caused sudden changes in my mother's life the last seven months and truly didn't want to bring any more pain and suffering to her. So, I kept quiet and went about my morning just as she did.

I made sure to turn the nozzle in the shower all the way to the left. The steam filled the bathroom disguising the mirror with moisture and heat. Once the mirror became clouded with steam and I was unable to see myself in the reflection, I began to undress myself. Afraid to look at my own naked body, the heat protected me from facing the girl who would've looked back at me. A mixture of dried blood and body fluid caused strain on my delicate skin as I peeled the fabric of my underwear down to my ankles. The realization that his body fluids and my blood dried together must have been the sick work of the underworld; the thought of it felt demonic. Pulling my band tee up and over my head I felt the bruised bones on my back from his weight. Stretching my arms over my head and out of my clothing I felt sharp, surging pains through my rectum, uterus and stomach. The pain hadn't subsided but only gotten worse. My eyes began to water and both hands began to tremble as I opened the shower curtain. Scorching hot water touched my skin but goosebumps surfaced. I was still in fear, and without hesitation lowered my body onto the shower floor. With my bottom on the tub and arms hugging my knees, which were tucked into my chest, I rocked myself back and forth in attempts to soothe the nature of my inner and out pain.

Time had passed and the clock was ticking, I still had to be in first period at 7:45am. Though, I wanted to lay in bed all day, I felt I had to be strong when so badly I wanted to be weak. Standing up slowly in the shower I began to wash away the dried fluids which brought upon a smell I'll never forget. His sweat, ejaculation, and my blood flowed down the drain with ease. The symbolic cleansing of my body wasn't enough for me; how badly I had wished ridding the emotion and connection I had to this man would drain out of me all the same. I imagined the hot water burning all impurities and sin away from my soul. This technique failed for I no longer had a relationship attached to my soul.

Pulling back the curtain and stepping out of the shower was as if I had stepped into a new reality which commanded an acceptance. While drying myself I said, "today is a new day."

58

Without hesitation I continued with drying and moisturizing myself. I dressed in loose clothing, the restraint of blue jeans and tight band tees which was my usual casual go-to style was a thing of the past. I wore an old pair of soccer sweats and an oversized black tee. I brushed my hair and teeth in my bedroom to avoid any accidental glances in the mirror. I was so ashamed of myself I wouldn't dare encounter the person who'd be looking back at me. Doing my best to stay invisible, my joyful mother knocked on the door.

"Marissa, hunny, Good morning sweetheart. How are you?" Her voice carried an innocence and sweetness long gone to me. Although it brought a sense of hope into my realm it was something I became intimidated by now.

"Good morning momma, I'm almost ready for school. I'll be out in a minute." I replied in a hurried, worried tone.

Momma replied in a respectful tone, "Okay doll."

Her essence was so kind and warm while I was the opposite of that now. How badly I wished I could have been honest with my mother.

Momma had fixed me a plate of scrambled eggs, jellied toast and a glass of orange juice. Could I bare to stomach any food right now? I had no appetite nor did the thought of food cross my mind. I had always eaten whatever my mother fixed for me on random and to turn away a meal would've been a reg flag for her. Making my way into the dining room, I sat down at the table thinking of a way to avoid conversation with her. The new wardrobe I sported was alarming enough. The only thing I could think of to evade dialect with her was to stuff my face with eggs; alas the taste and mush in my mouth reminded me of Jacks tongue forcibly down the back of my throat. Just as I had disassociated in the Fairfield hotel the night before, I did the same at my dining room table while eating mommas' breakfast. The most primal and basic care of my mother was now too, tainted with Jack's energy. Momma politely questioned my gagging. I think she felt insecure about her cooking which was in no way what I had become sick over. Grabbing my piece of toast and finishing my glass of orange juice I excused myself. "I should get going to school, I'm running late." I said while taking an awfully big bite of jellied toast. Disgusted with what bacteria or lingering residue might reside on my lips, I didn't kiss my mother goodbye. Again, I know my actions hurt her to some degree, but I felt I had to protect her.

The crisp morning air rushed my veins the moment I stepped out the front door. As if the wind carried a message upon its wings, Jack texted me. "Ida is suspicious of things. I think its best we take some time off from seeing each other. I love you Cheeks, talk soon."

Ida is Jacks wife whom they share three kids with, one being only six years younger than myself. Jacks message left me confused with emotion and thought. Jack left me genuinely hurt not only because of the night before, but for the reasoning that he had abandoned me when I needed his comfort most. I had questions left unanswered followed by a massive secret I had to bare the weight of.

By the time I arrived to school, I was the least bit interested in anything other than my own drama and suffering. Some might say this is typical for teenagers, but this wasn't common for me. I was never this type of kid or student, I enjoyed engaging with my teachers and classmates. The only thing on my mind was Jack. During my first period, I continued to disassociate and pose as if I was participating in the lesson. I must've been deep in the shadows for no one had taken notice or interacted with me. The baggy clothes and undone hair were fulfilling its purpose of concealing me.

Re-reading Jacks text, I still hadn't known what to

say. I didn't love this man, but I had an anger inside of me that he had used and abandoned me. I needed closure at least, how did he expect me to go about my day as if nothing had happened? Whether it was my ego or will, by the time second period had rang I became jaded. My second period of the school day, I was a teachers-aid with another girl named Grace, who I'd chat with often. Grace and I completed light work for the teacher during the lesson each day, but this day, in particular, we didn't have much work to do. She took notice of my clothing, my attitude and the blank stare on my face. Grace wasn't involved in any girl groups or cliques and I felt she was a safe person I could trauma dump onto without my personal conflict spreading throughout the high school. I shared how a thirty-seven-year-old man picked me up from school the day before and took me to a hotel room; I confessed the physical pain I was dealing with and emotional pain from him now abandoning me. Grace didn't say much, she barely looked like she was listening. "Maybe she really is anti-social" I thought to myself. Although a part of me felt a little better after sharing this with her, we parted ways as we did every day.

As the school day continued, I walked the halls surrounded by peers yet feeling most alone and trapped in my own head. That was until the school yard duty, who was so tall that he blocked the sun, approached me, "Miss Hardy, the principal asked me to escort you to his office, please follow me."

A million scenarios as to why I was being called ran through my head; at this point it could've been anything. I had been in a season of trouble and it wasn't stopping anytime soon, that was for certain.

Principal Beck was sitting at his desk with his office door open, seemingly calm and chipper. "Hey there, Miss Hardy, why don't you shut the door and take a seat." Suspicious of his demeanor and wondering what the reasoning for the request of my presence was, I timidly followed his directions.

"Hi, Principal Beck" I say.

"Miss Hardy, how are you doing today?" Principal Beck says.

"I'm fine, a little curious as to why you called me up here." I reply.

"Well Miss Hardy, you see you're not in any kind of trouble with me, but you may be in trouble with yourself. A student expressed concern over your relationship with an older man. Now your personal relationships are none of my business, but the claims this student is making about your personal relationship with this older man is concerning."

My heart jumped and my brain froze. Grace may not have been popular or a gossiper, but she always did what was right. I should've known better than to tell the one person who was a teacher's pet what I was going through. Alas she did do the right thing, but for my sake at the time, I was feeling jaded and knew if Jack heard I had opened my mouth about any of this he would kill me. And after feeling the strength and force this man had the night before, I believed him.

"What? Who spread this rumor?" I say with some confidence.

Principal Beck looked a little offended and replied, "Well I can't say, but they let us know you had confided in them about some injuries you sustained from this man."

He leaned in and said, "Look, I know you've had a tough year with your peers which is why I brought you in today. Is there anything or anyone you need protection from?"

I glanced down and thought for a minute, but the pain from my uterus surged through my body just at that moment and it was a definite reminder of what would happen to me if I said anything. So, I protected myself by protecting Jack.

"No principal Beck, I think whoever told you is just making rumors about me again." He looked disappointed but accepted my answer.

"Well Miss Hardy I'll see you out the door then." I felt a little saddened by how things went, a part of me wished my principal dug deeper. As I write this chapter as a twenty-five-year-old adult I respect the space he gave me, but it was a moment I wasn't brave enough to handle and I needed an adult to be brave for me. I had yet another opportunity to share my truth but neglected my own voice. Another confrontation which was an act of God reaching his hand out to rescue me from my own suffering, I turned it away because of fear. Living in fear became my downfall and I continued to dig a deeper hole inside and around me.

The school day couldn't have been over soon enough. Leaving campus, I pondered on how to reply to Jack. The walk home allowed me to realize that if I could make it through this day alone, I could make the rest of my days without him. Being on some type of watch list now by my principal added to the paranoia. There was little doubt in my mind, I had to completely cut things off with Jack. The moment I got home I sat down to write him back.

"Jack, today my school's principal called me up to his office about you. I denied everything, but I think its best our friendship and whatever else this is, ends. I'm in pain today, I have school and need to focus on finishing this year out. I think its best you focus on your wife and children." I felt proud of the maturity my text relayed. It not only cut ties on my end and gave me closure but gave him a way out.

As if he had been waiting by the phone all day, Jack replied instantly.

"Cheeks, I told you I loved you. I just need to work things out with Ida, can you please wait for me? I am trying my best to be with you so hold tight. Besides you are mine now, and what I say goes, do you understand?"

The immediate feeling of imprisonment to this man came over me.

I replied, "Well, I can't compete with your wife and I don't want to, Jack. I'm only sixteen and in school, if my mom finds out about you, I'll be in trouble."

The desperation I had towards Jack to leave me alone was ever-present. This message must have struck a cord with him because he called me instantly. I refused to answer, but again and again my cellphone rang with his name popping up on my screen. After ten minutes of unanswered calls and a flood of texts in-between, I found some type of strength to block Jacks number. I felt good about this and knew it was the right decision. His motives and energy towards me were possessive, controlling and manipulative. I couldn't bare to stand anymore of his torment. He continued to become an obvious danger and threatening person to me even though I felt some responsibility to uphold with him.

He no longer was someone who supported me like he once did. He no longer cared for me like I thought he once did. The underlying desire was not to love me, but to take control over me, which was clear to me now. Now I understand that on top of Jack being a pedophile, he is also a narcissist. Someone who is a narcissist when faced with any type of rejection will not forget or forgive you. They will use whatever happened as a reason to do horrible things to their victim; it's the reason they sexually abuse you, it's the reason they physically abuse you. No slight goes unpunished with the

64

narcissist; my request for solace was a slight. If the narcissist chooses to "set things aside", they'll eventually use any grievances against the victim, months or even years down the road. This includes blackmail, stalking, harassment and threats. My attempt in setting a boundary and moving on from Jack was the beginning of years of terror which follow me to the present day.

I had no idea the wits and will Jack had about keeping his eyes on me. But he used his knowledge of technology, access to the dark web, and twisted mind to find out everything about me from this moment onward. I never once gave Jack my email, but by the time the sun set; a full 24 hours since the initial rape, he had sent me a long, dramatic, terrorizing email. The fear I felt was deep. It was a deep realization of not just the physical power he had over me, but the mental control. The simple fact of him having my email address fucked with my head just enough for me to try and make sense of his email.

A piece of the email read:

"A man smarter than me said that forgiveness swings both ways. For closure to happen you should forgive yourself. I am not solely responsible for everything so I should not receive any blame."

another email followed moments after saying:

"Marissa, you are treating me like a child and acting like one too, and now you don't expect me to act out? How do you think it's fair I don't resort to threats or taking matters into my own hands? You haven't responded to my kindness and blocked me. You are proving you can't be straight with someone who has proven to you time and time again he is there for you and has your back. You crushed me when you didn't need to."

65

Reading his email was a fair warning of the ball and chain which was attached to me now. There would be no escaping the hold Jack had on me or his obsession.

Chapter 7

Just a Kid

Even though I walk through the
darkest valley, I will fear no evil, for
you are with me, your rod and your
staff comfort me.
Psalms 23:4

A huge part of Still Fucking Alive is acknowledging the loss of innocence and allowing myself to recognize the transformative experience that unfolded from every action and thought between myself and others by speaking my truth after nine, almost ten years of silence. Yes, this is my life story translated into a book for all to read but the real lesson is in the understanding that everything happened for a reason and continues to happen for a reason. My darkest days became my reason for strength, my pain became my purpose.

Now, not every moment lived in my sixteenth year was riddled by Jack's harassment and my father's abandonment, but the subconscious fear and worry lived through me at freewill, ultimately controlling me. Along with drinking, I began to eat without restraint. Drinking and eating allowed me to avoid and fill the void in my feelings which distracted me from what mental stress I was under. With each pound I gained, the Marissa who had been used and abused began to disappear. This version of myself, I literally and figuratively grew into my trauma. I subconsciously felt that if I became overweight Jack would find me unattractive and leave me alone; this wasn't the case. No matter how many numbers or accounts I blocked, Jack still found a way to harass me. His emails usually began with him apologizing for any previous harassment, then went into some type of romantic poetry about his undying love for me and finally ended with an ultimatum which revolved around black mailing or threatening me.

Jack once signed off an email with, "So I ask you this, do you want love or blood?" with attachments of nude photos he took from the time he had raped me. I know what you're thinking, why not go to the police and show them evidence of a grown man possessing child pornography, confess to the hours of rape I experienced and now the blackmail?

Well, I did. I went to the Roseville Police Station April of 2014. Walking into the Roseville police station to report a crime was intimidating yet I waited two and half hours to give a statement. A young officer approached me and said to follow him, no real introduction, just another day on the job for him; meanwhile it was a significant day for me. The officer seemed kind, although it was really an attitude of not taking me seriously.

We sat in an interrogation like room where I shared what was happening and what has happened. The officer took notes and asked some questions, but overall brushed me off for two reasons; one being that Jack was using random numbers and emails, which the officer said could be anyone and two, he thought I was a prostitute. Yeah, you read that right, the police officer thought I was a prostitute. I want to make it clear that Jack had never given me money or any gift outside of alcohol.

The Officer gave me a case number and told me the

next time I want make a report, to do it in the right county. Because Jack was living in Sacramento county and the rape happened in Fairfield, I guess I was supposed to file a report against him these areas. To this day I still don't know if this is proper protocol.

I was at a loss for words, how the simple fact that I was sixteen and Jack was thirty-seven didn't seem to alarm the officer at all. After exhausting three long hours at the police station, which had been extremely defeating and embarrassing, I once again lost hope.

What is it with men who hold a title with such ego, but ultimately end up useless? Now this doesn't go for all men but this time in my life all I had experienced was the harm and disappointment from men. I needed safety and protection; I was a victim looking for a hero to fight for me because I had lost the fight in me.

I truly started to feel that I was in the wrong and maybe all the things others said and felt about me were right. When I say I started to feel this, I felt it to my core. And once you repeatedly hear things about yourself, you believe them and ultimately become them. Between the overeating, drinking, marijuana consumption and self-isolation I was in a pit which became all too familiar. This was my life now. I fully accepted that Jack had a right to invade my life in every sense and there was no way out.

My mother caught on to my weight gain and habits; she must have noticed the boxes of Oreos in the trash or bags of Doritos laying around my dirty room. Or maybe it was the report cards sent home with attached notes from my teachers. My GPA was failing and by the end of my junior year of high school, senior year was already on thin ice. I didn't care. Any sense I had about my future or self was gone. My mother chopped up my failing grades to the trauma of my father and didn't necessarily check for any other causes. I learned how to use victimhood to my benefit and milked out as much of it as I could. This would become a toxic habit and scapegoat I would continue to use throughout the next seven years.

Summer of 2014 came and with the support of my old coach paying for me to participate, I was able to play in a soccer tournament with my teammates. I hadn't touched a soccer ball in months, but the team needed players. I remember being out of shape and not nearly as great as I had been, but I still performed excellent. Soccer had missed me, and I most definitely missed soccer. The Sunday of my last round of games my father decided to come. Aside from his ill feelings towards me he did love watching me play. That Sunday morning, my father drove myself, Marie and my mother to my game in the bay area. He sped the whole ride there, once even attempting to race another man in the same BMW as us. Unfortunately, my father's ego for showing out on the way to his daughters' soccer game got us pulled over. The traffic stop didn't take long but thirty minutes on the side of the road meant thirty minutes I didn't get to warm up properly.

When we finally arrived at the field, my team was finishing warmups. My coach started me in the first half against a very aggressive team. The game was tough not only because of the competition, but because of the mental and physical blocks I had due to the irresponsible actions of my father on the way there. By half time, the game was tied 1-1. My coach's pep talk was all about high pressure offense. It had been a long time since I had been able to play and the outlet soccer provided for me had been missing from my life for so long, I took out all my aggression, anger and pain on the other team.

With five minutes to go in the last half, I had the ball and with all my force I charged for the opposing sides goal when I collapsed. My knee gave out and I was unable to get back up on my feet. Right away I knew something terrible had gone wrong. Lying on the grass as my teammates surrounded me as the sun beat down on my face was as if spirit had intentionally reminded me, I had hit rock bottom.

My teammates all yelled for me to get up and thought I had just tripped. I sat up and the pain struck me again but harder. Tears began to fall from my face as I looked at my disfigured knee. Upsettingly, the only person I wanted in that moment was my dad. He came onto the field and picked me up. No matter what was going on between my father and I, his instincts were still present in that moment. Again, I was facing a deafening importance in life. The anger I had towards my father for making me miss warmups which led to my stiff muscles which than led to my injury was obvious, but the instinctual way I sought out his comfort and how he had rushed to be by my side was also, obvious.

The sadness I felt knowing that I had injured myself was more overwhelming than the pain which consumed my knee and spread throughout my left leg. Dad carried me off the field and brought me straight to the car. No goodbyes to my teammates or coaches, that was the last time I saw them all together. After thirteen years, my soccer career was over just like that.

With a straight leg across Marie in the backseat of dad's car, my knee began to swell and within thirty minutes I couldn't tell the difference between my thigh, knee and calf; it all morphed into one. Every bump and turn caused a pain which was almost unbearable, but I knew I needed a doctor immediately and suffered silently. Thoughts of shame and embarrassment came over me on our drive. The one weekend I was allowed to freely step back into my power was now gone, this time for good. It felt as if September of 2013 was happening all over again as the heart break set in. I had become so accustomed to things going bad for me and had no tools on how to be kind to myself.

Finally arriving to the emergency room, my mother got out of the car and retrieved a wheelchair for me. It was a Sunday evening, and the emergency room wasn't busy at all, I was seen right away by a doctor who made an indefinite statement about an ACL tear. The doctor sent me for an MRI to get a closer look at what damage had been done.

The doctor came into the hospital room with news we had already known, my ACL was torn and would need surgery but not only that, I had torn my meniscus, flipped my patella tendon and tore my MCL. Basically, my entire knee was blown out and in need of complete reconstruction. The doctor wrapped my left leg up in an ace bandage and secured it with a knee brace which had me looking like something out of a cyborg movie. The doc threw in a prescription for Norco's and sent me on my way. This was the beginning of my summer and I now had full access to prescription pills.

The summer of 2014 I spent my time on the living room couch, icing my leg while popping three to four Norco's a day. The pain was usually subsided after the first pill, but my body became addicted. Between mixing my pills with vodka and being alone most of the day except for Jacks daily email harassment, I was becoming a lonely addict and had no idea. My mother continued to work, and Marie spent her summer like every other thirteen-year-old.

I slipped into an addiction that I was completely unaware of until I had gotten sober at the age of twenty-three. Although the addiction to pills only lasted as long as my prescription did; I suffered from withdrawals which included mood swings, nausea, anxiety and depression.

I don't recall hardly any of my summer going into my senior year, but I do remember the one time I saw Jack. Eventually out of boredom and desperation I responded to Jack and told him about my injury. He gave me a degree of attention which I was yearning for at this time. Jack invited me to his home for the afternoon. He said his family would be home and it would be a nice afternoon for me to get out of the house. His family being his wife, her girlfriend and their three kids. I agreed to visit; I didn't think anything bad would happen being around his family. It did cross my mind as to what he told his wife and how she thought it was acceptable that Jack was bringing a sixteen-year-old over to hang out. Maybe he didn't tell her my age or maybe she was just as creepy as him, nonetheless Jack was going to pick me up and bring me to his home in West Sacramento for the afternoon.

I made my way down the apartment stairs on my crutches towards his truck. The moment Jack saw me he hurried out to assist me, the look in his eyes was if he was guilty of my injury. Maybe it was the fact half of my lower body was casted, but he seemed to genuinely care for me or maybe it was the fact he hadn't seen me in months, yet the endearment was deep and obvious in his eyes.

The car ride over I could feel my pain meds kick in which allowed me to relax some. Seeing Jack again was as if nothing had changed prior to our last encounter. Thoughts of what happened between his wife from the last time to now did cross my mind, but I didn't have the courage to ask. I assumed all was well and this was a sincere meet up with pure intentions. As we pulled to the front of his house, he warned me to keep "us" on the downlow. This confused me because there wasn't and hadn't been an us. But I still agreed and went about getting out of the car.

Jack lived in a two-story home in a quaint neighborhood past the rice fields in West Sacramento. It was modest and looked like the everyday suburban, American home, but what was inside of that home I'd come to find out.

Jacks only daughter, Sydney opened the front door for me, "Hi I'm Sydney" she said with a big smile. She was only ten years old at this time and was a splitting image of Jack.

73

She introduced me to her older brother Jack Jr. who was thirteen at the time, the same age as Marie. He wore big glasses and had autism; because of this he was a tad socially awkward and didn't care much for my presence but was interested in my full-length leg cast. Behind Jack Jr. stood Joe who was six years old at the time and was excited to meet me. Unsure if Jack had mentioned me to his children, their familiarity with myself confirmed he did.

The house smelled a little stale, like it hadn't been cleaned in a long time and was hardly decorated as if they had just moved in. I took notice of Jacks office under the staircase and the computer which he sent a flood of emails to me, as well as the living room where Ida sat comfortably with her girlfriend. "Did he bring me here to show me off to Ida or become her new girlfriend?" I thought to myself as she stared me down. Her demeanor was as if she was in high school the way she thought of me as her competition. Not once did I feel her concern that I was in high school and her husband had found an attachment to me. She oozed jealously and showed it through the way she dominated the territory in her living room. To say I felt unwelcomed would be an understatement. To this day, I'm not sure what Jack told her about me or what he didn't tell her about me, but whatever he did tell her made her not to fond of me.

This day was especially weird because the moment I sat on the couch opposite to Ida and her girlfriend, Jack left. Neither of us knew what to say to one another. I didn't particularly know why I was there and neither did she.

I'm still not sure why Jack brought me to his home or where he found the balls to do such a thing, it was risky on his part. What makes most sense to me, is that his own wife was just as trapped and manipulated as me if not more.

Jack eventually returned and had a mischievous look on his face. The reality of me, in his home, with his wife probably got him off in some sick way. It had only been an hour of me sitting in the living room awkwardly when he had requested that I come check out his office. I never knew what Jack did for a living, but I had a hunch it was in I.T. His office was covered in Star Trek memorabilia, The Joker and dust. It was clear he was the nerd I thought him to be. His office was a mess which indicated to me he was working on many things at once but what stood out to me the most was the four file cabinets which stood behind his desk. He explained to me how he used two different computers, one for work and one for play. Both piqued my interest.

I asked him, "What do you do for work Jack? I don't think I've asked you this yet."

Jack replied, "I help companies set up their electrical and Wi-Fi." This response didn't satisfy my curiosity.

"Okay and what do you do for play?" I said with a smirk, attempting to play into his game.

"Well, I use the dark web to trade, sell and buy things I can't get on the regular market. And every now and again I do side work for people who need my help." He says unapologetically and stern.

I had so many questions I didn't know what to ask or where to begin. The way Jack went about delivering information, he knew exactly what he was doing and what I was attempting to do.

"Woah, I wasn't expecting that." I say a little timid.

"What kind of side work do you do?" I ask Jack.

"Well Marissa, if I told you, I'd have to kill you." He pauses, smiles and waits for my reaction.

I refuse to break eye contact or move a muscle in my face, I could feel him trying to intimidate me.

Jack continues, "I can hack anything. Email accounts, home cameras, cooperate cameras, text messages, deleted video and picture, iCloud. Whatever needs to be handled I handle it." He said this with confidence because the intention behind his response was to let me know, I had been and was under surveillance.

I didn't reply to him and resorted to using my knee as an excuse to leave. "I think I should get home soon, my knee is starting to ache."

Jack laughed and grabbed his key from his office desk, "Alrighty then, let's go." He said with an ingenuine grin on his face.

Saying goodbye to Ida was nothing special, she waved good riddance from the couch with a fake smile. This visit had felt like a fever dream but also a warning. It started to make sense as to why Jack had brought me here, he wanted me to see how much control he really had and what he could do. I was scared but, acted as if none of this had even phased me.

On our car ride back to Roseville, Jack was extremely confident. He went on about how exciting that was for him, how badly he wanted me in his office with his wife in the other room and how I'd make a great stepmom to his children; whom I had hardly even interacted with. All of this made my stomach turn. I was reminded of how the relationship between Jack, and I was all for his pleasure. What I initially thought was friendship or someone who genuinely cared for me was just a creepy old man who got his jollies off by being evil to the degree of manipulation, stalking, threats, abuse and harassment.

He made sure I knew what he was capable of and it frightened me. The sun was still up and the heat from the summer day began to cool the closer we got to my home. I couldn't wait to be home and away from him, how this man kept coming into my life at my lowest points was his specialty. I was his easiest prey, and he knew just how to lure me in. Thoughts of how much Jack knew about my life flashed through my mind. If he could see my messages or emails than he for sure knew just when to strike. I felt so naïve for falling into his trap again.

Jack pulled into the handicap parking space outside of my apartment making a joke as to the privilege he had because I was a passenger. Again, he had this way of knocking me down while pretending to lift me up. I reached for the car door handle when I heard the doors lock. I looked at Jack and he stared at me with a menacing gaze as if he was deciding what part of me to physically go after first.

He said, "You are so beautiful, I've missed you so much and I love you more than you know." Then proceeded to grab my face so hard it twisted my upper body in the opposite direction of my lower body. I screamed so loud with pain in my voice; my knee had been jerked and instantly surged with pain.

Jack thought I had screamed because of his kiss and slapped me across the face so hard I pissed myself. This would now be the second time a man has hit me, and my body reacted this way.

Tears rolled down my face and my body shook as I said, "You hurt my knee. I'm sorry I screamed."

I was so heavily conditioned at this point to apologize after being abused that it was second nature to me. Jack looked down and saw the darkened fabric between my legs.

"Oh, wow you are just a kid" he laughed and unlocked the door.

In complete shame with dignity far in sight, I got out of his truck on my crutches. Jack took off before I even made it halfway up the steps. I cried each step I took, feeling completely sorry for myself and damned for the position I was in.

Chapter 8

The One I'd Chase

He gives strength to the weary and increases the
power of the weak.
Isaiah 40:9

The cycle I found myself in was addiction, abuse and apologies. The addiction subconsciously made me feel as if I deserved the abuse. Whether it came in the form of physical, mental or emotional abuse, I felt I deserved it. I didn't know what addiction was, even though I had grown up around it and was now an addict myself; I didn't know what abuse was even though I was experiencing it. I began to think these things were normal and represented love.

The physical pain from my face and knee overtook the emotional pain I had felt inside of myself. It almost felt good to have a distraction. As I write this, I am realizing this is when an addiction to physical pain and self-harm came about.

Once again, after coming back from seeing Jack, I had dirtied underwear which I needed to tend to. This was a lot harder than the first time; I had to unstrap my leg brace while keeping my leg stiff as a board. Sitting on the edge of the tub

I pulled back the velcro from the brace which was so tightly secured; the throbbing pain surged through my leg as the outside pressure had released. Taking a deep breath in and reminding myself "it's just pain you can you do it", I was able to gather the strength and finish undressing my soiled clothes.

I felt the spirit of an elder take control of my body as I cleaned myself with a washcloth. I learned how to sooth myself and take care of myself after the cycle of abuse. I had felt defeated and broken which was a feeling I was getting all too comfortable and familiar with. Some say that this is true for women and men in an abusive toxic cycle; to feel comfort in the process of it all. To an addict like me it became a drug.

After I had finished in the bathroom, my nightly routine of popping a Norco and having a drink began; this felt like a reward. A reward for handling the physical abuse today, woohoo, look at me, aren't you proud? That's the energy, which was behind it, I wore it like a badge of honor.

I laid across the living room couch numbed from the inside out when my mother came home from a date. She looked so beautiful and happy, we bonded most nights in the living room watching shows together; our favorites were Californication and Nurse Jackie. We laughed and cried and talked about my father a lot. We both missed our family but at least we had each other. I never once mentioned Jack to her or what had happened earlier that day. I wanted to forget it all and go on as if nothing had happened.

If the darkness of my truth wasn't real to my mother than it wasn't real to me and that is how I convinced myself that all of this was okay. I reasoned with the thought that, if she can move forward from losing her marriage than I can move forward from today.

The hot summer days alone in the apartment going into my senior year were a daze. The only thing I had to look forward to would be the surgery for my knee. Every day was the same, Jack continued to harass me, and my father was still out of my life for the most part. It was now July and time moved slow, wasted on the couch.

My knee surgery was this week, just five and half weeks after the initial incident. I don't remember feeling nervous or scared for the surgery. The was going to use pieces of my hamstring to reconstruct the ligaments and tendons that were either damaged or completely shredded.

The morning of my surgery my mother had gotten the house prepared for my return. This was my first surgery and I expressed to my mother that I just wanted to be comfortable afterwards.

I only expected it to be my mother bringing me to my surgery but, to my surprise my father showed up with Marie and Harper. They came to show their support which was sweet and all but really, they were just stopping by before they went on vacation. My father had intentionally planned a vacation with my sisters the week I had surgery. Obviously, I wouldn't be able to go, and he knew that. I did my best to ignore his ego and my sister's excitement, but I couldn't shake it. Their presence made me afraid whereas I had been at ease before they had shown up. I felt intimidated by their presence as well. An overwhelming sense of shame came over me as my father looked at my broken body, I felt the judgement and thought "does he feel sorry for me or think I deserve this?"

Now that I am older, I realize his dreams and dedication to my soccer career were now too, broken. Dad was my loudest fan, he loved going to my games and cheering me on. My mother and father both put a lot of money and time into the sport for me and this surgery and recovery seemed like a definite answer that it was all for nothing. I guess it was good for all of us to be there together as I closed this chapter in my life. Sustaining an injury like this going into my senior year meant in no way would even junior colleges scout me out. I had to accept this as the nurses came in to prep me.

My first time receiving an IV drip, the needle gave me relief; I really liked the feeling of fluid pumping through my veins, but the IV drip didn't compare at all to the feeling of the anesthesiologist putting me out. I remember looking up at her as she looked down on me.

"Okay Marissa, I want you to count to ten." The anesthesiologist says. Looking at the fluorescent lights above me and the masked up surgical team around me I began to count.

"One, two, three" My breath became lighter, and I felt softer. "Four, five" my voice began to drift and the euphoric feeling of passing out and losing consciousness began. It was desensitizing and one of my favorite feelings ever. As sadistic as that sounds, it is true. Most addicts have a favorite way of passing out or getting high and this would become the one I'd chase. "six. seven." I was out.

Something about being under anesthesia people either hate it or love it; I loved it. I woke up to what felt like someone from the surgical team pulling the breathing tube out of my throat. All the while I was reminiscing on going unconscious and wishing for an emotional and mental team that could fix me, like the doctor and nurses had just done to my knee.

I was the highest I had ever been in my life as they wheeled me back out to my room where my family waited. They all gathered around me with amazement in their eyes as they looked at my bandaged leg. I still hadn't taken notice of what my body looked like but seeing the expressions on their faces I got an idea of how messed up I was. I couldn't feel a thing at all and started talking like a woman on street drugs. My sisters recorded me in good humor and fun as I mumbled things like "I want asparagus and cottage cheese."

Thankfully that was the only thing that came out of my mouth and not the mound of secrets I had been keeping.

The nurses came in to put another full length robotic looking cast on me. My father and sisters waited long enough and after seeing that I was awake, they were ready to leave.

Mom looked at dad and said, "Can you meet us at the apartment and help me get Marissa up the stairs?"

Dad looked at me and then back to my mother and hesitantly said "Sure, okay, we can do that. I'll see you guys there."

My mother waited with me until the anesthesia wore off and I was ready to get up. Unfortunately, I became nauseous and started to feel the pain of the surgery. Which delayed our departure from the hospital about another hour.

After some time, we were cleared to go home. A nurse wheeled me out to my mothers car and helped me get situated in the front seat. I reclined myself all the way back and did my best to sleep on the way home. Making a stop at the pharmacy to pick up more pain medication and all I wanted was to be home. I was wondering what was taking my mother so long inside, was it the line? Had the pharmacist not filled my prescription yet? Momma was desperately trying to reach my father and didn't want me knowing his phone was ringing with no answer.

She got back into the car with my prescription and said, "Hun your father isn't answering. We might have to do this on our own."

I should've known better, but I thought my dad would've been there for me during this time of need. Which was just foolish because when had he been there for me in the last ten months? As my mother and I pulled into her parking space I begged her, "Please try to call dad again. Maybe he's on his way here."

We called and no answer again. Momma looked at me and said, "Marissa we got to do this together one step at a time okay?"

I was so angry with my father; how could he do this to me again. This felt personal; either he blatantly forgot because his lack of care, or he was intentionally trying to hurt me.

Momma opened the front door and made sure our path was cleared before helping me out of the car. Watching her franticly move made me burst into tears, it was the first time since she and I had been on our own that I felt she was really a single mother. When I imagine my life and think of being a mother, I'm not alone; there's always a partner in mind when I envision this dream. Experiencing this moment with momma broke my heart not just for me, but for her. I know how badly she had wanted and wished for my father to be there, but he wasn't.

"Okay Marissa, you lean on me as much as you need too, okay?" she says. Now, momma weighed about twenty pounds lighter than me with little muscle. She got down in a squat position and lifted me out of the car with all her might. Seventy five percent of my weight was on her while the other twenty five percent were on my crutches. Together we moved strategically from the car onto the pavement.

"Okay that is over, now we gotta make it to the stairs sweetheart, okay?" my mother said.

She reminded me how I wasn't doing this alone, and

neither was she. Using my crutches to make my way from the car to the apartment stairs wasn't easy.

In good grace, she held onto my side and said, "Lets pray before we go up the stairs. God's going to give us the strength." I needed all the strength I could get and replied by nodding my head at my mother.

"Dear Heavenly Father, please give Marissa and I the strength to make it up these steps together. Please be with us and secure her safety. In Jesus name, Amen."

A short and sweet prayer which reminded me that I was capable of anything even while partially physically incapable. With my mother on my left side supporting my inoperable leg and crutches under both arms, we took our first step up the concrete stairs. We didn't quite have rhythm or a strategy at first and I hit my left foot. I cried out loud in pain, but Momma said with passion and strength, "Marissa, you got this. We have to keep going, we can cry when were finished."

Now this may seem insignificant, but this walk up the stairs with my mother was a defining moment in our relationship and faith in one another.

We continued up each step one at a time. Taking a moment in between to breathe and regather our strength. By the time we had reached the last two steps, she and I both were drained and feeling intense emotion.

"Only two more honey, we can do it." my mother said. She began to pray out loud and like magic I was standing outside of the front door.

I said to momma, "I love you, thank you mom for helping me."

This moment gave her confidence from within that she

didn't need my father and that she was capable of much more without him. And just like clockwork, her cellphone rang. My dad had finally called us back right as we had gotten to the top. She didn't answer and continued to help me inside of the house and onto my spot on the couch.

What a whirlwind of emotions this was, but finally being able to rest on the couch with my leg elevated, I was wrapped in gratitude for my mother, her cozy home and the peacefulness she brought upon me. We rested together and went about our life that day without once mentioning my father. I was so exhausted and out of my wits from surgery and pain medication. All of my energy was now focused and dedicated to healing. I had about three weeks until school started up again and I knew I had to get better for my senior year. The road to recovery was calculated for two months on crutches, 6 months of weekly physical therapy and a total of eight months for a full recovery. There was a long road ahead, but as long as I had my momma, I knew I could do it.

Recovering from this surgery meant I had a definite excuse not to see Jack. I could hardly help myself to the bathroom there would be no way he could physically see or harm me. This injury, as much as I had cursed it, saved me from the wolf that waited for me.

But this didn't stop Jacks emails, nothing could stop that. His emails were always six to twelve paragraphs long; how someone could put so much energy into someone who paid them little to no attention baffled me. I wondered how much of his day he spent obsessing over me or where he found the time to do so with a wife and three young children. But Jack had grown into the ultimate stalker.

During my recovery, I spent most of my time on my phone, scrolling through Instagram and Facebook while watching TV, all the while being high on Norco's. My mother was working all hours of the day; it was summertime so anyone I could call was usually out doing a summer activity with a group of friends. It was lonely, but my consistent silent use of pain medication, marijuana edibles and alcohol made the time go by. Momma never questioned me much. I think she was at peace knowing that I was just at home. She really gave me a lot of grace and space; whether that was intentional or not, she didn't pressure me to do much with my day. Now I know this sounds like bad parenting but instinctively she knew I just needed to be still, which I was.

Alas, I had no father figure which I needed desperately during this time. Jack was a phone call away, but I couldn't trust him. It was a gamble, and I knew I didn't have the same feelings or wants as him so it would be a waste of time for the both of us. But he had persisted so much as I went about my own life.

That was until I began to receive a flood of texts and emails from random numbers and addresses, again. This was the first time I had gotten a message from "a group of people" who remain anonymous to this day, yet my instincts told me it was Jack. The message read:

"Stop hiding behind the bullshit you've created and face us. We know about Jack and you aren't innocent hoe. We will expose you to your family and classmates if you don't start acting right hoe!"

Now, this left me with so many questions. But I knew Jack had ultimately pretended to be a group of people threatening to blackmail me. I hadn't slept around at my high school, but I was deemed a rather loose girl because of the drama that unfolded the beginning of my junior year. The word "hoe" held weight to me, and Jack knew this.

I also questioned how he or they or whoever would go about exposing this because it was still a fact that I was only sixteen and he was now thirty-eight. So, whatever this was, it was a scare tactic, this I knew for certain. But my curiosity took over and I replied, "Who is this?"

The response took hours which led me to believe that whoever was doing this had a second phone and wasn't brave enough to bring it out on command. Hours had passed and in that time my thoughts and emotions went back and forth from being scared to pissed and sometimes even saddened that yet again I was dealing with a bully.

My phone buzzed with another message from this anonymous number, "You don't need to know, hoe. We know about you and what you did to that old man. You best learn some respect."

This response was almost comical, how dumb did Jack think I was? What human in their right mind would defend Jack and then proceed to tell me about respect? To see his desperate attempt at backing me into a corner to message him was pathetic. But my ego stepped in and I messaged Jack on his legitimate phone line. I attached a screenshot with the messages and wrote:

"Hi, so apparently the word is out about you and I. I'm getting harassed by this random number. Do you know anything about this?"

Jack replied immediately and said, "Hey Cheeks, it's good to hear from you. How's your knee? No, I don't know anything about this. They're reaching out to me too! I thought this was you."

His games were beyond me. I knew he was attempting to fool me, and I knew in the depths of my soul that he was behind it. Jacks' response made my stomach turn, I wanted to throw up right then and there. How far would this man take this sick manipulation? Knowing he had access to multiple accounts, numbers and had no shame in posing as a third party was extremely disturbing to me.

I left Jack and the "anonymous" number on read, but both Jack and this "anonymous" number continued to bombard my cellphone. The delusion of it was something I could hardly wrap my head around, to the point were I was at a loss for words. Jacks resume of crazy was getting longer and longer. I became numb to his antics; I didn't freak out or get scared, it just became "this is Jack being Jack."

I had learned to live with this absurdity and the only way I knew how to cope with it was through shutting my mouth, drinking and using.

This new game Jack started made me feel angry; at what lengths is this man willing to go? Would he ever give up and move on with his life so I could move on with mine?

Chapter 9

A Promise Kept

When pride comes, then comes disgrace, but with
humility comes wisdom.
Proverbs 11:2

My senior year of high school was around the corner.
While most of my peers were going in with a significant
other, some type of plan for life after high school or maybe
even just a good friend; I was going into my senior year with
a casted leg, a stalker and a substance abuse problem. It is true
in life when they say all things, good or bad come in threes.
Although, the sound of my 'senior year' was enough to get
me excited about life again to a small degree.

Unfortunately, I don't remember a lot from my senior
year, whether that is credited to my substance abuse, trauma
brain or simply because it was eight years ago; there isn't
much I remember from this year at all, except for a few key
things. The first being I turned seventeen just a few days
before school started. My mother's brother-in-law, Steven,
suggested we go to a Chinese restaurant up in the hills.
Without my knowing my mother had invited my father, but he
failed to show up due to a new girlfriend he was engulfed

with. My father's pattern of not showing up became a thing I had gotten used to nonetheless it all hurt the very same. The kindness of the people who did show up for me, like my Uncle Steven and my mother was just enough love I needed that day.

Coming into the age of seventeen had a freeing energy around it. Although I was still considered a child, I felt bold enough because I was "almost an adult" and whatever I did (in my mind) good or bad, I could blame on my age. Maybe freeing isn't the right word, I think daring suits this version of myself better. I recognized this about myself and decided I was going to live it up this year and forget about the last year. With physical therapy and weight bearing exercises added to my agenda for my knee, each day I gained a little more confidence as I shredded remaining pieces of physical trauma and remembrance.

I had gone into my senior year as if I was already graduated. I coined the nick name "Party Hardy" for myself and began hanging out with new groups of people who wanted to experience this time in life the same way I did. They say you shape into the five people you hang around the most. I quickly adopted people's personalities and habits as my own. This was what I did to fit in. And soon I regained a new status amongst my classmates which was a party girl. I liked the way it sounded, I liked the idea of being involved in what was going on socially with my peers and I liked that I now had drinking buddies.

To put it nicely I became 'loose' my senior year; from my thought processes to the way I handled schoolwork, it was all one big game to me. I began to completely lose myself. Becoming superficial in the way I treated myself and others became a personality trait. My mother, so innocently, was just happy to hear I had friends, but what she didn't know was what kind of friends I had due to my many lies.

What my mother saw from the outside was that I was busy and happy. The times I told her I was studying or working on group projects, I was really hanging with boys or out running amuck with my girlfriends. I had learned from my experience with Jack how to live two lives and that being manipulative meant I had control over both narratives.

I was about halfway through my senior year when my mother began to date a new guy. I was really happy for her, she seemed happy to be exploring something new. Most weekends she would stay at her boyfriend's house which was about forty-five minutes from where we lived. Some weekends Marie and I would tag along but for the most part I had the apartment to myself, which at seventeen was a big deal and I took full advantage of it.

Once I learned my mother's routine, I mentioned it to my new girl friends at school. One girl suggested to have a lingerie party at my mother's apartment, and I thought that was the coolest thing I could do. I didn't have any lingerie and hadn't thrown a party of any kind without the supervision from my parents, but I thought why not?

Walking into school Friday the news was out and by lunch time my peers were all coming to me for details. I felt important and wanted, which was something I hadn't felt in a long time from my peers. So, I ran with it and invited the 'coolest' kids.

After school I went home and hung out with my mother as she prepared to go to her boyfriends for the weekend while also retrieving any information I could about her weekend plans. She had asked me what kind of plans I had for myself and I replied, "just a sleepover with some friends."

She believed me; up until this point she had no reason to not believe me. As she pulled out of the apartment gates my girlfriends from school were pulling in. All of us in our lingerie with enough alcohol to supply a bar, we were ready for the night. I didn't have a head count of how many people would show up, but I mean how many people could fit into a two-bedroom apartment anyways? Well, word had gotten out not only to my school but a few others and by 10pm my mother's modest apartment had thirty half naked boys and girls in it. It was fun at first as people drank, smoked on the balcony and took plenty of selfies but then a few rowdy boys showed up.

I'm not sure if it was the fact that I had 30 people in the apartment or the window breaking but the cops came knocking at my door. I was intoxicated and didn't know exactly how to deal with this situation, but I made sure to tell the officers my mother was gone. The officers shut down the party and called my mom out of dead sleep. The disappointment and frustration in her voice I could barely process because of the alcohol but this was the night my mother had seen another side of me. Needless to say, I was on restriction the rest of my senior year.

I had taken all the blame and shame for this incident and was the only kid who had gotten in any kind of trouble from their parent. I went from being one of the coolest kids back to a lame within seventy-two hours. But I didn't care. I chose to be oblivious and go about my partying like nobody's business even if that meant I did it alone.

Being on restriction the last semester of my senior year led me a lofty boredom which made me feel the need for some excitement. Mentally I chased a high I was all too familiar with which was Jack. We hadn't spoken to each other in sometime and I was lonely, I knew he would be there for me. I mean he hadn't left me alone yet, I had multiple unread emails from him; I thought he must be waiting for my response, right? He was. Reaching back out to Jack was different this time. I knew what I was getting into and thought if I was just 'fun' then he would be too.

I saw Jack almost every week the last semester of my senior year. Whether he took me out to eat or took me for a drive it was enjoyable. Because I had come with different energy and didn't question Jack, he was happy. What I hadn't realized is he began to really fall in love with me, something I still didn't want or desire.

The week of my graduation Jack expressed his excitement for me; not because I was graduating but because I was soon to be of legal age. Jack professed his ideas of us being soulmates and how on my eighteenth birthday he wanted to get me a car and an apartment, he went on about leaving his wife and family for me. In a sadistic way I found comfort in this because I didn't have a father to provide for me or even one who wanted me in his life to the extent of dropping his past. But the terms and conditions that came with it were the fact that I had to be in a committed relationship with Jack. I truly didn't love him back and knew this was a dangerous idea.

My graduation night Jack was waiting for me. His plans were to take me out and celebrate which I didn't want, I wanted to be with my graduating class. If it weren't for my father and Marie attending my graduation, I probably would've left with him, but they were my excuse to not see him. He didn't take to this to kindly and lashed out at me. Luckily for me, this was now my excuse to cut him off for good, and I did.

Highschool hadn't been easy for me, a lot had happened. By the grace of God, I found hope from making it out of the mess which was my junior and senior year. I felt the next chapter of my life coming in; I didn't have a plan nor any idea of what was to come next, but I knew in my heart no matter how bored, lonely, hurt or down on my luck I was; I'd never reach back out to Jack. It was a vow I kept to myself and have stood by to this day. Although he continues to stalk, harass, blackmail and threaten me; I haven't caved back into his games and manipulation. This is my first time speaking about Jack and although the trauma still follows me, this is healing me in ways I had never imagined. Being able to finally speak my truth from a healed, levelheaded place is an act I never could've imagined for my sixteen and seventeen-year-old self.

This chapter is dedicated to her. She kept a promise to never go back and that version of myself kept it. Today I uphold the promise of speaking my truth.

Chapter 10

Pacific Heights

Above all love each other deeply, because love
covers over a multitude of sins.
1 Peter 4:8

Graduating high school, making a vow to myself to
never speak to Jack again and completely healing from my
knee surgery all came in one swift motion. Although I felt
free in so many ways, I had felt the aftereffects of all this
trauma which included the ongoing addiction, learned
behaviors and a constant dance between disassociation and
derealization. I had myself a strong cocktail of issues but
chopped it up to what post-graduation felt like. I had no plans
for what was next or what I wanted to do. It wasn't until two
weeks after graduation that my mother asked me, "So, what's
your plan?" I hadn't even thought of college or getting a job
at all.

I replied, "I don't know Mom. I really have no idea."
At this age, I hadn't traveled outside of California and grew
up with the notion that I was just a California girl and that
was the best and only thing to be. What the world had to offer
was nowhere in my mind.

My mother replied with the kindest tone, "Why don't

you come work for me at the deli? I also found a trainer up there we could go to."

When I graduated high school, I was overweight, out of shape and broke so this seemed like a sure first step in the right direction.

"Okay Momma, when do I start?" I say.

"Well, today is Friday sweetheart so how about Monday." My mother replied.

I'm sure there could've been a multitude of other options for me but looking back this was something I could handle. An honest job, making and serving food, Monday thru Friday, 8am-5pm working for my mom and then going to a personal trainer from 6pm to 730pm. The structure alongside dignity of this new routine brought a sense of personal fulfillment and purpose as well as bridging a closer relationship with my mother.

The deli she managed was about an hour away from our home. Rising in the early morning with her I learned how to start my day with tea and rouge. This was my first real job, so I followed the lead of my mother's actions. She taught me how to meal prep lunch, snacks and dinner because "money gets wasted when you eat out."

What became my favorite part of this routine was the hour drive to work. My mother and I listened to new music, old music, had therapy sessions for one another and enjoyed the scenic views together; it was as if we had created an evolved version of what delivering bread early in the mornings felt like. We became best friends this way. Although, when we arrived at the deli which was situated in-between a canyon across from the county jail and right in the middle of all thing's country loving, momma became 'manager'. She made sure to get her point across that I was no different than any other employee and it's important to work hard and follow the rules as others do.

My first few days of work were challenging, but I learned quickly and was soon working at the same pace, if not faster than the other employees. I took pride in my job and enjoyed every second of it. Making my mother proud made me happy. During my lunch breaks I swiped through the dating app Tinder for fun; mainly looking for new friends. Nothing had come of this yet, but I stuck to my routine of swiping on my lunch breaks. After a long day of working on my feet, it was time to clock out at 5pm.

The trainer my mother found was an exit away; we changed out of our work clothes and into our workout clothes before making our way to the gym. Momma had signed us up for a bikini competition. Something my mother had done in her early twenties was now a sport she wanted to pass onto me. I was thrilled about all of this. The positivity of working, exercising, getting closer to my mother and the routine of getting out of the house was great for my mental health.

By the time Momma and I got home we were exhausted, but still found the energy to prep and prepare for the same routine the next day. This was our thing, and it was a good thing, her and I. On the weekends I began to go with her to her boyfriend's home which was secluded in the hills on a beautiful property. I had my own room there and enjoyed being in nature. Something about being surrounded by trees and overlooking the valley was special. Mommas' boyfriend was a funny guy who adored her and made her happy; her happiness inspired me to find my own happiness.

Life began to have a sense of normalcy and following my mother's footsteps in healing was good for me. Although, I didn't particularly acknowledge the work I had been doing myself; I still made it a point to move on from my past. One Sunday morning, I had received a message on my dating app from a guy named Andre. Andre and I spent the afternoon, evening and late night chatting online; he was nerdy, interesting, kind, worldly and had a softness about him I hadn't felt before. The connection between Andre and I felt familiar; like connecting with a friend after many years of separation. Between my new job, workout schedule and the routine my mother and I had; Andre seemed to fit into my life like the final puzzle piece.

The following week Andre and I chatted on the phone during our lunch breaks, on the way home from work and every night once we were both in bed. He had an effortless swagger within him which I accredit to his New York upbringing and foreign background. Andre was not like anyone I had met before; he worked for a tech company in San Francisco and seemed to enjoy it. But even he, was restricted to the confines of the rat race. Our conversations were more than "what do you like to do?" we talked about our traumas and what we wanted to be.

It had only been three weeks since Andre and I had begun talking and we were ready to meet one another. At the time, my mother had found an apartment big enough for Marie, her and I. It was three bedrooms and had a lot more privacy. This new space felt like a real home whereas the last apartment was riddled with Jack and my father's energy. We had a fresh start. Andre wanted to meet and so did I but the move from one apartment to another pushed us out about another week.

Things hadn't worked out well for Marie when she was living with my father, he left almost every night or wouldn't come home for days due to his obsession with his new girlfriend. Thus, my mother had worked tirelessly to get us into this three-bedroom apartment; a place we could all call home.

Once we were all settled, I felt it was a good time to

meet Andre. I reminded twenty-three-year-old Andre how I was still two months from turning eighteen, but he paid no mind to it and felt we should meet. I didn't care either, I guess old habits die hard.

Friday, June 19th, 2015 Andre drove from San Francisco to Roseville which is about an hour and thirty-minute commute. I told my mother I was going camping with some girlfriends for the weekend and I'd be back Sunday evening. After my experience with Jack, I was fearless but also ready to get out of town. Andre seemed safe, trustworthy, kind; I wasn't entirely worried about him in the first place or maybe I was desensitized.

The afternoon Andre picked me up I made sure to walk a distance from my mother's place with my weekend bags in hand as if I was waiting for a bus to come by. I did my hair, makeup, dressed in some rock rival jeans and wore a cute top that accentuated my breasts and waistline. I waited for him on the side street for about ten minutes when I noticed him; he drove a white four door Volkswagen with blacked out rims and tinted windows. Andre sported glasses which reminded me of Clark Kent, a New York Yankees ball cap, and Jordan's; head to toe he was a New Yorker. I hadn't realized how tall he was either. He stood about six feet three inches. He was thin and tall, as if he had been stretched out, but I liked it.

Andre smiled from ear to ear when he saw me and gave me a big hug, "Hi, it's really good to finally meet you." He says.

"It's good to meet you too, you're so cute." I say with a big smile.

Now, at this point we were just friends, but it felt as if we were already each other's mates. Andre took my bags and put them in the back seat before opening my door. He was a

100

gentleman, he didn't try to kiss me or make a move, Andre was simply happy to see me. This moment feels like a time capsule to write about; it was my first taste of freedom and with someone who I felt so deeply connected to from the start, I felt my soul coming back to me.

Our hour thirty-minute drive from Roseville to San Francisco was everything I could've imagined and more; we listened to music (he had great taste), we talked about our family, what interests us, what made us who we were and where we wanted to be. Of course, I didn't dare share anything about Jack or what trauma happened the fall of my junior year of high school.

I loved riding passenger in his car, he laughed at my jokes, and I laughed at his, we held each other's hand; it was perfect. By the time we made it to the San Francisco bridge, the sun was setting, and the city looked like something out of a movie. I hadn't really been to San Francisco on my own and this was a complete fairy tale for me. Andre pointed out landmarks and seemed thrilled to have his own gem in a big city.

He lived in an apartment building on top of a hill in Pacific Heights which is one of the more expensive neighborhoods in San Francisco overlooking the ocean. We parked underneath the building and went up to his apartment on the top floor; the building was old, but modern. I could smell fragrance, marijuana and cigarette smoke in the elevator. His apartment door was tucked in the corner of the hallway and it appeared to be a small unit, but when we stepped inside, his place opened like a grand ball room. Floor to ceiling windows with a great view of the city.

Andre brought my bags to his bedroom which looked as if maids had cleaned the space just hours before, but nonetheless it was neat. I got a good sense of the person he was, organized, tasteful and lively. Unfortunately, he had some stomach issues and had to use the bathroom right away. I'll never forget the slight embarrassment he had when he excused himself to have a bowel movement. While he was gone, I made myself comfortable by unpacking my bags and changing into sweats. When he came back into the bedroom, I was on his bed scrolling on Instagram. To my surprise he had confidence as he joined me on the bed. He asked if he could kiss me, and it was magic the moment our lips touched. Then he looked me in the eyes and said, "Can I eat you out?" referring to having oral sex with my vagina.

I had never experienced oral sex before and was a bit shy because, "What did I smell like?" "What did I taste like?" I had no idea, but I was on a high of luxurious freedom, so I said, "Okay you better do a good job" and he did.

I remember taking account of where I was, who I was with and what was happening in this reality. My body relaxed and I allowed myself to enjoy it. But I'm not sure who enjoyed it more, myself or Andre. It was as if he had been waiting for this moment his whole life. He stayed in-between my legs for about forty-five minutes, it was romantic as the sun went down and our environment went from day to night. When I had finally reached orgasm and he came up, there was a union made between us. Andre proceeded to tell me how beautiful I was and how my lady parts were perfect in every way, which I was happy to hear especially after the amount of abuse I had been through; this was healing and why I feel it is important to share.

Andre made dinner reservations for us at a nearby five-star restaurant and said for me to get ready. I put on a new dress and did my hair in a side bun, light make-up and heels. I had never been on a fancy date and didn't know what to wear or what to expect. Having no expectations, I feel is what made the night even better.

I can't remember the name of the restaurant, but it was

intimate with candle lights and hideaway seating. Growing up I was never taught how to order off a menu and my pallet was basic. Andre ordered the goat tacos, I ordered plain chicken. His choice in food opened my eyes to how experienced he was. He ordered both of us a Margarita. This was my first time drinking at a restaurant. Andre didn't care about rules or the normal flow of things in life, he did things on his own accord, which I admired.

Holding hands across the table and sipping our drinks while we waited for our food, he says to me; "I see a lot of potential in you." No one had ever said anything like this to me before or at least in a long time.

I blushed from my cheeks to my feet and said, "What do you mean?"

Andre replied, "I see how things between us could work out for the best because of the person you are."

Now, this shocked me. What did he see in me that I hadn't seen in myself? I so badly needed that validation and reassurance more than I knew at the time. My longing daddy issues, trauma with Jack and complete loss of worthiness and innocence the last two years sucked the life out of me. I had no sense of myself so when Andre said this to me, I truly had no idea what he meant. But if I were to be the perfect mold of a girlfriend than this idea of who I was to him was something I was willing to live up to.

The rest of the weekend we went about our time like two love birds. Andre gifted me some New York attire; a Yankees ball cap and t-shirt. He claimed me as his that weekend, but this was still my first relationship, and I hadn't realized how serious Andre was about me. I think I inspired Andre in some way to do what makes him happy because shortly after we had met, he quit his job. Why? I'm not for certain and I'm not entirely sure what he had planned to do next, but he was free and so was I in many ways. We both needed each other's spirit during this time in life.

Andre brought me back Sunday evening like we had planned and there was nothing more special to me than our drives. We did this all throughout summer every Friday he would pick me up and every Sunday, he would drop me off. I'm not sure Andre knows how special those car rides with him meant to me. At this time in my life, Andre meant everything to me.

Part Two:

The Heart

Chapter 11

Hoping for More

Cast all your anxiety on Him
because he cares for you.
1 Peter 5:7

From June 19th, 2015 up until the week of my birthday, August 6th 2015, I saw Andre every weekend. During the weeks I continued to work and exercise, my life felt perfect in every way. Except for the fact that Jack still bombarded me with texts from random numbers, pretended to be other people to get my attention while sending horrible vulgar emails and stalking me daily via the internet.

I knew I was developing strong feelings for Andre and I'd be eighteen soon, and when that time came, he and I knew we wanted to be together openly and officially. But I couldn't fully commit without resolving this situation with Jack. Although Jack, somehow knew about Andre and began to stalk his social media. It was insane to me that a man with a wife and three children made it his life mission and obsession to harass me in hopes of me giving into him.

I thought ignoring Jack was the best solution and had hopes of things dying down, but unfortunately, they only got worse. Although I worked out of town and hadn't told anyone where I was working, Jack still found me. First, he sent roses to my work and the letter attached to the bouquet was written in French. Something I took hard notice of because I knew he had never spoke French, in fact his wife, Ida, was Mexican so if anything, he'd speak some Spanish. Andre however spoke French and sometimes in our text messages he would say something in the language. Did Jack have access to my texts? This petrified me. The note translated to:

"Dearest Marissa, I love you so much and cannot wait for your 18th birthday. I have a big surprise for you and cannot wait to share what I have been working on for you. Please reach out to me soon so we can discuss the details. Forever yours, Jack."

Oh, how I wanted to crawl into a hole and die right then and there. I hated this man so much and how dare he say these things. In no way did I want anything from him and the horrible reality that he signed his name off with "forever yours" made my stomach turn. I wanted Jack out of my life for good. I was terrified by the fact he knew my work address, I was terrified he wrote the letter in French and I was most terrified of what this surprise was.

Although Roseville PD had failed me once before I now had proof of Jacks creepiness, so filed another police report. The next day I skipped work and made my way to the police station. Again, I waited hours before finally meeting with an officer. From the start, the officer didn't believe me nor take me seriously. The officer said to me that this is all an allegation because "flowers and surprises are no real threat." This angered me because how is a gesture like this from a grown man not alarming? How are my feelings not valid? Being rejected by an officer discouraged me yet again. In my mind if the law wouldn't believe me, no one would. Would I have to just accept that this perv would be in my life forever and there was nothing I could do?

I hadn't shared any of this with Andre, he was so

innocent, kind and sweet. My feelings for him were growing exponentially, but there was little integrity on my end because of this big secret I kept.

Two weeks had passed since Jack had sent me the flowers and letter when he decided to show up to my work. I'll never forget, I was working the front counter when I saw him approaching the glass doors. My heart skipped a beat as I watched Jack enter my place of work. He was incognito just as he was, the day he raped me at the Fairfield Inn. He approached the counter while taking off his black sunglasses as if I didn't already know it was him.

"Hi Cheeks, what's good to eat here?" Jack said.

"My name is on the nametag." I said while pointing at my nametag which read, "Marissa".

"All of our food is good here." I continued to say in hopes to get this interaction over with. I dreaded my mother coming out of her office and seeing this odd interaction with a man she had never seen before. A lot of our customers were locals, so to see an out-of-towner in the restaurant meant that my mother would most likely strike up a conversation with him in good faith.

Jack leaned down towards the counter with his elbows on my register and his back end sticking out like a promiscuous girl. He said to me in a low stern voice, "You mean you're not on the menu?"

This sent shivers down my spine, but I stood my ground and replied, "I ask that you don't lean on my register and please give me some personal space. Now I can take your food order, or you can leave." Jack pushed himself back up to a standing position and had a menacing grin on his face.

"I was in town and stopped by for a bite to eat, I guess

the customer service here isn't so kind to its patrons. I'll be on my way out; I hope you enjoyed your flowers. I'll see you next time, Cheeks." And Jack walked slowly towards the door with his head down. As he was stepping out, my mother came out of her office.

"I saw the cameras, who was that man?" Momma said in a concerned voice.

"Some creeper, I had to ask him to leave." I replied to my mother.

She asked about what he said to me, but I couldn't bare to tell her. So, I began to cry and go into full on victim mode. Although this was an act at first to get me out of trouble, the tears and fears became real. I hadn't cried like this since the first time he raped me. My anxiety levels began to rise, and my hands began to tremble. My mother took me back to her office so I could have space and pull myself together.

This incident was incredibly triggering and emotional for me. So many factors were in play now; he knew where I worked, he made it a point to drive almost two hours from his home to where I was to see me, and he had no problem doing this on camera. Jack was not afraid, which in turn, made me more afraid. It showed me how he very much was still involved in my life whether I was okay with it or not; he would be a part of my new life on his own accord. I knew I couldn't work at this place anymore and if Andre can quit his job, so could I.

I wanted to wait until after my 18th birthday to quit which was now only a week away. I knew once I turned eighteen, Andre and I would be official and open about our relationship which meant the possibility of us spending more time together. The week couldn't have gone by any slower. I was looking forward to finally getting my driver's license which meant all the freedom I desired as well as getting out of town and away from Jack. Turning 18 was also a little scary because I had no idea what 'surprise' Jack had in store for me, and this was a day he always fantasized about; me being of legal age was the highlight of Jacks perverted mind.

I had no real plans for my upcoming birthday except for Andre coming to my mother's apartment. I told my mother about Andre and she was happy for me, unfortunately she relayed the message to me that my father would be making an appearance which honestly, confused me. Dad and I had no relationship at this point and him coming to my birthday felt fake. But we can't always get what we want and aside from what I want, the controlling men in my life were to do what they want, however they want, whenever they want.

Alas, the day of my 18th birthday came, August 6th, 2015. I woke up to a flood of "Happy Birthday" messages, but my only concern was going to the DMV for my driver's license appointment. In the state of California, you can get your driver's license without having a permit after the age of 18. I passed my test which was most important to me that day. Andre was excited too because this meant if I got a car, I could drive to see him now. The rest of the day was filled with drinking and smoking plenty of weed. My mother had planned a dinner at the apartment and invited a handful of my friends to come over.

Andre arrived about thirty minutes before everyone was getting ready to leave. I had already packed my bags earlier in the day and awaited his arrival; I was thrilled to see him.

Meanwhile, Jack was blowing up my cellphone in hopes of seeing me, his attempts became pathetic. Sometimes I wonder if Jack ever thinks about how much of a perverted loser he was during this time of his life.

Andre came in to meet my mother. She was pleased to meet him, as were my friends and Marie. Things were going great, and we left before my father arrived.

Andre and I made our way to San Francisco with the biggest smiles on our faces, it felt so incredibly good to be free with one another. I had no idea what was in store for us next except for the simple fact of us having one another. Andre made it clear on our drive that I was his girlfriend since the day we met, June 19th. I remember feeling surprised at this because the whole time I figured he was just courting me. But in his eyes, I was his, from the moment we met. This gave me butterflies beyond belief. This day was as if my whole life had now officially changed.

When Andre and I got back to his apartment in San Francisco he had my birthday gifts waiting for me. First, I opened a card which was tropical themed, and it read:

"Happy Birthday babe! A ticket for me, a ticket for you, we're going to Hawaii."

Andre bought us two tickets to Hawaii for my birthday. I had never been gifted something so grand and special and this was just what was inside the birthday card. What was in the box he wrapped up made my heart warm. I had always worn Andres watch when we saw each other and he gifted me my own, it was beautiful and shined in solid gold. I couldn't believe my eyes. How could a twenty-three-year-old kid afford something like this?

Andre put the watch on me and as our watches had synced so did, he and I. Time and synchronicity became necessary for all what mattered in my life, and Andre mattered. But how long would our time last? Some say time is an illusion, some say time is what binds the past and the future, but I define time as the most mystical yet obsolete part of life. In time, I've created memories, love, and sweet moments like this one. The one element of time I've come to learn is, times consistency was the only part of my life I could count on.

Meanwhile, Jack's time had run out, but he continued to message me the entire night of my 18th birthday. I ignored the messages like I had been but the one which stopped me in my tracks of celebrating in San Francisco with Andre was a photo of the Bay Bridge. He had knowledge of me being in the city and again I asked myself, how? Jack was like black mold I couldn't get rid of then and still to the present day behaves this way. Underneath the image of the Bay Bridge wrote:

"I left my heart in San Francisco."

Jack was and remains pathetic to me; how he tried to mask his extreme narcissism, stalking, perverted actions and delusional mind with romance is almost comical.

Understanding this made it easy for me to move on with my life as I knew that this would be a skeleton in my closet until Jack left me alone for good. I had finally found the strength to say no and move on, I had gained wisdom to know what was right and wrong, lastly, I found joy and confidence inside of me to begin a new life. And I wasn't going to let anyone get in the way of that.

Andre and I fell more in love each day, but the secret of my past still haunted me. I knew I had to confess this mess to Andre, which wasn't going to be the easiest on me due to the fact I hadn't told anyone close to me, anything about this man.

It was now fall of 2015, and I was spending most of my days and nights at Andres home. We weren't officially living together but there were a greater number of days and nights in San Francisco than anywhere else. Our love was sweet and adventurous, but I couldn't be fully transparent with Andre; I always had my phone facing down because I feared what messages would pop up. And after a couple of months, I couldn't stand it. I needed to share what was eating me alive inside.

I told Andre everything; from how Jack and I met, my fall from grace after the rape and even the lingering messages I was still receiving from him. I told him everything and I'm not certain his true feelings about this bombshell I dropped, but Andre was there for me. He listened and was empathetic towards me and the situation.

Telling a twenty-three-year-old guy this type of information was easier than I expected and I'm not sure if it was his age or immaturity, but it didn't seem like much of a big deal to him. We had the conversation, and it didn't bring us further apart or closer. Nothing came out of it except now he knew. I wasn't expecting Andre to save me, but I was hoping for more.

It seemed as if no one was educated on sexual abuse or assault up until the "Me-too" movement went viral in 2017. Women and men opened up about their experiences with sexual assault, abuse and rape. Andre had no knowledge or reference of this type of stuff because for one, he had never been a part of it and two, no one openly talked about this before.

I, myself, didn't understand what it meant to open up and share a piece of information like this to someone else. Even after the multiple attempts, I still hadn't grasped the severity of it all until years later.

Chapter 12

Red Eye

Above all else guard your heart, for everything
you do flows from it.
Proverbs 4:23

Consequently, my relationship with Andre developed a victimhood-saviorhood dynamic. Andre seemed to have had life figured out between the stability within and without of himself. He nurtured me into a free spirit and gave me stability again. Our relationship continued at a rapid pace, I spent most of my time at his apartment with him. He took me camping, on hikes, out to fancy restaurants and taught me how to shop. The concept of time and money became distorted in my mind because there was never a question of the two. I truly did love Andre, but the subconscious dynamics of our relationship and connection stemmed from trauma and codependence. I had all the red flags and he seemed to have none. My naïve 18-year-old self truly thought that life as a 23-year-old was this easy; now that I am 25, I understand that this wasn't exactly normal.

Through the fall and into the winter of 2015, Andre and I were glued at the hip. My mother's side of the family began to know him good and well; he came to family gatherings and we celebrated Thanksgiving together. We were a solid couple, which I think shocked almost everyone that I had found such a perfect human. Shortly after Thanksgiving, Andre had invited me to join him in New York to meet his family and spend the holidays there. Now, I had no knowledge of what it meant to live in New York or spend a month there on holiday, but he was willing to pay for it all. Andre paid for almost everything in our relationship, so this was normal at this point. Andre grew up in the Hamptons, where his mother and father still lived. His parents had been divorced for as long as I had been alive. I really didn't understand what it meant to own a home in the Hamptons.

We flew Jet Blue December 20th, 2015 from San Francisco International airport to JFK on a red eye, Andre figured this was best, so we could sleep on the plane then enjoy our first day together in the city. I was nervous for many reasons, including the cold winter weather, and meeting his mother. Andre described his mom, Adele, as an eccentric woman who was a little wacky with a French accent. For some reason this all intimidated me because I hadn't met anyone perceived to be like her before. But I was soon to meet her as she was the one who would be picking us up from the airport. She was right on time, pulling up in her navy-blue Audi.

She parked her car and jumped out like a little kid, "Hello Andre! Ahhh Marissa, so sweet to meet you beautiful girl!" she said with the biggest smile.

Adele had an unconventional fashion I had ever seen on someone before, granted she was an artist in New York city; I now had a sense of where Andre got it from. We packed up the car with our luggage and set forth through Queens past Brooklyn and into the east side of Manhattan just a couple blocks above Times Square. Adele and Andre were gracious hosts in explaining where we were, landmarks and what kind of people lived in the areas. Seeing New York for the first time wasn't only overwhelming but, showed me a

115

whole new side of life outside of myself, trauma and what I came from.

Life wasn't all bad growing up, my parents instilled everything valuable and built the foundation of character for me at a young age to end up in a grand place like this. In fact, if it weren't for the versatility and diversity, I had become adapted to, I wouldn't have been built for this new experience. Reminiscing on this saddened me for a moment; I almost felt guilty for going about my own way without my parents. It was as if the distance had created a deepened connection to my family. We had never traveled together or talked about any destinations outside of Sacramento except for colleges; to be out on my own in one of the biggest cities in the world hit me like a truck. Or maybe it was the fumes and excitement of New York City, but I became nauseous. I texted Andre this and he replied jokingly, "it's my crazy Belgium mothers driving."

I giggled at his response; he had a way of making fun others so casually I hadn't hardly seen harm in it.

Slowly but surely, I became like Andre throughout this trip. I admired and loved him so deeply, I followed his example. His mother took us to her place which was on the top floor of a 32-story building overlooking Turtle Bay. The door man helped carry our luggage up to her apartment. When Adele opened her door, the home filled with visceral, abstract and intuitive art pieces as well as furniture that suited her style. Things were put together so perfectly it almost seemed simple and effortless. I really hadn't seen any of this as wealth just a part of who Andre, and now Adele, were.

Andre and I unpacked and rested a bit in the guest bedroom; it was still early in New York city about 8am which is 5am California time. I wrote in my journal about my experience thus far which included how the flight was, what it was like to be in New York City and Adele's driving, which

116

Andre and I had been joking about earlier. Andre and his mother wanted to catch up in conversation while I wanted to catch up on sleep. She had a full day planned for us which included seeing Times Square and Madison avenue, all of which were decorated just like the movies during the holidays.

Andre had me completely smitten; I hadn't really been drinking like I used to, and lifes' troubles were nonexistent in this reality. Being with him was as if life was set in stone. He always had dinner or lunch reservations ready, knew what we should wear, what time our driver would be waiting for us and especially always had music ready to set the tone. Andre was the ultimate romancer and planner, which left little room for me to think for myself.

Adele and I locked arms while shopping through the prestigious galleries and brand name store fronts on Madison Avenue while Andre took our photos. I had just met this woman, but she took me under as if I was already her daughter-in-law. The kindness and openness felt all too surreal, especially when we made our way to Times Square. Andre had taken me by hand, and we led the way; at this moment I became aware of the energy shift in Adele. She wasn't involved in my personal space because she wanted to be, she was involved in my personal space because she had to be. Her envious energy towards me because of her only sons' admiration for me felt most uncomfortable but, was covered by her ability to smile and laugh with us.

Our night came and went and my first day in the big apple was much more than I could've imagined. Although when we got back to the apartment Andre and I were not ready for bed; I wanted to see the local nightlife and he had friends in the area he wanted to see. Adele stayed at the apartment while he and I left. We went to China Town and all around that night, drinking, schmoozing and enjoying whatever the city had to offer. Meanwhile Adele was back at the apartment going through my personal journal. I didn't know this at the time, but she said her reasoning for it was to be closer to me.

The following morning, things were different between Adele and I; she knew more about me than I had ever told her, and Andre had fallen more in love with me as if the essence of New York City at night casted a spell on him. Alas, it was our time to go out to the Hamptons which was about an hour drive up the island. Adele was driving and out loud I had mentioned something about my stomach hurting from the drinks we had the night before. Adele looked at me through the rear-view mirror and said, "Are you sure it's not from my driving?" and in that moment, Andre replied to her in French, something along the lines of "You'd only know this from looking through her journal."

After the two of them fussed about it in a language I couldn't understand, she apologized to me. I couldn't help but wonder why the theme for adults in my life all surrounded a lack of boundaries and respect for me. The rest of the ride was very awkward to say the least.

Andre tuned the silence with some music, and we continued on our way to Montauk, where his father lived, and Adele's second home is. He had always talked about how his father lived a much more modest and simpler life than his mother. Pulling into the driveway I saw that to be true, yet the estate was still so effortlessly finished I had a sense that meeting Connor, Andres dad, and his second wife Laura would be different. The sendoff with Adele was a bit awkward, but nonetheless we made our way into the snow-covered path which led to Andre's childhood home. Standing at the door tall, dark and handsome was Connor. Meeting Connor was like meeting an old friend, he and I connected immediately.

Andre, Laura, Connor and I sipped wine next to the

Christmas tree while learning all about one another. Laura had a daughter of her own and two grandchildren, who joined us almost every night for dinner up until Christmas. Life seemed so perfect; I had a family of my own now. It still hadn't hit me what type of life he came from because it was just who he was, and I truly loved Andre. It was now Christmas Eve and we had fallen so deeply into one another, we talked about marriage and a future. Now, we were only dating for six months at this point, but together we pictured a life led by the example of Connor and Laura who were two love birds in themselves.

That was until Jack had emailed me dozens of times with Andre CC'd. Jack was completely delusional and expressing this through email, threatening both Andre and I while also professing his love for me. The email read:

"I have waited. I have grown. I took my time to be a better person and you used that time to get closer to him. You have left me with nothing to cope with and offer no form of encouragement and given what I know right now I doubt this will never happen. The only time I have ever gotten a response from you is through negative actions which I hate doing but it is caused by you. My poems, my dreams, my stories all false. Marissa, you truly are an evil person, you did this to me. I hope Andre sees this. She fucked me over for you and she'll do it to you. Just her nature. Merry Christmas."

Seeing this email brought a chill and sickness to my body all too familiar. Again, I was reminded of how narcissistic Jack was. I was terrified of what Andre's reaction might be. But this was the night where Andre became aware of how serious this burden I had been carrying was and how real of a threat Jack had been to me all these years. Together Andre and I read the email and discussed it. His calm and collected attitude towards Jack allowed me to be calm.

This wasn't the fairytale Christmas story, but in an

odd way it was for Andre and I. He saw me at my lowest this night and in saviorhood fashion, comforted me until I didn't feel the pain. It was deeply disturbing how Jack had emailed us both, but Andre had a confidence about this situation that he and I would be just fine. We talked about staying out of Sacramento and creating a life away from Jack's territory. It was almost romantic how this went from my problem to "our" solution.

Andre and I spent three more weeks in New York; going to parties with people from old and new Hollywood, to building snowmen with his nephews; we continued to live our life as if Jack had never existed. Although the psychological effect of this led me to be a drunk almost every night. Andre was now twenty-four and the both of us had yet to learn how to hold any type of composer while consuming. This led to many sloppy and forgotten nights, but nothing a little coffee and morning rendezvous couldn't cure. Andre and I were so blind to the ways we chose to cope and recover as a couple. Every time we replaced communication with a vice it was as if we added straw to a camel's back. But the reality is that you don't notice when it is one grain or one missed conversation at a time, you only notice when it is finally broken.

We were both naïve to the circumstances of our relationships dynamic. And Andre still had secrets, the biggest one being where he really came from. It wasn't necessarily my business, but it did explain a lot of the lifestyle he and I lived. Andres family had brought the biggest American soda brand from the states into a European country. I had a completely different vision of who I was with but now the dynamic between us shifted. I loved him for who he was, and he loved me for who I was, but at the end of this who were we? This was now a journey we had set out on to discover and our reasoning for commitment within the relationship. Blindly, Andre and I had stepped through a metaphysical portal of self-discovery unaware of what was coming on the other side.

Chapter 13

Feminine Honey

For everything in the world—the lust of the flesh,
the lust of the eyes, and the pride of life--- comes
not from the Father but from the world.
1 John 2:16

One thing to be true of my late teens and early
twenties was the notion that most of the things I had gotten
myself into I didn't know I was in until I had gotten out of it
or gone through it. Happenings seemed to transform from the
words on my lips into a reality of great proportion. I had
learned how to forget instead of forgive. I became extremely
unaware yet subconsciously relied on habits and adaptations I
learned, but most of all I had no real foundation to my being
anymore. A huge portion of who I was, was riddled in trying
to be something I was not due to a lack of self-love and a
misconception of where true love stood. With this, lived an
underlining substance abuse problem arising yet again,
unhealed trauma and a deep insecurity. All of which I had
been unaware of; distractions whether they come in the form
of a person, pattern or how I chose to live in the present
moment withdrew me from my center.

Nonetheless it was now 2016. I had made it out of my hometown, was with someone who was just as lost as me; the ignorance was all to blissful. The lack of real communication between he and I became filled with things, places and substances in the form of alcohol or marijuana. That was until our trip to Hawaii came along.

April 20th, 2016 Andre and I were on a plane headed to Honolulu. I had no responsibility or idea what this vacation had in store except, for the two pills containing ecstasy I packed in my contact lens case. Andre had no idea I brought drugs on the airplane and I didn't necessarily think about the consequences of doing so. Andre and I both smoked marijuana before our flight and were as happy as we could be leaving San Francisco for the Hawaiian Islands. Not a care in the world for either of us. We'd be staying at different five-star hotels across three islands, excursions to fill our days and dinner reservations paired with partying to do at night.

We landed in Honolulu, got "laid" as the locals call it, received our luggage and drove to our beautiful beach front hotel in our rental car. I felt like a princess the way he treated me, life was incredibly good and incredibly easy. It was as if God was rewarding me for making it out of the dangers of my past. We made our way up to our suite and jumped on the bed like little monkeys; neither of us could hardly believe that this was real. To be young and experiencing life this way was magic. To feel the ocean breeze dancing on my skin while looking into the eyes of my first love as the sun set on one of the most beautiful islands in the world was a moment I'll never forget. These moments in time allowed me to forget any type of reality which my brain was imprisoned to while also healing my soul.

I was still clueless about what kind of money it took to make this vacation happen, but I did know where it came from. My only contribution was my smile, and the drugs I brought along. Shortly after we unpacked, we made our way to the beach in search of a restaurant to eat at. Of course, we went shopping at the most expensive stores; funny thing is I didn't know how to 'shop' at this point in life and Andre took pride and pleasure in picking things for me to try on. It was a romantic gesture in my eyes. I was lucky to have experienced a relationship in this way, but nonetheless it was a double edge sword soon to impale me.

How did I attract a young man like this? Now that I am twenty-five years old, I realize how rare it is that a twenty-four-year-old kid was willing to do this for me when I was only eighteen.

We ate fish tacos and kept it causal for dinner our first night. As we got ready to go out to the clubs in Waikiki, I prepared our pills. They were in perfect shape and ready for consumption. I sat down on the bed with my hands behind my back and asked Andre to sit down next to me.

"Babe, I have a surprise for our first night." I say. Now Andre wasn't accustomed to me giving surprises and by the look on his face I could tell he was smitten by my gesture already.

"What kind of surprise?" he replied with a sweet smile while looking out our window.

"Close your eyes and put your hand out." I say.

He puts his hand out and I place one pill in his hand while putting the other one in between my top and bottom teeth. He opens his eyes, looks at the pill and then looks at me, then looks back down to the pill.

"I wasn't expecting this, what is this?" Andre says.

Taking the pill out of my mouth I say, "It's ecstasy,

have you done it before?"

"No, not until tonight. Let's have a good time babe." Andre says.

"I intend to." I say with a mischievous tone.

Andre and I took the pills and washed it down with a bottle of water followed by a Hawaiian travelers' favorite alcoholic beverage, Mai Thai. We made our way to the club before the pills kicked in. By the time we arrived at the club and heard the flow of music, the drug crept on us gently as we danced towards the middle of the floor. I wore a short pink dress with heels, I can't remember what Andre wore, but he and I both danced the night away. So much that the locals took notice of our good energy.

A girl, with tan skin and curly-sun-kissed hair approached me. She and I danced in the middle of the dance floor as if no one was watching. Mid song she grabbed my hand and said, "follow me."

She brought me to a bathroom stall and said, "I'm Morgan."

I replied, "I'm Marissa. What are we doing in here?"

She responds, "Have you ever done coke?"

Shocked, I respond, "What's that? No, I haven't."

Morgan pulled out a tiny bag with contents of white powder that shimmered a bit when the light hit it just right. I had never done cocaine before and wasn't exactly sure what to do, what it was or what to expect, all I knew for certain was that I was open to it and had no problem following this strangers lead. For all I knew at the time, it could've been meth, heroine or fentanyl but I wasn't aware of what those drugs were at the time, let alone cocaine, which Morgan was now preparing for me.

With the tiniest spoon I had ever seen, about the size of a finger nail she fixed me a heaping dose of white powder.

"What am I supposed to do now?" I ask.

"Cover one nostril and snort it in with the other." Morgan says while laughing at my naivety.

With one big snort and inhale I ingest all the contents on the tiny spoon. Immediately a satisfaction and rush I had never felt before, but instantly craved, came over me. I liked it, a lot.

"Can I do another?" I say to her.

Morgan laughs and with a big smile she says, "Oh you like it? Yeah, you can."

I was experiencing my first coke high, it was everything I had wanted out of a high. I didn't think about anything else outside of myself and this tiny bag. I was instantly hooked to this drug; from the secrecy of it, to the process of doing it, the way it made me feel nothing and everything instantly. I loved it.

Morgan and I left the bathroom and I guess I came out a little more loose than usual because Andre immediately rushed me with concern. I told him what I did, his main concern was where I had been the last ten minutes. Nonetheless, Morgan and I had bonded far more than just drug buddies, she liked me, and I liked her. By the time the music had stopped, and the lights turned on Andre and I invited her back to our hotel room not realizing she was with two men.

Looking back this could've been a very dangerous situation considering we were on drugs, had no idea who these people were and not to mention the fact our cash and belongings were lousily sitting out in the hotel room.

All five of us went back up to our room a short walk from the club, not a clue about what we were going to do when we got back; that was until the two men took off their shirts. Morgan got completely undressed while Andre and I stood there in disbelief. Looking at Andre, looking back at our guests and then back to Andre I begin to get undressed. It was almost 3am and my drugs were nowhere near wearing off, but my clothes were.

The two men, Morgan and I began to kiss and feel up one another on the bed; I had no idea what Andre was doing or if he even cared. It just felt right. But in an instant, Morgan got up from the bed stuck her hand out again and said follow me. I thought we were going to do drugs but no, she wanted alone time with me. On the bathroom floor she laid down and signaled for me to join her. I had never been with a woman before or even knew what to do, but I knew what I liked... so I did just that to her.

Andre and the two other men must have caught on or maybe their curiosity brought upon the action of them barging into the bathroom as I was between her legs. But that didn't stop me, I had my first taste of the sweet feminine honey and in no way was I going to let men ruin that for me or her. All three men continued to watch as Morgan and I transformed into one orgasmic tantric being. This moment was the peak of my high. It felt so damn good to be free without a care in the world.

As Morgan came into full climax, she must have realized there was an audience because soon after her cum was on my lips and tongue she got up from the floor and looked almost embarrassed as if she hadn't intended for this

126

happen. Maybe it was regret and shame, but we both put our clothes back on. Andre was in the middle of saying his goodbyes to the men, but not before I had gotten their Instagram's. I figured, if we had already seen one another naked, we could be friends, right?

They left the hotel room one after another in a single file and as much as everyone else felt awkward, I hadn't. The high of experiencing sex with a woman as well as two different drugs for the first time had lit a fire inside of me. This took Andre back a bit, he had never seen this side of me. We didn't exactly discuss anything about what had just happened; another example of how we had no communication skills whatsoever.

Andre and I went to bed with two big ignorant smiles on our faces. We still had seventeen days between Honolulu and two other islands; this was only the beginning for us.

The following days I learned how to surf, we swam with sea turtles and even rode horses to a beautiful waterfall and in the same day went zip lining and topped it all off with a helicopter tour of Maui. Life was good and we were tan, there's something to be said about being young and in love for the first time. You do what feels right, not thinking of other possibilities except for the here and now. Which is beautiful and delicate although when heavy drug use and alcoholism are a part of it, the relationship becomes revolved around quick highs, withdrawals and unstable come downs. The foundation becomes weak; insecurity, jealousy and most of all ego disrupt any type of intimacy, including communication.

The high of our trip lasted into the summer, fall and winter of 2017. I had become sunken into my new addiction with cocaine, completely dependent on Andre financially and ego ran me ramped. The combination of all of this led to Andre leaving me one night. The day he left I felt like I was

127

dying inside. I called him to talk, but when he answered he was already halfway down to Southern California. He had packed up and moved himself far away from me. This moment was utterly shocking for me, it was as if my whole world was gone. I cried for days in my mother's arms; another man I had depended on, trusted and loved abandoned me because of me. I was reminded of that familiar feeling of abandonment, feeling ultimately unworthy and thrown away.

After about a month of sorrow, I decided it was in my best interest to fill myself up the only way I knew how to. The perfect opportunity for me to let loose was the night of my younger sister's 16th birthday party. January 27th, 2017 Marie and her friends were at the house which gave me an excuse to have my friends over. It was about 9 PM by the time I was drunk, smoked out and had already consumed plenty of cocaine. It was the first time I hadn't thought about Andre since he left.

By 1 AM, I was blacked out and alone with two other boys in my room, I was under the impression they were waiting for a friend to pick them up. But I was wrong. Both of them sexually assaulted me, one even putting his penis inside of me while the other took photos and videos. I remember not being able to move, I remember both of them touching me and I could barely feel it because my body was so numb from the cocaine.

My friend Ray had walked in. Ray was shocked by what he saw and closed the door, leaving me with the two boys. Ray didn't know what he walked in on and him being gay, as he says, made him feel intimidated and uncomfortable to say something to two straight men. I'm not sure how much time had passed after that because when I woke up I was alone. My nose and head hurt, and when I sat up to reach for water, I felt the familiar pain of rape harbored in my vagina. In a panic I reached for my phone and saw about 30 photos and videos of the boys assaulting me.

I felt completely impure and taken advantage of, I remember seeing my almost lifeless body on video and mourning the piece of me that died. I remembered how Ray had walked in, so I called him to try and piece together what actually happened. Ray said he didn't know what was going on or what to do and seeing what they were doing to me traumatized him. Ray went on and apologized, telling me he would be by my side the whole recovery process even mentioning if I were to press charges and needed a witness statement, he would do that for me. I thought long and hard about this, but the reality is, just over two years ago the police believed the molesting pervert over me and I didn't think I would get any type of justice this time either.

I decided to confront the main attacker who was involved, we went to the same junior college. He was on the football team and I was on the soccer team, so we commingled quite a bit before the incident and had a lot of the same friends. I was looking for some clarity and comfort, but that would not be the case. It happened to be after class and before practice in the parking garage when I approached him, shy and nervous. He had no clue how I was feeling about the situation. And his energy was very much standing tall in ego.

I said, "Hey Brian, can I talk to you about the other night?"

He responded, "There's nothing to talk about." This shook me. I wasn't ready to sweep this under the rug like everything else, so I got defensive.

I replied with an attitude and exclaimed, "Well there is because you raped me, and I was drunk!"

That wasn't very smart of me to say, he became very loud and with each word seem to have grew towering over me. He spoke so fast telling me how I was a dumb slut who didn't know what she was talking about, to keep my mouth shut and stay away from him. It was as if he repeated all of my past traumas in a few short words. I ended up apologizing to him; that was a mindfuck. Up until this point in my life, men had used, abused, harassed, threatened, assaulted, blamed and downright acted as if they controlled me.

Did I attract this energy? Did I deserve this energy? As time went on, I began to believe the words that had been said to me and what happened in my life because I thought I deserved it. My feeling of worthlessness and insecurity grew greater than any other feeling I had known. I became emotionally and mentally ran down. In desperate efforts, I called Andre on my way home from school, I needed him. Alcohol and drugs weren't doing it for me especially because I had schoolwork, practice and class taking up my drug use time. So instead of leaning on substances I leaned on my ex. And in victimhood fashion, I told him everything that happened since he had left and in saviorhood fashion, he empathized with me. Reassuring me of things I didn't believe to be true of myself, but I took them as a pretty lie I could hold onto. Hold onto because I had nothing left inside. So terribly I wanted to crawl in a hole and die, and this is would be my first attempt at just that.

Chapter 14

Are You a Believer?

Whether you turn to the right or to the left,
your ears will hear a voice behind you, saying,
"This is the way; walk in it."
Isaiah 30:21

The day had past sunset, and I made my way to the Fair Oaks Red Bridge. I sat in my car contemplating how I would jump. It wasn't until I saw that the bridge was clear that I found the confidence to take my fateful walk to what I thought would be my death. I hysterically cried from the car until I found myself looking at the shallow water below the bridge. Right before I was getting ready to climb over the railing, a woman came out of nowhere. She must've been an angel and with three simple words she snapped me out of it.

"You're not okay." She says.

Instantly, she made me feel seen and validated. I continued to sit on the bridge and cry. I didn't know better, and I believed I was an impure, worthless piece of meat in capable of fixing myself. Because I lacked the ability to speak my truth, I also lacked the ability to properly heal and do the right thing by setting boundaries with myself and others. A dark cloud of shame, regret and guilt followed me for a long time after that moment on the bridge. Feelings of being a failure, even at killing myself rushed over me.

There's a Seinfeld episode where Jerry Seinfeld says, "The thing I don't understand about the suicide person is the people who tried to commit suicide, for some reason they don't die and that's it. They stop trying. Why don't they just keep trying? What's changed?"

Now, I love dark humor because it helps me look back on moments like this a little easier, but when I heard this joke, I understood how he and many other people really don't understand.

I'd like to answer him now. First, the State's 5150s you, which is a 48-hour hold in the psych ward because you're a danger to yourself and/or others. But if the local police or hospital doesn't know, then the second reason and most common is because for someone to get to the point of wanting to kill themselves, it is extremely painful, physically and emotionally. They feel so completely worthless, like a failure and undeserving that the only way to get relief from their suffering is to be gone from this earth. Now, the suicidal person has probably tried all kinds of drugs, alcohol to the point of blacking out, self-harm, dangerous behavior and an extreme sex drive to self-medicate their suffering. Because at that point in life, they didn't know better. What changed in their mind wasn't much more than feeling like a failure, feeling stuck on earth and in their own body, as well as, being rejected from the other side. A few thoughts, feelings and moments I've experienced myself.

Jerry goes on to ask, "Is there life any better now? No, in fact it's much worse because they found out one more thing they suck at and that's why these people don't succeed in life to begin with. They give up too easy."

You know, he's not wrong. Suicidal people do give up easily because they've been a victim to their own suffering for

132

so long and hadn't learned how to become a fighter. Although, the first time I heard this joke wasn't until after my third suicide attempt and rehab, it did make me laugh. But only for a short minute. The laughter felt programmed. No, this isn't a Jerry slander moment, just an example of how we've been conditioned to not take people suffering from suicidal ideation or trauma seriously and when it is taken seriously, we get thrown into the state ward or heavily medicated. When in reality, we needed to be seen, heard and validated. This growing number of suffering humans need family; supportive family and friends without being judged. I believe the woman who simply said to me, "You're not okay" was brave enough to speak a truth that my family and friends couldn't or wouldn't.

The taboo around saying to someone "you're not okay" has caused a lack of integrity and a lack of leadership in our homes, relationships and community. It is not just the suicidal, depressed alcoholic that isn't living with integrity and suffering. It is the people who witness it and don't say anything. This isn't to say others don't try to help, but most of the time when they do it's to little too late.

I mention my loving mother which she was, yet she so badly wanted to believe everything was fine. But even if she did say something would my shame, regret and guilt allow me to speak my truth? No, it wouldn't.

I know this to be true because as I write about my personal experience, I am discovering things about myself during these past events. The suicidal person isn't interested in offing themselves. They are interested in the death of ego, shame, regret and guilt. They want an ending of an identity they unknowingly built for themselves, inflicted by imprinted trauma, neglected past life lessons, basic nature/nurture adaptations and habits. From the moment a human is born, their precious and pure being is soon to be affected by these things. In a beautiful way, it makes us who we are if we can

133

overcome it, for I wouldn't be writing this book or have any sense of my essence if I didn't. No matter who your higher power is, he gave us all one thing, free will. And with that, we make mistakes, learn lessons, experience seasons of life and become who we are meant to be.

My experience in this lifetime has been nothing short of feeling misunderstood, layered in complexity and unique in self-discovery. The true self of my being. I wouldn't be the 25-year-old woman I am today without these experiences. I know my 20-year-old self is proud of who we became. Although more of this story will unravel between the ages of 21 to 24. I want to acknowledge and apologize to my younger self for the harm and suffering I put her through. I want to remind my younger self that we are safe now. We are worthy of a good life.

The following months after my suicide attempt were blurred by countless drug and alcohol blackouts. I had befriended Sacramento's favorite cocaine dealer, but in his eyes, I was his cash cow and arm candy. I used him for drugs and a good time, and he paraded me around downtown Sacramento like a trophy. There were multiple times in my addiction that he got me so out of my mind and tried to make moves. I was always able to make a break for it, except for one time.

This day I hadn't used cocaine for a couple of days and was feeling the need for it due to withdrawals. I had no money in my account and an empty nose, but I knew how I could supply myself. So, I called my dealer. He was always happy to hear from me and came to pick me up right away. On the car ride from Roseville to Sacramento I was getting high off his supply. I rode shotgun while he delivered powder around town for a couple of hours. He parked his car and asked to eat me out. The thing about cocaine is, it makes you incredibly horny, at least for a woman. So, I allowed him to. In a sense, this day I traded my body for drugs. During my

134

addiction there have been a couple of times including this one where I had crossed a line, a line I never thought would've been crossed. By the time I got home, my come down off the cocaine brought upon the realization of the trade I had made.

The combination of the come down and the mental realization I had, caused my moods and emotions to swing very hard and intensely. I remember feeling angry, disgusted, used, empty and impure. But as a good addict does, I hid the truth and covered up my lies. No one knew this side of me, and I hadn't truly recognized it until many years later either. People in my personal life are just finding out as they read this book. I was thought of as a party girl, easy and a good time, but the secrets I've kept hidden inside of me for all these years, my closest friends and family will be learning about for the first time. I had most certainly lived two different lives. My first life being the one that everyone saw and my second life which was this. Dark secrets I kept to myself for almost a decade, even in romantic relationships.

Spring of 2018 Andre and I began to reunite. There was no way I was going to tell him about the truth of the life I had been living. He had spent the last year traveling with a group of people facilitating spiritual retreats using psychedelic medicine and sacred plants. The summer of 2018 Andre began a road trip from New York to California and by fall of 2018 we were living together.

His time apart from me gave way for a delusion of how he could fix me because I was special, kind and sweet, but looking in the mirror I never saw that... I was no longer that.

In a second chance at love with him, my character was built on victimhood, ego, drugs, alcohol and manipulation. Let's not forget about sex to replace any real communication or true love. I did have love for him, but I don't believe I was actually in love with him.

135

Now this is where things get interesting.

In saviorhood fashion and wanting to help my now, 21-year-old self, Andre consistently spoke, acted in and thought in the spiritual teachings he had learned while traveling with his prominent tribe and spiritual community. His energy was different and harder for me to manipulate. We fought and argued over just about anything because of this. I was very stubborn and rebellious and put up every reason why I didn't want to be involved or crack open my subconscious and super conscious. My number one reason being that I would have to face my bullshit and take accountability.

It had been two months after my 21st birthday when he decided it was time for me to take the leap whether I wanted to or not. He and his good friend, Chacho, attended my college soccer game. At the end of my game, they both greeted me with big hugs and smiles, Andre said he had packed a bag for me because we were going to a weekend getaway in southern California. This wasn't unusual especially for Andre to plan something and pack my bags. With excitement, I got in the 1997 red Land Cruiser. We were about two hours into our car ride when Andre confessed that this wasn't one of our normal weekend getaways, and that he was taking me to the tribes' spiritual retreat. So badly he wanted to fix and help me. And so badly I wanted him to just let me be.

This was the same retreat and people who opened Andres subconscious and superconscious through the traditional use of plant medicine and integration of light. This light being the same light that shines on our shadows and darkness, exposing our inner child, essence, soul and trauma. I pleaded and cried so badly for him to turn around, but he had already paid the $1,500 it cost, and in his words, I needed it.

There was no changing his mind. This spiritual weekend retreat is guided by mystics, psychics and healers who administer a sacred plant I will not name, but is referred to by the community, tribe and people who have done it as the Adam and Eve plant. Why? Well, when Adam and Eve ate the apple, they became conscious human beings. Their first conscious thought led them to realize that they were naked, which lead to Adam and Eve covering up their naked bodies.

The Bible says God came down and asked them "How did you know you were naked?" And thus, the conscious, mindful human was born. This plant has the power to unlock not just parts of the brain and subconscious, but past lives, the shadow side, reveal to you your inner child and take you to realms you couldn't just imagine, touch or see in this dimension or reality.

I was about to experience this and give my will to a much greater force. We arrived at a large cottage style home in the middle of the woods around 10 pm. The only light that shown was coming from the moon. I was still in my soccer uniform and had a horrible attitude as I entered what would be one of the most spiritual settings I had ever known. At this point, I was completely trusting Andre and Chacho that I would be safe. I stood aggressively and insecurely in the doorway.

Out of the left side of the house stood a man about six-foot-one, dark skinned and dressed in all white. He asked me to come into the bedroom, I had absolutely no idea what the fuck was about to happen at this point, but I had so much adrenaline I was prepared to fight if I had to. I entered the room, which was candle lit. He was sitting on the bed with a woman also dressed in all white, when he asked me to sit in a chair at the foot of the bed.

I could hardly see the woman's face, but she radiated a beauty I had never experienced before. The man and woman I am going to refer to them as Judah and Leah. Judah looking into my eyes from across the room… I could feel him looking right through me. As if he could see past everything done to me and right into my heart and soul. He was looking at my dark side, searching for my lost spirit.

I must've looked so miserable because that was the first thing he had pointed out. I'd hardly known this man for three minutes and he was not into small talk one bit. He told me how I lacked integrity, stability and responsibility. He went on to say I was totally living in ego, victimhood, denial and deceit. That I was an expert on self-sabotage and judgment because of unresolved abandonment issues. And lastly, he went onto say, "I am not your father."

An anger arose in me. How is this strange man going to tell me who I am and why? I know who I am, so I thought.

Judah told me during this weekend session, that I was going to go deep within and purge until I found the key to my essence. At this point, I had felt so completely exploited and afraid by this man I began to cry, which at this point he then pointed out the victimhood that I carried deep inside of me for far too long. Judah said to shower and change into my white clothing because the rest of the group had already started downstairs. Started what? I thought to myself. I was soon to find out.

This spiritual tradition is centered around an ancient, sacred plant used by a tribe in the heart of Africa for many centuries and it was now in my life for a reason of healing. Dressed in all white, I was ready to begin my ascension to a higher level of consciousness by descending down the wooden steps that led to the basement. The candle lit basement had enough light for me to recognize that there were 11 other people laying down on the floor, the 12th cot was waiting for me. Before I settled into my resting position, Judah asked me to kneel.

He then asked, "Are you a believer?"

I replied, "Yes."

He gave me a spoonful of what tasted like earth in the purest form. I had a liter of water next to me and swallowed the spoonful whole. In this moment I knew that I had ingested this sacred plant. What I didn't know was how much I was given in comparison to others or how long it would take for me to feel anything. I remember laying my head back and saying a quiet prayer to God for protection.

At this point, I didn't know where Andre was, as he was holding space for this weekend session. Holding space in a setting like this is a responsibility; space holders are of service. Not only to the man and woman facilitating the session, but the participants. Space holders at one point have previously experienced the plant. Because participants are orally purging, having out of body experiences and possibly speaking with light beings from passed, future or higher realms, space holders are there to keep that energy balanced, as well as clean our puke bowls. Space holders are on the same amount of this sacred healing plant, but because they are not in the circle of light, they do not experience the ceremony like the participants on the floor.

Although the basement candle lit room was filled with about 20 people I had felt alone. Feeling alone in a crowded room resembles feeling like a stone stuck on the bottom of a riverbed, a feeling all too familiar. Questions like, "Is my existence recognized? Am I contributing to the life around me?" come up. As a sunken stone, you watch the water run down the flowing river, but as a stone is positioned stagnant so was I in this moment. What my stone-self failed to recognize was that maybe I was positioned in the bottom of this figurative riverbed to find the meaning of grounding. My fears and insecurities were far too strong in this moment to do anything other than give my will to God, follow my faith and trust my guardian angels. Closing my eyes, focusing on my breath I begin to drift into a deep meditation.

They played music in the room which consisted of the harp and drums, but what took me by surprise was the recordings of an African tribe singing in a language I did not understand. Their voices carried me into a deep lucid dream. The plant was now working. The plant becoming one with every cell in my body, it began planting seeds for my journey. With each breath, my lungs filled more and more, and with each exhale I fell deeper and deeper into the meditative lucid dream sleep. Still conscious enough to hear the beautiful tribal music and harp symphonies consuming the room, filling each soul as we all began our journey.

The harp is known throughout religion and spirituality as the instrument of truth. The harp is depicted in art surrounded by angels in cathedrals, murals, movies and paintings. If there is a group of Angels, there are harps around. The music was so soothing yet exhilarating. I still to this day have never heard anything quite like it.

My body was still, my mind was still, but my spirit was off for a journey to another place. The plant opened my super and subconsciousness, third eye and soul. The visuals and downloads I received on this journey I'd like to go into depth with now.

Chapter 15

Mayas Veil

I will instruct you and teach you in
the way you should go; I will
counsel you with my loving eye on
you.
Psalms 32:8

My soul started out by traveling to a realm as pure and white as heavens clouds. An owl approached me; this owls soul belonged to my father. My father in the form of an owl had a cloak of protection hanging from his beak. Looking into my father owls' green eyes, he motioned for me to turn my back to him. At the top of my spine, right on the axis, he secured this cloak over my shoulders. The cloak was made of Stardust and when the light hit just right transformed from translucent to a kaleidoscope of colors.

Father owl said to me, "This is your cloak of protection. Do not be afraid, you will suffer, but we would not know love, will or nirvana without this first. Your heart needed to break in order to grow."

He flew off before I could say anything. This first vision woke me out of this realm and back into the ceremonial room. Sitting up to write down my experience felt like I had a weighted blanket on my chest. I turned to my side, opened my journal and began to note my experience. My vision and strength in the physical realm were completely distorted and weak. I drank some water and laid down on my cot. It amazed me that I saw my father in the form of an owl even more so, that he was the one to bring me protection after many years of feeling unprotected by him.

The music still filling the room loudly, rocked me back to the spiritual realm like a newborn child in their mother's arms. My sense of time was completely gone when experiencing the plant. I do not know how long it took for me to fall back deep into the spiritual realm, but it seemed as if it was instant.

Back in the spirit realm, in a white space, with my cloak of protection on, I realized I was back in the place I had just encountered my father owl. This too, amazed me, I was brought back to a place I had just awoken from. Any other time I have dreamt I've never been able to go back to the place I had just come from. But, I was on the plant now and I was exactly where I was supposed to be along my journey. I didn't know what the sacred plant had in store for me, but I did know that it had a path that I was to continue to embark on. Consciously wondering what to do next or what was coming next, I wandered around this plane, pure white abandoned space.

Coming into my vision I began to focus in on what appeared to be my childhood home. About 20 yards in front of me, the home was sitting in clear view. I began to walk towards my childhood home and the closer I got to it, it started to open like a doll house. I'm not sure if you, the reader, can imagine what that looks like, but its opened faced. My childhood home looked just as I remembered, all the furniture was the same, even down to what photos hung on the wall. The more I looked around with wonder of it all, I began to feel waves of sorrow, abandonment, and deceit. My

142

childhood home became bleak. I heard it crack right down the middle, separating the left and right side of the house. Splitting into two, the separation was so terribly loud and disruptive, followed by an eerie quietness. I knew exactly what this had represented.

A loud cry came from one side of the split, broken home. Crying, afraid and alone in a highchair I see my younger sister, Marie. This vision brought me back to my earliest memories of life. Marie was born when I was 3 ½ years old. To me, she was the most perfect baby. Marie looked completely opposite of me, she had light skin, colored eyes and blonde sun kissed hair. When Marie was born, she was now the baby of the family. I always adored her though. She was so cute and sweet, filled with so much energy, purity and life.

Although Marie and I were still considered the babies of the family because Joan and Harper, our two older sisters were five years older than me and only 14 months apart between each other. By the time Marie came into this world, our world, roles within the family had already been established. Where I stood was in the middle, not so much a big sister and not really a little sister anymore. This caused a power struggle between my three sisters and I. An unspoken power struggle, for attention and survival in our home.

Although in this realm which was my current reality, seeing Marie carrying such pain and suffering while sitting in her highchair on one side of the split home got to me in a way I've never considered before. Her life was all about being brought into an established family. She had no ego or expectation, only pure love and joy for having a family. But when our parents split and the two eldest were gone and my mother and I sought safety; Marie was left in a broken, lonely, fragile home. The sense of family and togetherness had disappeared in the blink of an eye for her. The image of her that I was currently seeing in this realm was something I had never thought of or felt, it was a trauma I unknowingly carried as well as she.

Awakened by this revelation I wrote down in my journal, "Be the big sister Marie needed, be the big sister, I needed."

After this realization and revelation, I begin to feel as if knots were unknotting from the depths of my belly. The energy and force were so strong, I physically purged. In my opinion, this is one of the best parts of taking the plant. Physically purging the trauma that you've been carrying inside of you is one of the absolute best feelings I have ever felt. I do not condone purging on a regular basis, but in a spiritual setting under the guidance of ceremonial practice, it is necessary.

Sitting up and crawling to the front of my cot; the emotion, burden, guilt and regret exited my body with every heave, with every droplet and projection of my vomit. That release is something I have never experienced before. I had previously felt release from crying or screaming in the past, but this purge was about 10,000 times more relieving than any emotional release I had experienced prior to this. I couldn't control the amount of water releasing from me. In a bowl wider than the width of my body and as long as my shin bone, I filled up ¾ of my puke bowl. It was as if I could feel subconscious entities leaving my body. After this glorious purge, I held my head over the bowl. Looking at my own vomit, was like looking in a mirror. All the things my soul had been tainted with now lay still in this bowl.

Now back in my resting position lying flat on my cot, it was time for the group to decode our experiences. All twelve of us shared with the group and the facilitators. Each person had beautiful revelations at the same intensity as I, if not greater. Judah helped each of us decode our out of body experiences. He was very direct and to the point, no bullshit.

144

Leah, who I had met in the bedroom just before descending the basement steps into the ceremonial room was also on the floor with me. She was six months pregnant at the time. Her way of interpreting her experience was unbelievable, beautiful and frightening. After we all shared what the last hour and half was like for us, Judah distributed another dose of the plant.

This time in the form of a capsule. I was given six capsules. The capsules were easier to swallow than the first spoonful of raw plant. There was no taste of earth. Laying back down, the music started up again. It took a little longer for the pills to become activated, but I listened and focused in on the tribal music. My senses were extremely heightened. I began to notice that the recording they were playing was actually a recording from a live session with the natives in Africa who harvest this sacred plant and created the spiritual practice and ceremony of using it. I noticed laughing, babies crying, people purging in the background of the drums and harps playing. How interesting and comforting I thought.

This observation revealed to me how in touch Judah and Leah were with the plant, practice, tribe and spirituality of it all. To have a recording of this which would last all forty-eight hours of ceremony must have meant that they were initiated with the tribe. This wasn't your average westernized yoga instructor and burning man hippie facilitating a ceremony. It is the real deal. My current reality and the groups collective consciousness were interconnected through music to this tribe. For protection purposes, this tribe is not to be named.

My body, mind, and spirit began to drift deeply into a lucid state of being. This brought me back to the realm where my spirit began to continue its traveling journey. In this realm, I was greeted by the Dove of Prosperity. She guided me to a forest surrounded by hundred-foot trees. Here, she left me to wonder. Walking through this forest and the enchantment which surrounded me, I was blown away by the realness of it all. The colors were vivid, the sound of water running in the distance, the smell of fresh air, the taste of rain on my tongue and the feeling of a soft wind caressing my skin was all too real. I was no longer on planet earth. I knew this place was real and that my experience was that of another dimension. I could touch plants and feel the texture, I put my nose to flowers and inhaled their scent; I was truly out of my body in another reality. Where exactly? I don't know. But what I do know is that it was as real as me writing this book, as real as you, the reader, reading these words.

I encountered a woman with a white veil over her face. She said to me, "Pull back my veil, I want you to see me."

I carefully grabbed the edges of her white veil. It was smooth and delicate like ancient silk adorned with beautiful stitching which depicted a scene of angels. As I gracefully pulled her veil back, her beautiful face came into light. She looks at me and says, "My name is Maya, I am the Mistress of Creation."

Stunned, I did not respond. Her beauty was enough to make anyone freeze, but what she said made me realize what I had just done by pulling back her veil. In historical terms, she was an opposing force balancing good and evil. Maya's veil represented the illusion that clouds the reality of our being. Pulling back her veil, I was able to see the balance of the two forces, good and evil, joy and suffering, creation and destruction. My ability was to now consciously choose which direction I wanted follow. It was a Matrix red pill or blue pill moment. I had seen past the veil which blinded me for so long. And the gag is, to not choose or place judgment on either side, but to walk the line of duality, remaining harmonious and balanced. Maya had gifted me with the responsibility of accountability, consciousness, choice and duality.

146

And with that, she vanished in the wind. The forest around me had a different feel to it prior to when she had arrived. The Dove of Prosperity was circling above me waiting for me to continue my journey. I was still processing what just happened; I had woken myself up to take note in my journal of the experience with Maya. Back in my body, in the ceremonial room, I scribbled what I could manage. I drank more water and asked for a hand to the bathroom. My legs were so weak, it was as if I had never walked before. A woman who was participating as a space holder helped me up. Holding onto her waist and shoulders she guided me to the toilet. This moment had felt more unusual than the one I had experienced in another spiritual realm, reality and dimension. My human body and human need to urinate felt so foreign to me. I had felt as if I was a visitor in my physical body. This is also the responsibility of the space holder; because people on the floor are leaving their physical bodies, space holders literally hold space, so entities or foreign spirits are unable to enter our beings while we are not present.

I had to talk myself through this process. "Okay Marissa, shut the door, lift the lid, pull down your pants and undies."

Sitting on the toilet seat which faced the sink and mirror, I had to remind myself, "do not look in the mirror!" I don't know what it was, but I was afraid to see myself. My fear had taken over me and pushed me off the pot and out the door in one swift motion, I can't remember if I wiped or even flushed, probably not. When I exited the bathroom, there stood my human being space holder looking as friendly as ever. I grabbed held of her tightly for safety and security. I felt like a newborn deer exposed in this reality. How anxiously I wanted to lie back down in my cot and drift away again.

Chapter 16

You Found Me

Let Him weigh me with accurate
scales, and let God know my
integrity.
Job 31:6

What felt like hours might've only been five minutes since I encountered Maya in the spiritual realm and higher dimension. I'm not sure what to call this place because it seems to be undiscovered and the ones who have been to this place aren't interested in discovering anything other than what is meant for them.

As I was being led back to my cot from the bathroom, I took a moment to lift my head up and observe the ceremonial room. Each participant in the circle of light was either out of their body, purging or trying to get comfortable on their cot. Space holders were sitting upright and overlooking each of us on the floor. As for Judah and the other mystics who assisted him, they were nowhere in sight. I've come to understand that the way Judah facilitates the ceremony is by tapping into our experiences, guiding us through what we encounter or see, all the while receiving downloads of his own; his work is very tiring. Judah and his associates must've been resting during our second round of plant.

Because my focus had not been on my almost inoperable legs which were jelly and my arms which felt weightless yet intensely difficult to operate, I dropped onto my cot, the moment the space holder had released me from her hold. I found myself going from a standing position to a laying position. It had felt as if my body melted as quick as ice in the Sahara Desert. I slowly and carefully situated myself to be as comfortable as I could be. The point of lying on a cot is to not get too comfortable so the participant can come back to the physical realm with ease. If participants were to be too comfortable, they would have trouble coming out of their deep meditative sleep from the spiritual realm and higher dimension realities.

Floating back into my lucid dream state, I found myself in the forest where I had met Maya. In this spiritual realm and higher dimension reality, I had my physical strength back. My veins were visible, as if I had done an intense workout. My health and focus were in better shape than the physical reality I just came from which wasn't hard to do considering I felt like melted ice and jelly. My physical health in the higher dimensional reality was better than I had ever felt in the physical realm.

The air that flowed through my nostrils was so crisp and clean as if I had never done cocaine. The oxygen filled my lungs effortlessly, as if I were a balloon, and each exhale was deep into the bottom of my belly.

The deep breaths I took in repeatedly brought a message upon its euphoric grace. I had come to know the breath of integrity. Prior to this, the word 'integrity' was not in my vocabulary; I truly did not know what the word meant or what weight the word held. The last five years I had been living in dishonesty, paired with a deep suffering of subconscious and conscious choices made in my daily life resulting in the consequence of not knowing who I truly was.

Integrity came to me in the form of breath to instill that with every voluntary and involuntary moment of my life the breath which is continuous and present in my physical body harbors the meaning of integrity. This was the binding of my spiritual lesson, into the depths of my physical body thus becoming a part of who I am in the physical reality.

I felt touched by spirit, within and without my merging of the two dimensions I was experiencing, physical and spiritual, were planting seeds for me to grow into after this weekend ceremonial retreat.

In the distance I heard, "You found me!" and instantaneously I knew it was my mother. The sound of her voice brought me immediate comfort. Although when she came into my vision, she did not look like my mother in the physical realm. She looked aged, almost possessing a demonized appearance. I was not scared, just aware of what I was looking at. With higher consciousness this made sense to me as to why she would appear to look this way. In the physical reality, my mother had turned the other cheek to a lot of situations for the sake of keeping the peace. This resulted in a lack of accountability, communication and responsibility. This isn't to say she was a bad mom. When in a higher consciousness of reality like I was experiencing, there is no wrong or right, only what is true or false. How or what the observer chooses to accept or see is up to them and their level of awareness.

It was, however, a quite poetic experience for me. The reason for this is due to the encounter I just had with Maya's veil. This experience would be my first test which was standing in front of me; my mothers' demons. I am not suggesting that my mother had evil inside of her or was an evil person, but it would be bullshit to say that every human is perfect. We all possess entities that inhibit us from being a great human all the time; whether that be caused by heartbreak, mourning or stubbornness, it is one part of what the human experience is about. In this spiritual realm, her demons appeared through her physical body. In my heart, I knew far past what I was witnessing, my momma was here for the purpose of healing. Whether that meant healing herself or me, my journey had brought me here.

Through psychic communication I spoke with the demons which possessed my mother.

"I want you to show me how life is. Rather than living in fear show me how light is made of integrity." I say.

The demon which possessed my mother replied, "Walk in light or walk in shadows, you have no inner stability. You know no direction. What you see in me, you see in yourself. How are you to walk the line of duality and fill your lungs with the breath of integrity if you cannot see yourself."

She was right, in the physical world, I couldn't even look myself in the mirror. The last time I had given myself a good look in the mirror was just before Jack had raped me and only hours before this encounter, I couldn't bare to be in the bathroom in fear of facing myself in the mirror. I had no stability or balance to walk this spiritual tight rope of duality and integrity.

This was the moment I learned the lesson of balance and reflection. To live in integrity, one must know their truth and remain true to themselves. There is no doing wrong or right, only what is true or false. To live in integrity, one must be honest about their past, shine light onto their darkness and embrace it. When one shines lightness onto darkness, it becomes light and thus light and dark become one. Without darkness there would be no light.

What I saw in my mother was merely a reflection of myself. Her brave spirit came to me in the form of a physically ugly demon to show me that there was nothing to be afraid of when I look at my reflection. I learned the valuable lesson that what I saw in others is what I see in myself. My mother had given me a handful of lessons during this experience and yet it all simply came down to accepting who I am and the truths which came with it.

The moment I came into acceptance, my surroundings changed. Trees which once casted shadows in the forest that surrounded me had disappeared, along with my mother. A glistening gust of light wind danced around me. It was a playful wind reflecting colorful layers of light.

I continued to breathe in deeply, taking it all in. I closed my eyes and with one hand on my heart and the other with my palm facing out, I became one with my surroundings. Because I had accepted myself, I had accepted all which was around me.

Becoming one with nature starts with becoming one within. The wind tickled my spirit, as well as my palm. As if the wind had somewhere to be, it left me as swiftly as it had come. When I opened my eyes and peeked down to my opened palm, there I held a gift from the wind, a diamond. I had never seen a diamond like this before. I held it to the sun above me and the path of ascension became clear. As if the diamond were a telescope into my future and a compass to guide me there, I now had a map for my journey.

During my astral trip I had not only been coming to face the entities of guilt, shame, abandonment, regret and deceit but I had been re-grounding stability into my foundation. I showed gratitude to spirit and continued on my path.

The never-ending forest was abundant and beautiful.

There were trees, plants, bugs, birds and all other types of animals thriving in harmony here. The light which now guided me led me to a garden. An oak fence ran the perimeter of the garden, as if someone had created this in the middle of the forest. Peeking past the fence and looking into the garden I saw young girls running around with bouquets of flowers for hair. I noticed they were sticking their tiny fingers into each other's heads.

"How odd I thought to myself." Still in curiosity about what I was witnessing, my younger self approached me. We knew each other so there was no need for an introduction. She had chubby cheeks, a nail sized gap between her teeth, long brown curly hair and a big round belly. I asked my younger self, "What are you girls doing?"

She tells me how the oil from their finger's seeps into the soil on their heads and destroys the flowers by tainting its nutrients. The young girls were poisoning each other. She goes on to tell me that sabotaging each other means no one is prettier than the others. Taken back by this message, I came to an understanding of the envy and jealously consuming my younger self and the other girls. It reminded me of the competitiveness that took place in my childhood between my sisters and I. This revealed to me the self-sabotage I did to myself and what jealousy and envy I held towards others.

The garden I stood in sprung beautiful young girls with beautiful bouquets, but they were poisoning each other. Was this the behavior I had shown my sisters and friends?

I asked my younger self, "How do we stop this?"

She responded, "Well isn't that why you're here? I don't know." Looking into my younger self's eyes, I searched for the answer. What did she need from me? The answer which came to me was that she and the other girls needed compassion and care.

I said to my younger self, "I can show you how to take care of yourself so you can all be equally beautiful and abundant."

I asked her if I could pull out the weeds, which infested her bouquet. She had concerns of me hurting and poisoning her. I reminded her this was an act of care and I was here to be a solution, not a problem. Reassuring her that although it might hurt for a moment, she would have a more beautiful and lively bouquet.

The action of pulling weeds from my younger self's head reminded me of the days my father would have my sisters and I do yard work. Our main duty was to pull the weeds which infested the backyard from time to time. I hated that chore, although this time it gave me relief. Being of service to my younger self, another human in this case, showed me the value of being of service and compassionate towards others was also being of service and compassionate to myself. Caring for others is caring for myself and lastly, but most importantly, my younger self needed me not just in this spiritual reality and higher dimension, but in the physical reality.

After gently plucking her weeds out, her bouquet was restored to an abundant beauty. She said to me, "Can we help the others?" and so we did. Each young girl became restored from the inside out.

This form of gardening brought me a core memory of the time I spent with my GG, Ira Vivian or Ivy as my great grandfather would call her. As a young girl in the physical world, we spent time gardening together. Now, to be spending time in the spiritual realm and higher dimensional reality I was teaching young girls how to help themselves and tend to their own garden.

I hadn't realized previously to this, how much of my relationship with my sisters were centered around competition, jealously and envy. This grew into my relationships with other women as well. To realign myself and rid myself of this negative energy, it was necessary that my younger self meet me here in this garden; to get to the root of the problem. It was necessary for she and I to connect, understand, resolve and heal each other. If I were to continue to be unable to find compassion for my younger self, how could I ever find compassion for my current self and others. She and I danced and celebrated in the garden with the other girls who I felt were my three sisters.

We laughed, played hand clapping games, jumped rope and told each other secrets. One of these secrets being that what I thought was my younger self was actually my inner child.

I hadn't heard of the term, inner child, before coming to the spiritual realm and higher dimensional reality. My inner child was now too, along with me on journey. I told my inner child and the other three girls about my previous encounters on my journey before making it the garden. I told them of meeting Mother in the form of her demons.

The girls said, "You mean the dead woman?"

I replied, "I guess so."

The four girls told me how that wasn't just my Mother, but that she had taken on a dead woman's identity when she was seventeen. They continued to tell me that she had healed herself when she found love and gave life to us, although when she faced heartbreak, she died inside, again. This information made sense in the physical realm; my maternal grandmother died when my mother was seventeen. Any previous judgement or anger I had towards my mother and her parenting style drifted away. She too, needed compassion and care.

In this moment I want to acknowledge my mother. I love you and thank you for doing your best. I truly hadn't realized how much emotion I negatively held against you until I recognized it in the spiritual realm and purged it in the physical realm.

This purge in the physical realm was different than the last. I awoke from my dream state and felt the need for my mom. For a split second, I felt what it was like to need your mom but can't reach her. I had to remind myself that she was indeed alive and that I would never take her for granted again.

Chapter 17

I Am Conscious

God made the two great lights, the
greater light to govern the day, and
the lesser light to govern the night;
He made the stars also. God placed
them in the expanse of the heavens
to give light on earth, and to govern
the day and the night, and to
separate the light from the
darkness; and God saw that it was
good.
Genesis 1:16-18

Laying back down into my dream state, I drifted back into the spiritual realm and higher dimension reality. Again, meeting with my inner child, the Dove of Prosperity and the diamond in hand, I was assured that whether it be physical or spiritual, I would possess my three guides.

I asked my inner child, "Where in the physical realm can you be seen?"

She said, "I cannot be seen, only felt. I rest in the center of your chest behind the diamond within."

This was now a new level of confusion for me. My inner child was sure to teach me more than I anticipated, but what was I to do for her? The responsibility of carrying my inner child inside of me felt like I became a new mother unexpectedly. I had felt blessed and happy, but the question of "How do I handle you?" or "What do I do with you?" was now at the forefront of my consciousness.

Judah had stopped the tribal music in the physical realm, which signaled for us to come back into our bodies for the next debrief as a group. I shared my experiences with the group and expressed my now troubles with the inner child. Judah congratulated me for connecting with her and said my only duty as of now was to integrate and protect her.

It was now Saturday in the physical realm and about 8 o'clock in the morning. We had all spent the last nine hours traveling to places outside of this room and ourselves. My long journey surprisingly had me feeling rested and at peace. All facilitators, participants and space holders went upstairs to enjoy a vegan meal, sunshine and personal time. After a night of purging and intense mental and spiritual work, you would think one might be hungry for a meal, I was most certainly not.

I met with Andre in the kitchen, he had a smile on his face that I hadn't seen before. I could sense he was proud of me for surrendering to the experience. It's important to note that space holders also hear the debriefs the participants in the circle of light have. He had knowledge of what I had experienced through the night. I was feeling extremely vulnerable and in a position of submission. I didn't know what to do with this idle time or how to interact with another human, my hope was for Andre to guide me like he always had in the physical world. Yet the thing about this sacred plant tradition is all who are involved are urged to know the value of autonomy. Another word which wasn't in my vocabulary at this time and something, along with integrity, that I wouldn't mature into until years later.

It was refreshing to see the house we were all in, in the daylight. I would best describe it as a modern cabin with 70s style roots. An artist must've owned the house because it was decorated like something you'd only see in magazines. The home was surrounded by trees, but I didn't feel the need to go outside this day. I was still heavily on the plant and adjusting to being back in my mind and body. It was nice to see Andre, he gave me a big hug, which I needed so badly.

"I'm really proud of you Marissa" says Andre.

"You know Andre, after all the pushback I gave you about coming here and experiencing this, I am thankful you brought me here" I respond.

The next round of ceremony wasn't until 10pm Saturday night. Andre and I spent the day recharging and snuggling with one another on the couch. He introduced me to sacred geometry and the way my brain was operating I grasped the concept of it within the afternoon. He and I discussed my journey to other realms, although I can't remember much of our conversation, I do however remember thinking, "Will Andre truly love me now? Will this weekend fix our relationship?"

My need for his blessing and approval stemmed from my lack of self-esteem, abandonment issues and boundaries. These issues underlined every notion of interaction between he and I. Because of the plant, I was finally conscious of it. There was not an ounce of autonomy in my being, I lacked the ability to stand on my own and be my own person.

In the late afternoon, Judah had called me in for a meeting; we discussed how I was responding to the plant and what I would be focusing on next. The direct tone we spoke with one another and the absence of emotion was as if I had learned a new language. My mind was now operating in a different way than ever before. I was slow to respond and held eye contact during conversation; I didn't fear judgement because I now accepted the experience I had surrendered to.

Going into the second night of the session, I knew what to expect and how to flow a bit easier. My ego dropped, my fears had lifted, and I had become fully surrendered to the happening of the sacred tribal ceremony.

The second night began like the first, with a heaping spoonful of raw, grounded up plant followed by a big swig of water. Instead of praying to God for protection this time, I prayed for an experience. I learned so much the first night in the spiritual realm and higher dimension realities, but this night I wanted to really live in these other places. Because I had known the possibilities of what could happen, I welcomed all possibilities.

As I laid my head back on my cot, I reminded myself of the things I learned the night before; my father's spirit protected me, Marie is here for me, have compassion towards my mother, to heal myself is to heal others and lastly, but most importantly my inner child is always with me, teaching me while I protect and honor her.

I began to drift away in my sleep far into a lucid dream. I knew it to be a far place because I could see and feel my spirit traveling. Supported by the beautiful musical recordings of the tribe playing throughout the room, all 12 participants, including myself were now in a deep lucid dream. I felt as if I could feel the others energy. I also felt that if I didn't want to feel their energy, I could easily disconnect from them. That interconnectedness of consciousness was obvious to all who drift.

This second night the energy felt stronger and intensified. In my spiritual realm and higher dimension reality, I found myself sitting on the dark side of the moon and next to me of course, sat my inner child.

160

She asked me, "Where'd you go?"

I looked into her eyes casually and said, "Earth, its behind us."

She says back to me, "Oh... you're still there? Why am I here then?"

In this moment, it came clear to me that I have not carried my inner child with me all these years, that I had forgotten her and left her in places all alone. It would be a continuous and conscious duty of mine to bring her with me at all times.

I replied, "I won't leave you here again, do you want to come with me on all my journeys? Not only in the spiritual realm and other dimensions but in the physical realm as well."

My inner child replied, "I do, it's lonely here."

I thought to myself, "Well yeah, we're on the dark side of the moon."

But an eight-year-old didn't need to be reminded of that. It was my duty to show her compassion and protection. We sat on the dark side of the moon, listening to the music from the physical realm and making moon castles. Moon castles are kind of like sandcastles, but with moon dust.

What's interesting about the music we were able to hear, is that although we were in a different realm, reality and timeline, we were still able to experience the sacred tribal drums, harp and song. Music possesses a frequency that can travel. I learned of this in this moment.

While I sat here with my inner child, I felt ever-present and at peace with her. Neither of us feared the dark because we had each other's light and warmth.

It felt as if we sat together for an eternity, when suddenly, I heard Judah say from the physical realm, "The black hole in front of you, do you wish to go?"

This truly amazed me. Judah's ability to know where we were in this universe while not being there with us blew my mind. And I thought this while sitting on the dark side of the moon looking into a black hole. Without saying a word, I looked into my inner child's eyes; I could see the fear in her.

She says to me, "I want to go by Rissa but I do not want to go there" Rissa was a nickname my family called me often as a young girl. Just the feeling behind this nickname reminded me I had a tribe of my own.

I say to her, "Of course I can, Rissa. We can stay right here."

I declined Judah's offer to go into the black hole, I was happy with where I was at, who I was with and what I had learned. Looking back, it was the first time in a long time I had been genuinely happy with myself. It was only for a moment that this feeling had lasted, but I wanted to savor every second of it. Judah didn't question me as to why I didn't want to go in the black hole either. It felt good to tell a man no and him actually respect it and move on with his life.

My inner child looked at the black hole in amazement and appreciation. Watching her stare with wonder at this marvel was the most outstanding experience I've had up to this point in my journey. As a child, I had the tendency to become overly excited and act without thinking and for the first time she and I observed. Looking at a Gods wonder, a universe wonder, a science wonder which is the black hole, a mythical space creature approached us.

162

Without any disturbances to this moment, we had advanced from the seventh dimension, to the ninth. This creature is known to many as a unicorn. This creature had no gender, it was a spirit possessing the form of a unicorn. My inner child was delighted as was I. This creature graced us with its presence and left us with a sense of wonder and possibility. To this day this wonder and possibility still lives inside of me. After our short encounter with this ethereal white creature, we noticed it left a horseshoe for us. My inner child did not hesitate to pick it up and dust it off. The electric blue horseshoe danced with diamonds and rubies. It was now adorned by my inner childs precious hands.

Judah lowered the music, and began speaking to the group from the physical realm.

"I want you to envision yourself as a bee" he says.

I envisioned myself as a bee and with ease I became a bee. He then asked us to fly into a beehive and find the queen bee. One of the most miraculous things about being on a journey like this is the ability to become anything you want and embark on adventures to the most peculiar places.

In fact, I found myself in a beehive on the Darkside of the moon as my inner child looked at me with a ginormous black hole at her back. You could say in this moment, I was tripping. But this moment felt as real as me writing this book. All five senses were active. I could comprehend the physical world and spiritual world simultaneously. Hearing Judah in the physical realm while I was living in the spiritual realm, as a honeybee, was all certainly new to me.

Flying into the beehive was like walking around Times Square on New Year's Eve. I had no idea what I was looking at, where to go or what to do. It was as if the other bees couldn't even see me. I tried communicating with them through dance. Yes, bees can communicate through dance.

Unfortunately, all the bees were busy and moved so fast. What was I to do?

"Think like a bee" I thought to myself. Well that made things more complicated. So, I took a seat on a honeycomb and observed the hive. I knew bees could also communicate through frequency, but what frequency was that? I tapped into the frequency of the hive, after all I was now one of them. And just like that, I joined their busy line of communication.

The queen bee who I was supposed to find I knew two things about; she was a virgin, and she was heard to be clinging to the wall of the hive. To my luck of the horseshoe, she was right next to me, sharing half of the honeycomb I was sitting on.

She told me, "Energy, vibration and frequency are the three keys to my existence: and yours. No matter where you are in this universe, never forget that you can become one with everything around you through your energy, your vibration and your frequency."

And with that experience I woke and purged ferociously. I couldn't believe what I experienced in that moment. Back in my body, in the physical realm, wiping vomit from my face, I looked around the room. The other eleven participants were in a deep lucid dream which oddly made this experience that much more real to me.

The way I had come back into my body and purged so grand, caught the attention of Judah. He knew something profound happened to me.

I felt the plant had completed its journey within my body. I laid back down, bringing myself to a meditation while placing my hands over my chest, I felt the warmth of my inner child inside of me. She was still with me. I rocked us back to sleep while singing her lullabies mama would sing to

164

us as children, we both fell into a deep sleep only this time we stayed in the physical realm.

After what felt like a few hours, we were woken up by Judah, "This concludes our weekend session, please take as much time as you need to get up."

I laid on my cot counting my fingers, toes, doing a complete body scan; making sure I still had all my body parts.

"Okay, I'm still here" reminding myself it was now Sunday. I sat up, drank water, grabbed my things and made my way up the basement steps. It was as if I was walking for the first time. My vision had vivid colors dancing across it, from all directions. In the physical realm, I was experiencing layers of light from another dimension. I made my way outside to the patio where I found Andre sitting on a daybed with Chacho. He greeted me with love and a smile, we sat while overlooking a valley with beautiful trees and lush greenery. Andre was sitting on my right, the sun directly in front of us. Staring into the sun and nature was like seeing the world for the first time.

I turned to Andre in confidence and said, "I am conscious."

My vision was clearer, my body was lighter, my imagination spread wider. I had no shame, regret, or fear living inside of me at this moment. I sat tall with my spine erect and both hands on my chest. I could still feel my inner child. She was warm, alive, and as present as ever in this moment with me. I had truly become a different type of human.

Andre and I snuggled under a blanket on the daybed discussing the second night of my journey. He was so proud of me and in amazement of what happened. I felt so sweet and pure again.

All the purging left me skin and bone. Two days of extreme vomiting and not eating, while only consuming water and plant will do that to you. As well as leave a smell. The bathroom opened for use and I felt it was time for a well-deserved hot shower. So, I got up and went to the bathroom.

This was my first time encountering a mirror in the physical realm. I was not afraid to see who I was. I got undressed in front of the mirror, looking at my thin boney self. Appreciating all my body had supported me through. I was beautiful. For the first time since being raped, probably before then to, I felt truly beautiful. It was as if I was seeing my body for the first time. There were no preconceived labels or insecurities about the way I felt towards my body. Just me and my naked body. Looking into the mirror I was tall, lean and a bit curvy. My imperfections became my perfections in that moment. I smiled at myself noticing every detail with great appreciation and love.

Taking a deep breath in, I took notice of my ribs and my hip bones as well as the breath of integrity which was still with me. Taking another deep breath in, I lifted my arms up and over my head. Stretching tall, my rib cage expanded, and every piece of bone was outlined. In this moment, I saw my angel wings disguised as my rib cage. With each breath they grew bigger and bigger. I began to cry, with tears running down my face and hands above my head, my angel wings had come in. This moment is and was so special to me. After so much time of hating myself, judging myself and feeling impure, I had finally felt okay. I took one last look in the mirror and got in the shower.

I wasn't sure which way the nozzle went for hot or cold; mistakenly I turned it all the way hot. The steaming hot water burned my skin, yet my body moved further into the stream. I closed my eyes and allowed this to happen. Once my eyes shut, I had visions of earth catching fire. A huge ball of

166

fire burning anything and everything to ashes. This vision didn't scare me. This version of earth, I felt, represented my body and all the harm done to it in the past. Once I felt this revelation, I took a deep breath into the steam as my skin burned from the hot water. It felt so good to vigorously burn metaphysical impurities this way. My intuition told me it was now time to allow myself to replenish my being.

I turned the handle all the way cold. I let out a scream from the shock this caused my body. The cold water felt like knives piercing my skin. My nervous system began to hyperventilate and the only action I could do in this moment was pray. I prayed for forgiveness and with all my being, I felt God's presence. The once cold harsh water became cool forgiving waters rushing over me. I had been forgiven.

This moment was so euphoric, I was hesitant to even turn the faucet off. I did so, carefully. I was even scared to pull back the curtain, after my experience with Maya's veil, who knew how significant my every day simple actions could mean.

Stepping out of the shower I put a towel over myself. Bundled up like a little kid, I could not believe what I experienced in the physical realm during the day and out of all places, the bathroom. I put my clothes back on slowly, the moment had come and gone. Feeling as if I was back in disguise, I was ready to re-join the other participants who had equal if not greater experiences than I just a few hours ago. I wasn't exactly sure how to communicate with anyone except for smiling. I could sense everyone was coming back into their bodies in their own way. I thanked Judah for the amazing weekend and said goodbye to the others as it was now time for me, Andre and Chacho to go. We packed up the red 1997 Land Cruiser together. I took leverage of having the backseat to myself; with all the windows rolled down, I snuggled into a huge purple tribal blanket, we called this the spirit blanket.

It was the beginning of Fall and the weather was perfect out. I had never felt more at one then this moment. I didn't care for my phone or any distractions, only this moment of lounging in the Land Cruiser through the windy roads surrounded by trees, listening to the Beatles- life was good.

Yet I couldn't help the uncertainty of being vulnerable; I had never felt so exposed. After a weekend session with the plant your intuition only desires to be in balance, harbor integrity and transparency. My intuition felt as if something was imbalanced. Now this car ride home was six hours, and I knew something was wrong; maybe it was my car sickness or not eating, but the pit of my stomach ached. Thoughts came across my mind like, "Am I victimizing myself?" or "Am I self-sabotaging already?"

The thing about cracking open your consciousness and opening your heart is, you better be ready to integrate and decipher between what is right and wrong, light and dark, balanced or imbalanced. Integration followed by action are by far the hardest mental and emotional responsibilities I took on up until this moment.

Chapter 18

Essence of Love

To love Him with all your heart, with
all your understanding and with all
your strength, and to love your
neighbor as yourself is more.
Mark 12:33

Once the veil is lifted and your heart is opened you
have conscious choices to make, a new language to speak and
a new sensitivity to life and its happenings. What I wasn't
prepared for (or even had a basic knowledge of) was the
reality of living in my truth to such a great capacity that it
would come to change my relationships, habits and beliefs.

These responsibilities can feel like a burden at first.
These emotions combined with my new sense of intuition
drove me mad on the car ride home. I didn't know how to
process this or understand it. This was the beginning of a long
period of confusion, identity crisis, drug abuse, alcohol abuse
and self-harm. My subconscious had just been cracked open.
And the way, the proper way, to integrate this gift is to be
sober, live in integrity and make positive changes in your life.

Now, because I had pulled back the veil any disregard
to my actions, thoughts or speech against the lessons I had

learned would come back to me harder and faster than dharma and karma usually moves.

This, I did not know, I would come to learn about this the hard way. But the knowingness I felt came to me as an unspoken rule on my car ride home. So, not only was I juggling this in my mind, but the simple fact of how impressionable my subconscious had been and would be moving forward. To say I was now in fear would be an understatement.

The beginning of my end is what was approaching. But like I said I didn't understand this fully. All I knew was fear at this time. And the best way I knew how to handle this rather than going through it, was to run the opposite direction. And I did.

The moment we arrived at our apartment from the weekend session I put on a face. I forced myself to be happy in this relationship with Andre, I forced myself to believe he was honest and had pure intentions. It was all an act and a lie, yet I convinced myself I was living in integrity.

At 21, I was now a perfect housewife. I thought to myself, if I could do everything the way he likes it, we will be fine, he'll love me and see that I am deserving of his love. I cooked, cleaned, and had sex for someone I wasn't in love with anymore. But, because I experienced the plant with him, I felt obligated to try.

No, things weren't always bad, but because our foundation was built on lies, deceit and a saviorhood/victimhood mentality it was all unaligned. The energy between Andre and I felt off the next couple of months at home. It wasn't until one day my intuition was barking at me like a dog. Per usual, I ignored it by folding laundry in the bedroom. He had come in our bedroom and tried to initiate some type of intimacy. Although, he looked nervous and

170

awkward. I wouldn't engage and he joined me to fold clothes; I could sense he wanted to say something, and I asked finally, "What is it?"

He set the clothes down and looked at me with guilty eyes, "I slept with someone else."

In this moment it felt as if my whole world came crashing down. I had so many questions.

"With who?" I replied.

He looked at me with an even more guilty look and said, "A random girl in New York and a prostitute in Vegas." "When?" I replied.

He responded, "Just before the weekend plant session. I told Judah, and he suggested to still bring you there."

I felt like everything from the plant session to my now integration was a complete lie. I had known something was off on the car ride home and this was it. My nerves and brain became completely out of whack. The façade I put on completely dropped and my ego had risen once again.

I lied and told him I had been cheating on him too. He laughed, smiled and hugged me. In his mind, we were one of the same. In my mind, I was going to make him feel my pain.

The entities I met during my weekend plant session were now out greater than they ever were. I guess you could say this was the beginning of my villain origin story. I hadn't truly resolved the issues with my entities in the physical reality. I just had a name for them now and unknowingly to my future we were about to meet the worst of them.

It wasn't Andre and I's lease that kept me in this relationship for another three months after this moment, it was revenge. Looking back, I could've and should've left. But I stayed, only to endure the worst heartbreak of my life. The smart thing to do would've been to just break up and go to therapy. Our relationship was dead and oozed toxicity out of every inch of it.

We both treated ourselves with weed, alcohol and shrooms, not to mention I went back to using cocaine only this time pairing it with ecstasy. The thing about the plant is, that I was completely unaware of, was that if you are not living in integrity and harmony within and without yourself than your entities and unintegrated dark side will come fist first into your life.

The last three months of Andre and I's relationship this most certainly was happening. Neither of us had the integrity to end things and in saviorhood fashion, Andre planned and paid for a two-month trip to Europe for us. I think he had hopes that this would save us.

A week before our trip and Christmas, I had been feeling so nervous to go. The whole week I was drinking and using, I felt as if this trip was a trap. My paranoia began, but nonetheless I started packing. Andre had left for New York a week prior, and I was to meet him there.

The night of my flight, I decided to pack a couple pairs of sneakers, one of these being a pair of White Air Force Ones. They had been scuffed up from all my inebriated adventures and I wanted to clean them. I remembered Andre had kept microfiber towels in his truck. I looked all through his truck for those towels so I could clean my dirty shoes. I opened the center console and found the towels I was looking for. As I lifted the towels out of the console, I found a pack of condoms underneath.

My heart froze. Staring at the box, was a reflection of our relationship. Lies, secrecy, cheating, but this moment was

172

symbolic for me. I had seen the truth right in front of my face, there is no denying that. I immediately put them back and went up to the apartment to call him. No answer. He replied to me over text, "I am at dinner, call you after. Are you ready for the airport?"

I asked him to please call me because it was urgent. He called and I asked him about the condoms. He said how he had never used them. "Wow, so unprotected sex" I thought to myself.

He continued to say "Don't worry about it, just get on the plane. We can talk about it when you get here."

I went on to say, "No, speak to me now."

He said no repeatedly and that he was at a Christmas dinner with friends. Throughout our entire relationship, he had chosen his friends over me. Anytime they were problems between us, he would go to his friends instead of me. This was the last time I was going to allow this to happen. So, I hung up the phone and missed my flight.

My first instinct was to drink with friends. I called a few girls and guys over. When my friends arrived at my apartment, I was down half a bottle of wine and unpacking my luggage. To my surprise the situation was water under the bridge to them. When I told them about ditching my trip with Andre, the solution was to go out and dance.

We all drank enough to put an elephant on his ass. All the while Andre was blowing my phone up, I ignored every message and call. I'm not sure what more I was trying to accomplish other than hurting him, but really, I was only hurting myself.

That night I bragged to anyone and everyone that I skipped out on my two-month New York and Europe trip;

looking back that was nothing to brag about at a local bar, I'm sure everyone there would've rather been on a flight to the Big Apple.

Although, it was as if fate had its eyes on me. A young man, by the name of Daniel, who I'd known through friends approached me. I was very fond of him in the past, a few years back during one of Andres and I separation I met this young man for the first time.

Daniel and I had only run into each other two times over the past two years, both times we were single and both times we had intercourse. Now, this third time had to of been fate, my mind had completely forgotten what had happened with Andre the moment I saw Daniel.

Daniel was tall with broad shoulders, a face which was sculpted from the Gods and dreamy green eyes. He made me feel beautiful and special from the first time we met. I had never forgotten about him and now here we both were. We caught up with each other, laughed and kissed; it always felt right kissing him. I admired how Daniel was always truthful about where he was at in life and what he was working towards.

He was now home from college studying for the MCAT to get into medical school. He was a dream and with each blunt we passed, I got higher physically and emotionally. That night we went back to my apartment, the one where I just unpacked my bags for Europe. We stepped in the house and immediately started making love. Sex and love had an obscure line and because of the abuse I didn't know any better. Although, it was the most genuine love and care I had experienced up until that night. The next morning, he left, and I was back to dealing with Andre.

I didn't tell Andre about my night of romance; he only knew I was hung over. Andre begged me to get on another flight, he tried to buy me every flight out to New York and even Paris, which was our first stop, but I refused. I was already falling for someone else.

The week went by and I was still in Sacramento. My now ex-boyfriend was on a lonely trip to Europe by himself. Meanwhile, I was in a fairytale. Although in Daniels eyes, we were friends with similar interest and likes, he had me smitten. We would get high at night and watch planet Earth or go hot tubing. Sometimes during the day, we would hang out with his friends at his parents' house.

When we were together life was poetic, sweet and loving. Most afternoons when he was done studying, he would play the piano for me while I sipped tea. Each day I fell for him in wonder and lust, just as I had felt wonder and lust on the dark side of the moon many months ago. We had conversations about the cosmos and earth. He inspired me like no one ever had before. He inspired me to study different sciences, read books, spend time in nature and become curious about the world.

My friends said I was living in a fairytale. But no one could tell me anything, and that's because I was the happiest, I'd been in months. I knew Daniel and I would always just be friends and occasionally lovers, but our connection was real, the stimulation between us was real and our conversations were real. We could spend hours with one another and not look at our phones once. I got along well with his family and was always welcomed; we became good buddies over time. Within a few months, he had set a standard for me on how I wanted to feel in life and love.

He opened my eyes to the excitement in learning, reading and creating good habits. When I was with him, I was as prime and proper as they come. He had no clue about my addictions, I was good at keeping that secret. No one really

175

knew. Not even myself fully understood the level of addict I had become. Although I did create new habits, like bike riding, running and reading, I still depended on drugs and alcohol heavily, I was a functioning addict.

Daniel saw me as a beautiful young lady, who had a different way of thinking and loving. We were always kind and sweet with one another. Although my friends saw me as a party girl who knew how to have a good time, he was the one person who got to see me in a different light; I felt my best with him. What I knew of myself is that I had been lying and living in deceit, but had the potential to be more.

I was dealing with my breakup with Andre behind closed doors. And even then, I don't ever really remember sitting down and quieting myself to process anything that had happened. I never thought about the relationship, how I wanted to handle the breakup or even the simple fact of me ditching an all-expense paid two-month trip to Europe. If there is one thing I did right during the winter of 2018 into 2019, it was to have enough self-respect to not go on that trip. I still had enough dignity to make the right decision for my own sanity and happiness. Andre and I did not speak for almost two months while he was gone. It was for the best considering I had already moved on.

Not that I was looking for someone or trying to use Daniel to get over my ex, but it just kind of happened that way. I felt as if I had found a new identity that was aligned with my deepest desires and wants because of Daniel.

There was one day we sat on the swing in Daniels mother's garden, and we studied the beehive nearby. It was stimulating not only for my brain but my heart. It brought me back to the queen bee I met on my trip with the plant. And I felt called to tell Daniel about it. He listened to me with excitement and wonder, he asked me questions that made me excited too. We discussed energy, sympathetic resonance, and the frequency of the bees.

I asked Daniel, "Do you think the same happens for humans? That we can respond to another human's frequency?"

He said, "Of course" and grabbed held of my hand and drew me in. As we looked into each other's eyes softly, never breaking eye contact. That was until he glanced down at my lips and then back into my eyes; I returned the same movement to him as he did to me. It felt as if Cupid had shot me in the butt; he kissed me. No other place I'd rather be in the world than in his mother's garden, with him. That night we laughed under the stars while smoking the DMT his brother made. It was magical and we just got lost in the universe together. You could say our archetypes of the magician and lover were out.

The rest of our evening was carried out by movies, popcorn and cuddling. This was the night I knew for certain I would never again go back to Andre. I'd never felt more comfortable and safe with a counterpart up until this point. In a way, Daniel saved me and became a forever friend through our time spent together. I don't know if he ever really thought about us more than friends, but I knew where the boundaries were. It's not until he reads this book that he'll know how much our friendship, shared love and time spent meant to me then and does to this day. So, I'd like to take this time to say, thank you, Daniel, for showing me how to look up; your genuine love and curiosity for life as well as the faith you have in yourself, inspired and healed pieces of me. You'll always be a true friend to me.

Part 3:

The Mind

Chapter 19

Accustomed to Chaos

We all, like sheep, have gone astray, each of us
have turned to our own way; and the Lord has
laid on Him the iniquity of all of us.
Isaiah 53:6

Months had passed since I had last heard from Andre,
until one morning; late February 2019, I received a call that
he was headed back from Europe to California. He expressed
to me that he was going to come and pack his things up. To
my knowledge, he had nowhere to go after our separation, but
he was always good at finding a place to call home. This
would come to be my sad reality. After years of a confusing
unstable first love, which oddly made me who I am, our time
together was now up. To make things easier for the both of us,
we lied to one another saying it was a much-needed break and
maybe things could work out in the future. We had just spent
the winter apart which was enough time to think about
everything. Deep down, we both knew this was the end.

I've come to realize now that my relationship with
Andre, as much as it had been spontaneous and an adventure,
he was another reflection of the sexual abuse and trauma that
lived within me. I was unable to give and receive love
properly. It did not dawn on me until years later that I had yet
again found myself preyed on by an older man. Andre is not a
bad person, but I do believe that his intentions of dating

someone much younger than him were tainted by desire and manipulation. And my intentions of being with someone older were misconstrued because of my abandonment issues with my father and the sexual abuse I endured of Jack; I had always been searching for a father figure in my late teens and early twenties.

When Andre got home, we were both distant from one another. Although we remained kind and respectful during his moving process. Our agreement was that I would live in the apartment until the lease ended. We sold most of the furniture, packed his truck up and within a week he was on his way to a new life. This time he was not going to come back.

I now officially had the apartment to myself; it was lonely. I wasn't quite sure how I was going to live without the person who supported me financially and emotionally. Not seeing his things around the house and knowing that he would not come back made our breakup real for me. The bills were paid, but now my drug and alcohol money were going to food and gas. Some days my bitter, lonely, depressed self took the money I had for food or gas and spent it on drugs and alcohol.

My days were filled by curing any type of hangover I had from the night before and picking up more drugs. Then followed by a night of using by myself or with one or two friends. This time of my life is a blur. Most of my early 20s are a blur; I don't have any accomplishments to put a timestamp on anything except for heartbreak, addiction and the plant. I was pretty much all over the place, not to mention, I was still in my integration process.

I sincerely cannot tell you or myself what actually went on in that lonely apartment every day, what I do know for certain is the partying, sex and crying that happened frequently. I felt it was normal and valid the way I had sought out to cope with my feelings and life. Mainly because it is what I had always done, only now I had a handful of people to join me. Looking back, I was being used by these people I once called friends. I hold no resentment because it is a lesson I had to learn, and these particular friends were only doing what they knew how to do; along with myself.

Although the feeling of being used in this dynamic was a very prominent reality for me. I had an apartment which was my own now and my drug dealer who was enamored with me. He always supplied me with free drugs if I let him join my friends and I. Not only were they free but they were the best in Sacramento. How do I know this? Because every cocaine dealer in this city I had picked up from. This isn't to brag or something I am proud of; it is the reality of my addiction.

Cocaine was a party drug for me, my cup of coffee, my emotional band-aid and what I used to avoid any self-reflection, accountability or self-respect. The spring of 2019 was a new level of addiction I hadn't yet experienced. The thing about becoming an addict is you lose any type of self-awareness. And with losing awareness, you become blind to what you really are and what you're really doing.

I don't recognize the girl I was back then because I am a healed woman now. Although, she was a whole lot of fake, hiding behind a glamorous lifestyle. It was at this time I had started to lose control and my addiction gained control over me. Countless times I'd get into cocaine driven arguments, sexcapades and downright dangerous situations.

My obsession with self-harm took arise with every come down I experienced. There were times I would cut or burn my arms to either feel something or feel nothing. Seeing my scorched skin or blood running out of me gave me relief. I felt as if I was releasing the pain inside of me as well as trying to drain my impurities. The scars which remained on my arms made me feel validated. I was a sick person in the head, and it's hard to truly describe what self-harm did for me. It didn't do anything good, but I convinced myself it did. Because I turned my back on the lessons I learned during the plant session, I was fully living in darkness. I did not trust the light anymore; I did not trust myself anymore. Because I had knowledge of the light and dark inside of me, and I rejected the light, I only saw the dark as what was possible for me. This is who I thought I truly was. I thought I had it all figured out now, I thought this is who I'm meant to be... darkness.

I fantasized about the way I would off myself. It was as if those thoughts gave me comfort. Every time I rode my bike, went for a walk, showered or laid my head down at night, suicidal ideation brought me peace. My mind became idle from the numbness of cocaine; the devils' drug spewed all my demons, entities, insecurities, guilt, shame and regret back at me without hesitation. In a way, I became possessed and was far worse than I was before I did the plant.

I had abandoned and forgotten about my inner child. And the only love I recognized was the love I had for drugs during all those lonely nights. I would try to stop buying drugs, whether it be cocaine, molly or weed, but either the pressure from friends or my own fragile will broke into temptation every time. This stage of my addiction was about self-medicating my past and numbing my reality.

When I couldn't stand to be alone in my apartment or if no one picked up the phone, I always went out for a bike ride and into nature. A small piece of me, which was barely surviving, was trying to pull me back from my addiction. This small piece of me only knew how to do one thing to get my attention and that was to go into nature.

On social media, family, friends and followers would see my posts and react in good spirits about how well I take care of my body or how they wish they could be where I was at in nature. Where I lived was a short bike ride away from the American River, and in my opinion this area of the

American River is the most beautiful part in Northern California. Others thought I took good care of my body because I was thin. What they didn't know was that I was only thin, because of the drugs. I lied to myself and would think something along the lines of, "Yes, I am okay because others believe I am."

My reality at this time was me running away from myself. I sought outside of myself because there was nothing left inside of me. Yes, I did enjoy my adventures. Yes, I loved to pull spirit cards in the park or find new hidden sanctuaries along the river. But, I was never truly present or sober. In fact, I was almost always delusional and under the influence. I was never truly at peace or felt safe in my own presence. I looked for answers in my lie of a life. I became so lost in the world I wasn't entirely sure what I was even searching for.

That was until I found out about the power of magic mushrooms. I had taken mushrooms before, but only with Andre under his guise. Before Andre had left for Europe, I saw him hide a couple of bars of chocolate magic mushrooms; I knew he had forgotten about them. He and his friends were not the least bit of strangers when it came to taking them. From hero doses to micro doses, he was all about the sacred healing of what a magic mushroom experience can do for you. Although, I still had no idea what integration, intention or doing the spiritual work meant, I was interested in beginning my journey with magic mushrooms. I was always scared to venture out on my own with mushrooms; the one time I had taken a little bit, more than the recommended dose, my demons and entities had me sitting on the window ledge ready to let go. There was so much inside of me that had come up during that mushroom trip because of things I did not heal. The consequence of this left me feeling suffocated and okay with killing myself.

Luckily that night, Andre had walked in right before I let go from the windowsill. Seeing the terrified look in his eyes, I paused for a moment on the ledge. In that moment, he had lunged for me with his arms wide open and pulled me back into the bedroom. That night he didn't take his eyes off me, watching me like a child. As a girl who constantly found attention and validation through victimization, this was good for me. In my mind, I had him where I wanted him, although in his mind I was bat shit insane.

Although I acted on my suicidal ideations in the past, I now wanted to experience magic mushrooms on my own, without a babysitter. I felt I had nothing to lose. After all, I was tired of cocaine in the midafternoon, and I wanted to save my hard drugs for the night while enjoying the day tripping.

I ended up eating half of a chocolate shroom bar that day which is equivalent to five grams. This was, not a micro dose. Combined with the previous night's tequila and a cocaine come down, I had no idea what I was getting myself into. This is an absolutely irresponsible way to take psychedelic mushrooms.

It was 1 PM and I set out on my bike along the American River. It was a beautiful day; the sun was shining, and a light breeze was flowing. I found a grassy spot to lay out under the sun and watch the clouds go by. The trip was relaxing and smooth. Things almost felt too peaceful for me. As someone who was accustomed to chaos, this peace I felt, began to feel very uncomfortable.

I craved the instant satisfaction of a quick high which was unrecognizable on mushrooms; I began to resist my experience. And this is not good, at all. I became fearless without judgment and harmful to myself without restraint. I walked under bridges alone, sought comfort in the depths of the forest around me. Now, this may sound like something out of a fairytale, but this part of the American River I found myself in, was homeless and crime infested. I had gone looking for trouble. A part of me wanted to be physically hurt.

184

My obsession with self-harm was now not only limited to what I could do to do myself, but what others could do to me. I wanted to die, I was heartbroken, and I refused to deal with my problems in a healthy way. I didn't know how to handle my problems in a healthy way.

Years of suffering and not once had I properly healed myself. When suffering and avoidance starts to add up like that, hope is nowhere to be found. I felt that if I got a head start on hurting myself no one could do as much harm as I could do to myself. The path of destruction and suffering was much more comforting and familiar to me. On this path, I was allowed to be who I thought I was. The moments I experienced out in nature were as lonely as the moments I spent inside my own apartment.

The magic mushrooms I took became not so magical. Everything became dark, real dark. A type of dark where you feel it consuming the inside of your mind, body and soul; the type of dark were the voices in your head start to become your only friend. The type of dark were a park, at 4 PM on a sunny afternoon, becomes so hopeless and depressing you began to dream about life on the other side and fantasize about ways to get you there. Because I had experienced another world on the plant, it was easy for me to have desires to end up back in that place, only this time permanently.

At the time, it was truly unfortunate that my integration process went down this path. Looking back, it eventually allowed me to understand what duality truly means. But, it does deeply concern me that although psychedelics are great for therapy, there are huge risks if the patient does not integrate properly. America is currently pushing for psychedelics to be used in modern medicine for psychotherapy and addiction. This does seem great in retrospect, unfortunately the meetings and conferences I have sat in on over the last year in 2022 and 2023, no one can properly answer me about what they are instilling in their therapies and integration process. This is very alarming considering that the integration process is everything.

The setting of the sun changed the reality of my headspace which urged me to go back home. On my bike ride back to the apartment, I convinced myself that my thoughts about suicide, death and despair were normal.

There are a lot of moments like this bike ride. Often times, I had normalized what experiences I had with rape, self-harm and intentionally putting myself in dangerous situations. I had become numb to the evils of the world and became an evil of my own. Although I grew up as a Christian, at this point in my life, I didn't know of a God or what any relationship with him looked like, like I do now. All faith and hope were lost. The personality I took on during this time in my life solely revolved around trying to accept the false sense of self I had.

However, I did feel that it was important to find inner peace and happiness for myself because I was tired of feeling disturbed. Instead of getting sober, which I should have done first, I found comfort in spirituality.

Into the summer of 2019, I began to introduce friends, family and followers to my new adopted lifestyle and beliefs. Again, I felt that if I had the approval and validation of others that meant that I was okay. I did truly believe in the spiritual teachings, books I read and insight I had received from continuous mushroom trips. Yet, I was living a life with no relationship to any higher power, the higher power I would someday get to know again as God. I'm aware this higher power has many faces and names around the world, but I got to know this higher power as God.

My hyper focus on spirituality kept me from not wanting to kill myself or experience suicidal ideation during the summer of 2019. It gave me reason and purpose every day. Although, it did contribute to my delusional ideas. I had become so blissful and ignorant in a way.

What I have come to learn is that practicing spirituality without a higher power, only feeds into the super conscious of your ego. When I was praying or manifesting, who or what was I praying and manifesting to? Like I said, I had no relationship with a higher power at the time. All this subconsciously fed into my ego.

Now, in life, a healthy balanced ego is necessary. To have a healthy balanced ego, one must be aware of the conscious cognitive shifts that occurs as a result of the polarity of ego and intuition. To have a healthy and balanced ego, it's important to have a sense of humility. A healthy ego can give you the confidence to accomplish goals in your life, take a leap of faith or try something new. An unhealthy, unmanaged and imbalanced ego will take a mind of its own. If one is not aware of this, the ego could be mistaken for intuition. A lot of people who go through manic episodes or psychosis often mistake their unhealthy, imbalanced ego for intuition.

Ignoring your true intuition is the act of not trusting yourself. To disregard the inner voice is to follow a path unaligned with your purpose. When I first began my journey into spirituality, I was a complete fool to this information. Information is a poor word to use in this case, I had a knowing of the within and without, the above and below, but I had no inner knowledge. I thought the point of spirituality was to find another path outside of a higher power, my intentions were self-serving. I had learned so much on the plant, which was almost a year ago now, but because of the secrets Andre and Judah kept from me during that weekend, I didn't believe anything I had learned.

Because, I was so foolish at this time of self-discovery, it did teach me many lessons, insight and dynamics to the human experience. I do, however, believe todays spiritual community, from my personal experience, are lost souls without a true knowingness or relation to a higher power like I once was. Now, spirituality is a practice in learning thyself, yet the ones we also learn from, myself included, are not figures to be praised.

That imbalanced ego tends to disrupt this path and in modern times it's very easy to allow this to happen. The toxicity that comes with today's culture, engulfs many without them even being aware of the conscious cognitive shift happening within them. Although I meant plenty good at this time in my life, I surrounded myself with what I thought were like minded individuals, yet it was all under the umbrella of egos essence.

Living fully submerged in an ego driven fantasy land, I felt what I was doing came from a genuine place. Again, this is because I had no higher power and the only counsel I took, was from myself. The right belief, right thought, right speech, right purpose, right passion, right community and right faith was far left in my case. Now everyone's beliefs and faith are different, and that is okay. The problem occurs when an imbalanced ego and self-serving purposes get mixed into it.

The journey of self-discovery is a unique and complex time in most people's lives. Once you discover that the key to it all is simply the right belief, thought, speech, purpose, passion, community and faith. The complexity of many drinks, many lovers, many spiritual practices, many drugs, many lives and many identities ease away. It is difficult to share in detail what this time in life was really like for me because of all the complexities I was experiencing and living through.

I do however remember the feeling of being empowered, free, magical and mischievous. Every day was special and unique. It was a life of carelessness, freedom of the heart, yet not the mind, a healthy diet yet a hidden addiction. Life was either swinging to the left or to the right; I was never balanced, nor did I have the spiritual strength to become balanced.

My dependence on spiritual tools like tarot cards and substances overpowered my own will. I was a prisoner in my own mind. The suffering I inflicted on myself was the only suffering I put myself through during this time of life, I had become addicted to suffering. Now that I am writing in a place of harmony, I look back and see all the times I could've helped myself by simplifying my life. Instead, I complicated everything to fill the void.

For a long time, my life story was about being the victim and what others had done to me, what I couldn't accept, what I couldn't forgive and what I couldn't let go of. I turned into a dependent attention seeker. Deep down, all I wanted was the true love of another, but my inability to truly love and look at myself for who I was wouldn't allow me to find that.

Chapter 20

Circles

As surely as I valued your life today, so may the Lord value my life and deliver me from all trouble. 1 Samuel 26:24

I was now 22 years old, thinking I had it all figured out. I had friends in LA to party with during the weekdays and weekends paired with a no fucks given attitude. Life for me had gone from being depressed, suicidal and alone to becoming what I thought as a spiritual being while living life in the fast lane. I thought because of the spiritual work I had done that I was now being rewarded with a glamorous life. Really this was just the devil working in plain sight.

I was single, 'spiritual' and sensual. That was until November 20th, 2019 the night my beautiful friend Gwen invited me to a Post Malone concert at the forum in Los Angeles. Gwen is a true friend in my life with a heart of gold and I absolutely adored her then as I do now. She recently started modeling in Los Angeles and was given VIP tickets to the Post Malone concert. This was something Los Angeles promoters did often to get beautiful girls in and around the scene.

I remember the feeling of not wanting to go because it was last minute, and I didn't particularly know any songs by the artist. Yet she convinced me because it was going to be a good night. With my make-up and hair halfway done and a casual dress on, she picked me up in her Mercedes. There was another model with her who was so fierce she actually scared me.

All three of us ready for a night of fun. Casual me and two gorgeous models, what a fucking life this was looking back. This would be the night where my life's story takes a turn.

This was the last night of Post Malones tour, which was held at the Forum. I was underdressed and not prepared for any of it, but I was happy to be there. The inside of the venue was grand and beautiful. All the greats of my generation and past generations played here. Thousands of people gathered here this night to watch their favorite artist perform, and I was taking it all in.

I most definitely experienced imposter syndrome that night. That feeling of "Wow I can't believe this is happening, who am I to be here right now?" you know... that feeling. Nonetheless, I was going to enjoy myself. The first hour I followed the lead of my long-legged companions. We ordered margaritas and pretzels because we had forgotten to eat anything before arriving; a carb meal was in order to make it through our night of fun.

In the VIP concession area, I took notice of a very tall, slender guy. He was by himself and looked a little anxious. We made eye contact a couple of times and every time I turned around, he was in my line of view. He was certainly my type, and I could feel I was his, too.

Our energy was friendly towards one another, but it

wasn't until he saw us lining up to go backstage that he made his move. As I was getting ready to walk off, he asked me, "Hey, who are you waiting for?"

In my head I thought, "Uh, Post Malone, dude…" but I responded kindly to his attempt to talk to me and simply said, "I don't know."

The encounter with this man came and left, or so I thought. I didn't give any mind to it because I was living my life carefree and if it was meant to be I'd see him again, or maybe another three times that night.

Backstage at the forum were celebrities, other performing artists, hard liquor and unimpressive display of food. We hung out while the opening artist preformed on stage, getting our buzz on and taking selfies. The hard liquor became empty as fast as the staff sat it out. So, us three girls went back out to the first concession area to get another margarita. There I saw this tall, slender man again, looking frantic. He was cute and kind of dorky to me.

"What is he doing?" I thought to myself.

Time was moving quickly; we had our drinks in hand and the girls wanted to go backstage. Our buzz was on, well I should say my buzz was on because it for sure was, along with my confidence. We were now just minutes away from seeing Post Malone come out on stage.

But, at this point, only an hour into being inside the venue I was intoxicated. The long-legged beauties walked fast, and I couldn't keep up. They walked in front, leading the way and with one head turn to look back at fans in the stands, I lost the girls.

The tall, slender, handsome, mysterious man found me the moment I lost my friends. There he was, looking down at me, while I, in amazement that we now ran into each other for a third time, looked back up to him. He was at least a whole foot taller than me, and I am 5'8". With a blunt in his hand, he asks me, "You smoke?"

I said, "No, thank you." and with a bat of my big brown eyes I said to him, "I can't find my friends."

Our eyes were locked, Post Malone just came out on stage when he said, "I'm Louie."

I responded, "Hi, I'm Marissa." and in one swift motion he grabbed me by the face gently and kissed me.

It was sweet, but I was shocked. I froze, and with a confident lead he said, "Follow me."

Without hesitation I did. He grabbed my hand, his hands were huge. I felt so small with him, he had to have been at least six foot seven. The connection was instant, it was as if we were kids on the first day of kindergarten and chose each other.

We just met, and this was a movie-esque moment for the both of us. He stood a whole foot over me and right behind me with his slender build while I stood right in front of him like a squished version; thick and short.

From the outside perspective maybe, we looked awkward, but we were two peas in a pod. Post Malone came out to perform, and the production was heavenly. It was as if the scene was set for the two of us. Louie and I danced and sang together. I was taken by surprise at how many songs I knew. To this day, that is the best concert I've been to. Everything was perfect.

Louie smoked a blunt behind me, we shared margaritas and I danced on him all night. We had the time of our life. Because he was so tall and standing behind me most of the time it was hard to make eye contact with him. Although we shared a similar frequency, the second time he and I made eye contact I knew he was going to be a part of my life.

The lights changed from a pink and orange ambiance to a dark blue hue. I turned around to face Louie and with my back to the stage, Post Malone began to sing Circles. If you ever get the chance to listen to that song, it pretty much describes our relationship together. We made eye contact for the second time that night and it was as if we had both been charmed. He hugged me and I had laid my head on his chest, ear to heart. His slender build made it so I could sink right into his frame. We connected like a puzzle piece.

We spent the whole concert together; I had honestly forgotten I even came with my friends until the concert ended. My phone was on 3% and I had no clue where they were. But Louie was with me. He was in a hurry to meet up with some friends so they could make their way back to Hollywood. Louie and I left the stadium together, hand in hand. His legs were so long, I practically had to run to keep up. He had a lot of energy; I think it was due to our unexpected night we experienced. Since my phone died and I couldn't order an uber he suggested I take a cab back to the place I was staying.

His friends were in the uber behind the taxi I was getting in. They were all yelling for him to hurry up. I gave him my number, he kissed me again before we said goodbye.

Our night ended there at the taxi, but it was just the start of where my story begins with him. I wanted to take time out of this book to share my life up until this point to really paint a picture of the person I was. It wasn't until what came almost two years later of being with Louie that I became who I am now.

This relationship taught me a lot, put me through a lot and without it there would be no, Still Fucking Alive. Before I continue, Louie if you're reading this a piece of my heart goes out to you.

During my taxi ride back to my place of stay, I kept replaying that night over and over again in my head. The driver asked, "Why isn't your boyfriend riding with you?"

I replied, "Oh, yeah. Well, he wanted to be with his friends."

"Did we come off as a couple already?" I thought to myself.

And this is when my fantasies about the possibilities of him and I began. My energy, heart, and mind were on level ten. As soon as I got back to my place on the beach, I made sure to charge my phone in case he texted me, which he did. Louie really wanted me to meet him at a club in Hollywood, but this was all new to me, so I didn't.

The next day Louie and I texted plenty. He asked me to go out with him for dinner. I drove to his apartment which was right off of Hollywood boulevard. I remember driving down Selma and seeing the Hollywood sign for the first time; it was beautiful.

I was like a puppy that had been taken to the park for the first time. It was about 6 pm so there was quite a bit of folks out. Looking back, the fact I drove from Malibu to Hollywood during rush hour goes to show how ignorant I was about Los Angeles even with something as simple as this. Or was is it that I had been yearning to be loved and would go to great lengths for it? I think it was a little of both, which would qualify me as a fool at this point.

Finding parking on Hollywood Boulevard wasn't

easy, but as lucky as I had gotten the night before, my luck struck twice right outside El Centro otherwise known as the lively, luxurious apartment building in the center of Hollywood. I found parking right outside the massive building; it took up four blocks on the boulevard. Louie said, he'd come out to greet me and bring me up to his place. As he was walking towards me, I was in shock yet again at how tall he was. I must have forgotten considering all the other thoughts and feelings I had going on inside of me. Louie had an interesting look, a clean fade on the sides of his head which flowed into a bun. He had a friendly and welcoming energy, like he had known me for years. His confidence about me took me off guard, which made it hard to read him. Although I was nervous, I was interested.

Even though it was the end of November, I wore a summer dress. In Los Angeles where anything is possible, especially Hollywood, you can pretty much wear whatever you want. Later I would come to find out that your style is your résumé in the city. Any who, Louie greeted me, walking with purpose and hugged me the moment I was in reach of his long arms. When he pulled me in, the shape and figure of my body felt like it melted into his. He was as thin as he was tall, but I loved the way he looked, I liked his style and to me he had a very handsome face which was set with big green eyes and nice plump lips.

We embraced each other; I think he was just as surprised as me that I actually showed up. He grabbed my hand and led me to the building. On our way to his apartment, he proudly gave me a tour of all the amenities and scenery around the building.

This place was like a resort. It had beautiful tropical plants bordering walkways, stunning residents hanging out around the complex, and beautiful bungalows on the first floor. I felt as if I was in an oasis.

196

I certainly did not expect any of this. I've never known anyone in Los Angeles who really had it like this. He talked a lot and talked fast; I think he was pretty nervous, but also excited. After 20 minutes of walking, we finally made it up to his apartment where I would come to meet some of his friends.

I felt like a fish out of water in comparison to them, but good people are good people. I wasn't going to let my insecurities get in the way of knowing them. Louie had some work to finish, he seemed a bit stressed, yet I remained unbothered.

Everyone in Los Angeles has some type of hustle and seeing them package up product wasn't a second thought to me; I took this as an opportunity to feel out the energy and check out his apartment.

The living room and kitchen were one big space, and the balcony overlooked the pool and hot tub which were both Olympic size. The largest TV I had ever seen was sitting behind the hot tub. It must've been thirteen feet tall and twenty feet wide.

After about thirty minutes of waiting for Louie and his friends to finish work, he was more than ready to go on a date with me. He must've been hungry or "hangry" I should say. He insisted on a great Italian spot down the street just a short walk from the apartment.

We arrived at the restaurant around 7 PM. It was a nice restaurant, and of course he already knew the best items to order. Therefore, I let him order for me. Our conversation at the table flowed easily and romantically. We talked about our experience together the night before and how great it was, we both shared pieces about ourselves which consisted of how we ended up in Los Angeles and what we were doing here. Although I was just visiting a friend, I wasn't a stranger to frequent flights and stays. In my early twenties I was on a bus or flight to Los Angeles at least three times a month just so I could party and do drugs. But I didn't share this truth about myself to him. Instead, I lied and stuck to my story of visiting my girlfriends.

I hid the truth from him because this wasn't a reality I was willing to admit to anyone including myself. During this time in my life and especially the time I spent in Los Angeles, I believed and only knew that what people had or did was all that mattered. I became a materialistic person and completely unaware of the simple magic of just being myself. I only valued myself by what I had, did, or accomplished. Not by my true character, which in turn, I did not value others in a genuine way, but only at the level I subconsciously viewed myself.

This would become my demise along with an unacknowledged substance abuse problem. In this moment with him, I came from a place of my then definition of love. I didn't want to disappoint this new guy by being a nobody. I lied about myself to him from this day onward and I had been lying to myself all along.

I was completely unaware of the consequences or how much this would actually affect my connection and trust with him. I was always okay at finding a way out when things got sticky or complicated because of my lack of integrity and honesty. Louie and I just met, and he didn't have a baseline of who I was or what I was capable of. And for myself, looking at him, neither did I.

Chapter 21

Death Wish

Remember, it is sin to know what
you ought to do and then not do it.
James 4:17

We both had our flaws, yet fate brought us together,
which now I know the reason for, but we will get there in later
chapters.

Our dinner went great and our exchange of
glamorizing our own lives had come to an end. He invited me
back to his apartment and of course I said yes. We only talked
for a little while longer back at his place, we kissed but no
sex. I knew I had a flight the following afternoon and I still
needed to pack my things, so I left his house around 9 PM.

We had such a nice time together that when I got into
the car to head back to Malibu, I already missed his company.
The moment I got to my friends' place, I packed up my
things, all the while messaging Louie trying to schmooze my
way back over to his place; convincing him was easy. Just as
quickly as I could pack my things, I was on my way to spend
the night with him before my flight back to Sacramento the
following day. This part felt like a rush of energy. It was now
11pm, and the both of us were looking forward to our night
together.

The fact I came back a second time had him feeling more confident than before. The Uber dropped me off and Louie met me outside to bring me up to his place again. It was about 11:45 PM now and all of his friends had left, it was finally just him and I.

I remember us going into his room and seeing his California king bed for the first time. We snuggled up with some liquor and put on Disney+, our movie choice was 'The Night before Christmas'. It was kind of cute because he did remind me of Jack the Skeleton, which I told him and without hesitation he said I reminded him of Sally. That was our first movie we watched together, he set the mood lights and provided snacks, it was as if we were having a good ol' fashioned sleepover.

The time we spent together flew by. It was now sunrise and Louie booked me a new flight home. We were in love already, so I thought, but I've come to understand that this was the feeling of lust and a byproduct of how addicts attach to others. Louie was a new drug to me. I couldn't help myself and neither could he. Once my new ticket was booked, we both fell fast asleep through the morning and into the afternoon.

I already felt as if I was home, as if we were a couple. And after that night, that's what it was between us. Instant addiction to one another and how this happened was beyond the both of us. The thrill of it all was electric.

I ended up staying with him for a whole week and we had a great time. From meeting friends, going out to the best clubs in Hollywood or hanging out by the pool; we had a blast in La La Land. And after seven days of pushing back my flight, I had to eventually go home. Our goodbye was upsetting, although I made sure to book a flight back to see him again before I left.

My mother who I had been living with at the time had no idea who I was with or what I was doing out In Los Angeles the last week. When I got home, my ego was inflated, and I hadn't really considered how I made her feel or the worry I put her through. All I told her was that I would be going back soon to meet with someone special. My mother would become numb to my erratic behavior. As unfortunate as it is, that's just the truth of what kind of daughter I was at the time. I wish I was better to my mother, but I cannot change the past. This is something I would also have to come to face during my journey.

I had worked the next two weeks and the only intention I had of spending my money on was what I could do in Los Angeles and the drugs I could take with me. Louie and I talked every day, all day. We couldn't go a waking hour without talking to one another.

The two weeks we were apart in distance was filled with 3 am phone calls, thousands of texts messages and plenty of daydreaming. It was now the second week of December. I told my mother I was going to see Gwen for the weekend when all I had truly planned for was to see Louie.

The short hour flight from Sacramento to Los Angeles, I drank wine. When I stepped off the plane, I was intoxicated, but the Los Angeles smog gave me an excitement for the city and what was to come like no other. I ordered myself an uber to Louie's apartment. Seeing him again was like meeting up with a best friend on the playground. Except for the fact he was 28 and our playground was Hollywood. As soon as we walked into his apartment, I unpacked my things into the closet.

I remember how things felt and what we did, but we never had a moment of sitting down to share our true stories, desires, dreams or goals. In his day to day, there was a lot of drama, business and partying. Almost every night we would go out to dinner and the club.

Louie and I walked to the club about four blocks away from the apartment and met up with his friends. It was a blast, we had bottle service, a table and the place was filled with attractive people. He smoked, I drank and ran off every now and then to do some cocaine.

I fit right in, except for the part where I would run off to do drugs. In Hollywood you could just do them. Some might give you a strange look, but it's nothing they'd never seen before. I didn't know this until I saw another girl do it. This was a scene I didn't have to hide who I was and what I liked to do. Louie and I danced, made-out and before I knew it, the club was shutting down.

On our way out, a girl from another table came up to me and said, "Come to Jamie Foxes after party!"

The funny thing about LA is people will say anything to get you interested in doing something. Louie kept walking and I was friendly to the girl as I was flattered by her gesture. But I declined her offer. When I got outside of the club, I found Louie and told him the funny and random encounter I just had.

And it was this moment, he yelled at me for the first time. He was so hurt and jealous about the interaction I had, that I was now at the will of his anger and aggression. Louie called me out of my name by saying things like, "Hollywood Hoe" and how I was "Just like every other bitch in this city."

I was to stunned to speak. In my eyes I wasn't doing anything wrong and the fact that it was so easy for him to demean me and call me out of my name shook me up.

His anger was so intense and uncalled for that it made

me think that I really did do something wrong. On our uber ride back home, I tried to touch his arm or leg, yet he wanted no parts of this by the way he was pushing my hands off him. I attempted to defend myself and get to the root of the problem, but he ignored me and shut me out.

I felt trapped in this situation and scared of the person who Louie suddenly became. I had never seen this side of him before. When we got back to his apartment, I desperately tried to defend myself and kept repeating, "I thought the interaction was innocent and wanted to share it with you."

This only made him angrier, his face turned red, and I was in tears. This was the night that he categorized me as nothing more than the names he so easily called me. We were not officially dating at all and I should have left him that night.

Just like I saw my mother deal with my father I tried my best to make Louie feel better. I tried comforting him even though he acted as if he didn't want it. I put up with this treatment from another man because of what I was taught, shown and to a degree, familiar with.

He truly couldn't have cared less about my explanation or apologies and here I was basically on my knees asking for forgiveness. After an hour of this back-and-forth game, I decided it was best to give him space.

As I got up from his couch to walk away, he says in a threatening tone, "Oh, so you don't want to be around me because you got dudes to text?"

I submitted to him out of fear. I was in a place where I questioned myself and didn't understand how insecure or what issues he had until this incident. His attitude, mood and personality switched so fast, it was as if he suffered from Jekyll and Hyde syndrome. It was most frightening the way his chest poked out and how he closed his fists at his side or the way he paced and the bad energy coming out of him. Yet the moment I walked away and stopped fighting with him and the delusions, he became what reminded me of a scared, abandoned child.

It was now 3 am, I was tired and had nowhere to go. So, I stayed; Louie never apologized or believed me, nothing had been resolved, yet he was so certain of what kind of person I was. Louie became insecure and had now villainized me into a whore as if my intentions were not pure. And this would become how Louie always viewed me, even though my kindness and sweetness is what attracted him to me in the first place; it was what he became threatened by.

The remainder of this night I submitted to him; I was timid to be anything else because of the mental and emotional abuse. Now that I am 25 and in a healed place, I have no tolerance for any type of abuse. I learned from previous experiences to submit to the abuser and try my best to diffuse the situation. Unfortunately, this backfired because my submission was taken as a sign of being guilty and the mark of red, he painted on me, stained me from this day forward.

The following day, I cleaned his apartment and fixed breakfast, my attempt at proving my worth to him worked because he began to soften up towards me. I did feel some relief knowing he had calmed down, yet now I was walking on eggshells.

I began to wonder why anyone would want to keep someone around who they felt was all those things he called and viewed me as. Yet, I stayed because I was so desperate for love and he sold me a Hollywood dream.

This would be around the time I became responsible for his happiness. Trying to make a delusional, aggressive, insecure man happy is like trying to mop the bottom of the ocean floor; and if the pressure from the ocean doesn't kill you, you'll end up killing yourself.

Louie officially asked me to be his girlfriend on January 1st, 2020. When the clock struck midnight on New Year's Eve, I was now his. I wasn't expecting this to happen considering I hadn't been living in Los Angeles yet. I put no thought into it and said yes.

I was now his, officially. With each meal out, party we went to, or club we attended, I became all those words he had preached into me. Isn't that funny how life works? Things between Louie and I never got any better, we never should've dated, but I wouldn't change a thing for the reason that this part of my life also made me who I am today.

Only a week into dating, I had quit my job back in Sacramento and moved to Los Angeles to be with Louie. I had no plan for myself, no job lined up or any idea what I would be doing down there aside from being his girlfriend. I put myself in a position where I was completely dependent on him. I subconsciously and continuously sought out what I was missing in my life, I deeply felt that this way of living was okay.

Louie needed me to be this way, and I accepted it. The verbal abuse didn't stop or lighten up. There were a lot of times where I would try to establish some type of respect or dominance, but it always backfired.

Louie was very exhausting day in and day out. He accused me of things that made absolutely no sense, yet he believed his own delusions and conclusions. There was no changing his mind. He controlled me through such intense manipulation, even as far as gaslighting me. I began to lose the ability to think for myself. This man had no control over his emotions and took everything out on me with his words and mind games. I had gone from living carefree and having

205

fun to shrinking myself for him and walking on eggshells. It is a death wish to compromise who you are for someone else. It is a death wish to be responsible for someone else's happiness, they will never be happy, and nothing will ever be good enough. You'll lose a piece of yourself every time.

Chapter 22

Thanks for the Idea

Peace I leave you; my peace I give
you. I do not give you as the world
gives. Do not let your hearts be
troubled and do not be afraid.
John 14:27

I began living in survival mode, which is when you change your thought, speech, and actions to adapt to a dangerous or threatening situation. Remember earlier what I said about having the 'right' speech, thought, action, passion, purpose, community, and belief? Well, the 'right' way for me was whatever would help me survive. Unfortunately, the survival mode I was in didn't recognize this. It wasn't until years later, when I sought professional help, did I understand what happened. Survival mode is the process of receiving a threatening signal, whether it be verbal or physical and doing what you have to, to protect the emotions of the aggressor. The aggressor being the one to send out that threatening signal in the first place.

That last part is a little confusing, I asked myself "Now why would I have to protect the aggressors' feelings?" The answer is that an aggressor who is catered to and constantly feels like they are in charge, keeps the victim out of physical harm's way. I hate to have to refer to myself as a victim here, but that was my reality. I had no idea what it even meant to be a fighter. This is a constant cycle I lived through and no one knew how bad it was. I didn't realize how bad it was until the day I sought help.

The cycle I was experiencing also involved what I call the "recovery" process. I'm putting this in quotations because it wasn't a real recovery, although at the time, I believed it was. All it really meant to me then was making up with Louie in desperate hopes that things would change and not resurface. Nothing was ever resolved or fixed, only stored in his back pocket for later torment and use.

Now, not every moment was like this. There were happy times, not completely happy days, but happy moments. It could've been a date night or making one another breakfast, but there were small happy moments which I held onto in between the bad times.

I did try to challenge his thinking with the intention of changing the way he thought. I would ask him very blunt questions like, "Why don't you tell me I'm pretty?" He would respond, "I can't let that get to your head" or "Why don't you make love to me?" And he would respond, "Because you don't deserve it."

I was constantly trying to prove my worth and love to him yet there was never any type of recognition or reciprocity. I wasn't a bad girlfriend; I definitely had my issues, but I did not deserve this. Comments and actions like this are what led me to seek love outside of our relationship. Again, I should've left.

To not live-in integrity, to have no stability, to lack a relationship with self and God, is the beginning of the end. This fever dream of a Hollywood lifestyle with him fueled a life of liquor, drugs, lies, suffering and desperation. A desperation we had both put on ourselves. Time from January

2020 through March 2020 was fast, abusive and unfocused.

Louie and I had been experimenting with magic mushrooms, LSD and DMT with each other. One night his bad energy oozed out of him like an infected pimple. And if that wasn't enough, his face began to terrify me. His laugh scared me, and the things he talked about I had no interest in at all. I felt so incredibly disgusted to be around him.

I had never experienced anything like that. His demands even while tripping put me in a dark space. His insecurities and ugliness came out; I had no way to escape so I tried my best to ignore him and sleep it off. I experienced many horrific visions and nightmares this night.

He was a fool with a deep unaware, obscure vision of life, community and love. This was clear to me now, and here I was trapped in Hollywood with him. The following day I made sure to take a hot shower and do some self-care. But, getting out of bed earlier than him or not spending hours in bed with him before I did anything else would typically result in him scolding me. So, I made sure to suit his comfort's before mine. This was how most mornings went. He'd turn on a movie, smoke a blunt and scold me if I dared get out of bed and start my day.

I had no interest in him early on in our living situation, I tried, but I always felt it in my gut that something was not right. I thought maybe I was the problem, maybe I didn't deserve love because I was not worthy of it. Maybe the ugliness I saw in him was an ugliness in me.

I finally got to step into the shower and have time for myself. Attempting to create a safe space, when the door burst open.

"Why are you in a rush this morning?" Louie says.

Startled and knowing whatever answer I gave was going to make him upset, I evaded conflict by not sharing the truth about wanting a safe space. I said softly, "Oh, the shrooms just made me sweaty."

And to my demise, he responded, "Shit me too, I'm hopping in."

I could never have my own space. It was clear to me he no longer nor ever saw me as just, Marissa. Never mind a human or friend. I was his property, and I was to be treated as such.

The guy I met at the concert was no longer around. The day we started dating officially, he completely changed- I changed. My identity was no longer present, my beliefs were no longer present, but all of my demons and entities were. I suppressed my feelings and desires with cocaine and alcohol. With each coat of mascara, I hid behind a mask. A mask and false identity curated for Hollywood and survival.

Day in and day out, I lied to myself. Day in and day out, I called my mom and friends from home in sadness and loneliness. Day in and day out, I posted on social media like everything was fine, but I was far from it.

The first week of March had flown by and all of a sudden it felt like an apocalypse had happened. COVID-19 just broke news and it felt as if the end of the world had begun from all that was being said. The two-week lockdown meant we were to stock up on alcohol, groceries, weed and for me, cocaine; Louie never did cocaine, but he did allow me to do it. We made sure we were going to get the most out of our two-week break from life, as if we weren't already doing that.

I don't remember necessarily being in fear of Covid. It seemed more like a break from the world the way our friend group took turns convening at one another's home to eat, party and hang out. The whole city shut down, yet the people did not. It was a good couple of fun nights, but of course it did not cure or heal anything between Louie and I.

Because we were spending time with his friends more often than usual, I got to know them and actually befriend a few. They were all different, unique, kind and sober. A lot of his friends had met in the previous years in AA meetings. So, I had to hide my addiction a little more than I wanted to, I wanted them to like me. What I failed to realize that if I would've been honest about my addiction, they would've been the first people to help me. One particular friend of Louies', named John; had similar interests as me in spirituality and life, we always made great conversation.

John was not my type, and I respected the dynamic of their friendship to not think about him more than a friend. Unfortunately, Louie's insecurities got in the way and he accused me of wanting to sleep with his friend, be in a relationship with his friend and that John was now my little boyfriend. These accusations were absolutely absurd. I didn't even have Johns' number, only his Instagram, as did everyone else we hung out with. But like I said, Louie never saw me as a human, only as his property.

One night there was a group of us that did mushrooms and DMT together. Louie, while in his trip watched me like a hawk. His jealous and insecure nature was so obvious and disruptive, I had no other option but to distract myself by baking desserts for our guests. I knew, in my heart, I was not doing anything wrong and there was no need for him to put this energy out there.

Unfortunately, John began to have a bad trip because of Louie's horrible energy and went back to his apartment one floor above us and down the hall. Louie was happy about this, almost like a bully who gets off on hurting others. I felt terrible about it but did my best to let it go.

About a half an hour later, we ate the chocolate chip banana bread I made, but unfortunately, we were out of butter and paper towels. Louie didn't have any in the apartment and since I was now hosting our friends, I went to our neighbor, John, to borrow some. I found him meditating and trying to understand why this bad energy was happening to him. It was only about two minutes since I had walked out of Louie's apartment and as I'm standing by the door, with John twenty-five feet away from me on the other side of the room, Louie aggressively walks up and says, "Oh! I see what's going on. Enjoy your little boyfriend."

He had followed me in distrust and assumed I was up to no good. His insecurities were becoming pathetic. I grabbed what I came for, said sorry to John and walked back to Louie's apartment bracing myself for punishment.

I found Louie spazzing out when I walked in, it was as if he could not control himself. Nothing had conspired between John and I, but Louie painted me red and there was no convincing him of my innocence. The only thing I could do now was to yet again submit to his will of terror. The cycle began again, and I know what you're thinking, when is she going to learn?

I became extremely discouraged; I had never had someone relentlessly treat me this way. I was still on shrooms and it dawned on me that I was the best thing to ever happen to Louie, which is why he became so controlling. His insecurities about himself is what ran our relationship to a dead end.

Our friends unfortunately picked up on Louie's bad energy and collectively decided to go home. That's how most nights ended; I was made to look like the bad guy every time. I knew this for certain because this pattern became so obvious that none of his friends ever really struck up a conversation with me after this, I was isolated. When his friends left, Louie began yelling at me with all of his might about the delusions he was having between John and I. He was so threatened by Johns' inner gifts and light. It made me think, is this the reason that he treats me this way? Is he threatened by my full potential? The argument became so ridiculous I couldn't help but laugh at one point. He did not like this one bit, it made him even more angry. Louie balled his fist and got in my face calling me every name in the book; every time I tried to open my mouth, he told me too "Shut the fuck up."

This experience was awful. I screamed back to him, "I wasn't even thinking about fucking your friend until now, at least he treats me with some respect! Thanks for the idea!"

Louie turned red in the face; he left the house to go God knows where, doing God knows what. I was just happy to be left alone. That was until he blew up my phone telling me how worthless I was. Instead of responding, I went about my night and showered than fell asleep on the couch, just happy to be safe and left alone. The next morning, he had acted like nothing had happened and so did I.

This was our relationship 80% of the time. Louie and I never resolved the John situation. Not because I didn't try to resolve it but because he wouldn't let any of his delusions, insecurities or jealousy go. This strife in our relationship taught me how I was unallowed to make new friends, even if they were his.

This unspoken rule in our relationship was one sided which hurt me as well. I was made to shrink myself and watch my words even more carefully than before. It was clear to not only me, but all of his friends that it was a dangerous game to connect with one another. Any extra conversation or complements was a warrant for a dirty side eye from Louie or a disgusting energy which radiated off of him.

My status wasn't Louie's girlfriend, it was Louie's property. At least that's how I felt from the inside out. In a mentally and emotionally abusive relationship, the victim is most likely experiencing isolation, degration and separation. I was isolated from friends and family. I was degraded by his words and actions. And lastly, I was separated from my true self.

The only identity I had now was Louie's girlfriend. The idea of that in Hollywood led me to cling onto Louie for safety and approval because that's all I was to anyone including myself. I couldn't hang out with any friends without his approval. I rarely saw Gwen, if ever.

With each disapproval and harassment, he won. I soon had no friends in LA I could go to. I only had him and was now solely reliant on him. This is quite the conundrum because he wanted to be the only person for me to rely on, yet he was completely unreliable and unavailable.

I guess this is how control works. What little he could do, he did only if I was "good" which is extremely hard to do when that person is constantly looking for the bad in you. Nothing was ever good enough and if things were okay, even for a minute, he was always commenting things like "Don't fuck shit up again."

Was I truly so desperate for love that I accepted the spoiled crumbs he gave me? Although, for an addict and alcoholic like I was, this was good for me. He didn't care or question my use because when I did use, I never left the house. The drugs and alcohol also felt better because they numbed so much hurt inside of me.

Cocaine numbed me and kept me busy- cutting lines, waiting for the drip, cutting and snorting more lines. Drinking allowed me to let loose and let go of any loneliness or sadness I was experiencing.

I got to experience a lot of Hollywood parties, clubs, culture and people, yet most of my nights looked and felt like this. I had no awareness of what habits I was creating and how I was slowly losing my mind and sense of reality. I don't know if my family had any idea or hunch about what was going on.

The times my family would ask how I was doing, I lied. I wanted my family's approval for two reasons; one being I didn't want to disappoint them and two, I didn't want them to worry about me. But the reality of it is, I left home to live in this big city with a guy I hadn't known for more than two months. I kept telling myself "I'm young" or that God put me in this position for a reason. Now, I do agree when you're young it is important to take risks and God did put me here for a reason much bigger than any boyfriend or what Hollywood could ever give me.

My path continued to stray further away from myself and my true identity. I had forgotten myself, but there was one person during this time that brought me back to my core, made me feel safe and had been a true friend; and that was Daniel.

Chapter 23

Safe Place

Come to me all of you who are tired.
You are like people who have
worked for a long time. You are like
people who have carried heavy
things, come to me. If you do that,
you will find a place to rest. I will
not tell you to do things that are too
difficult. I will not tell you to carry
anything that is too heavy for you.
Matthew 11:28-30

Now, Daniel and I did not talk every day, he was busy and for myself I was actually forbidden to speak to him. At one point I was forced to block Daniel because of Louies insecurities. This led me to resent Louie. I was in Hollywood suffering and the one person who I was able to be myself with and feel a sense of peace with, was now my boyfriend's biggest enemy. It didn't help that I was honest with Louie about Daniel and I's friendship. Louie couldn't handle me being fake friends with people let alone a real friendship. I began to hate Louie, and rebel against his demands. I began to think to myself, that if Louie was going to project his insecurities onto me and continue to label my thoughts and actions as whatever delusions he had going on in his mind, then I might as well act on these accusations.

This made perfect sense to me because if he already believed I was the cheating whore he made me out to be and continued to still be with me, why not actually become one? And aside from these thoughts I was very lonely. I couldn't talk to Louie about anything, whether it be simple day-to-day things or stories from the past, his jealousy, anger or hate arose and if not that, judgment.

The summer of 2020 came and by this time I was completely exhausted from Louie. I visited home for the first time in months, it felt so good to be home in Sacramento with my family and friends. I was with people who lifted me up when they saw me, something I didn't have with Louie. My friends had so many questions when they saw me, asking me what I was doing there or how I was doing; I never really answered their questions. I couldn't answer their questions because, I myself, didn't know the answer. It had been months since I truly checked in with myself, I no longer knew anything about myself.

My friends reminded me of who I was, especially Daniel. I knew he was staying at his parents' home in a special little town nestled right by the river. I always loved going to his parents' home, they had a beautiful garden, honeybees and were surrounded by matured sequoia trees.

Although, I was forbidden to see Daniel I didn't care, he was a warm light in my life and gave me hope and inspiration, safety and acceptance and most of all, we always laughed. One evening after dinner with my mother, I went over to Daniel's parents' house without telling, never mind having Louies permission. This was the first time I actually acted on any of Louies accusations.

The moment I stepped onto the family's property all my fears and anxieties had lifted. Being there again was like walking into an oasis as familiar as home. Daniel stood out on the front porch to greet me, he always dressed simple although sporting his fashion sense well.

"Hi Marissa" he says as I walk down the driveway to the front door.

"Hi Daniel" and just like that our connection was ignited. I'm not sure if it's because we hadn't seen each other as often as we used to, but it was always good to see him. There was never anything behind our motives as friends.

This particular night with Daniel, we sat under a tree in his mother's garden. It was completely covered by low hanging branches and leaves. As if we had entered our own secret hideout, we were comfortable on the ground surrounded by dead leaves and green grass. Times like this weren't uncommon for us. We shared a sense of wonder and appreciation for all things science, nature and mischievousness. The space under the tree he brought me to was like a womb of love, nurture and protection. I had forgotten about the outside world and was submerged and engulfed in this world with him.

We talked about life and what our dreams meant to us, I shared how I dreamt of one day writing a book and sharing my story with others. Daniel dreamt of becoming a doctor and serving in the military. I really admired how focused he was on his dreams. Sometimes I'd wish to not be in the shackles of my relationships so I could focus on myself and my dreams.

In our secret hiding place, time was nonexistent, our phones were in the house and the only light shone came from the moon illuminating in the night sky. This moment was a dream. This moment I had felt my heartbeat to his and in this moment, we connected eyes and as if his eyes had spoken to me, he asked to kiss me. I shook my head yes. Daniel leaned in and so did I, our chemistry was something sweet and special. I had always felt love for Daniel in a unique way and kissing him in this moment felt right.

I failed to mention I had a boyfriend; my entity of deceit was present. If Daniel would've known, I don't think he would've kissed me or invited me to stay the night. I acted in manipulation in my own way. I slept over and we watched movies, ate popcorn and continued to love on one another.

I couldn't have cared less about Louie. Louie had never made me feel this way in our relationship, never mind even asking if he could kiss me. In my mind, Daniel was worth it whether we were just friends or lovers.

The next morning, we took our time getting up and ready, drinking coffee and enjoying the cool morning weather. I left Daniels' house before 10 AM and finally dared to look at the messages and notifications on my phone from Louie.

My energy after leaving Daniels' house was re-centered, calm, confident and happy. I didn't care to argue or entertain Louie, so I continued to ignore the messages and go about my day. I had been shown what a healthy relationship and connection should be, at least what I had been yearning for. I had absolutely no interest in Louie anymore.

The evening came and I finally called Louie back. We ended up fighting and I broke things off with him. Anytime I had previously tried to separate myself from Louie, he suddenly became sweet like I always asked and begged of him. It wasn't unusual for us to fight, take a break, make promises and then start the cycle over again.

I barely knew how to keep promises to myself, let alone keep a promise to someone else. But I wasn't aware of this until about a year later. After about two months, we decided we would try to work things out. Louie had been good and sweet to me, and I believed the promises that he would change.

I booked a flight back to Los Angeles, on a broken dream, forgotten promises and a divided heart. I had found myself back where I had almost escaped from. I couldn't figure out what kept bringing me back, especially after spending time with Daniel.

The thing I now realize is that I was doing it all for the wrong reasons. My ego wanted to prove myself to Louie as well as show my family that I could make it in a big city. Which in fact, I didn't. Back then I thought I tried although looking back did I really? No.

It was foolish to think that just because I was in a big city, meant that I made it in life. I believed in the hype and façade. And so did Louie. We both were not only living unaligned in our relationship, but within our own personal lives.

When I landed in Los Angeles, he seemed different. I had never not replied to Louie when he would blow up my phone and the fact, I broke up with him meant he was on his best behavior. I thought to myself, "Is he actually trying? Are my assumptions about him wrong? Had I become the bad guy?"

I was no better than him now, in my twisted mind I really had to prove myself not only to him but to myself.

We came into an agreement that we would start over. We would get our own place and make a home together. Although I wasn't prepared for this, his lease was up in December and it was now September, so I had one month to step forward with him or break up for good.

No wonder he was on his best behavior. Because his

work was all under the table, he could not qualify for an apartment on his own and needed someone else on the lease. I was fooled yet again. This is the time I came to find out that the apartment he had been living in was actually an office space he and, his friends acquired for work, Louie wasn't on the lease only paying his friends rent. Which is fine, but he lied to me.

I felt weird knowing he lied to me all this time and did not share this information. Everything really started to make sense why he was so eager to get back together, make amends and have me living in LA full-time.

As this all unfolded in front of me over the next week, I was blinded by the extravagant dates, dinners, shopping, parties and fake love. I thought he was really wanting a relationship with me, but each day it became clear he was trying to win me over. And I allowed it because at this time in my life, my love could be bought, and my own vanity overpowered any sense I had.

In a selfish way, I figured I had Louie right where I wanted him. He needed me and I had control. Because he was on his best behavior, he would not question or harass me. Or so I thought. As I'm writing this, I see how much drama, spitefulness, control and manipulation took place. I should've walked away but something in me wasn't ready to or really even wanted to. A piece of me did want to give this a shot and make something work for myself down here… not with him.

Louie spoke in all or nothing terms about our relationship and officially moving in together. He and I had suffered so much in this relationship together that we felt moving in was the cure we needed to make things work.

I agreed to find a place with him and make it work. My mother and closest friends all warned me how bad of an idea this was. No one in my life thought he was actually good for me. All of the phone calls home made it quite obvious I was not happy. I told my friends and family about signing a lease with him and I understood their concerns, but this was what I was going to do.

I agreed to this life. I agreed to promises which were untrue to my divine path. I agreed to a lifestyle which caused harm and chaos into my life. I agreed to disagree with my inner voice. I agreed to suffering.

Louie had bad credit, and no job on paper so I would become the main provider on the lease. The red flags were screaming at me, but I continued to turn another cheek and follow his lead like a lost puppy looking for a place to call home.

As long as I was able to do cocaine and drink as I please, I thought I could handle this situation. But when I was alone and in deep thought, I always fantasized about the Marissa I was just a few months ago with Daniel. She was happy, had free will to be whoever she wanted to be. She wasn't abused or belittled for who she was or who she dreamt to become. The safe place in my mind were the times I had spent with Daniel. That is what kept me going.

Chapter 24

In the Lonely Hours

Trust in the Lord with all your heart
and lean not on your own
understanding; in all your ways
submit to him, and he will make
your paths straight.
Proverbs 3:5-6

Although my heart and inner voice were screaming at me, "No!" I agreed to signing a lease with Louie. So badly I wanted to stay in Sacramento, but in my mind, I kept thinking to myself, "I need to get out of my comfort zone."

The drugs did not help either, they say you shouldn't operate heavy machinery when under the influence; honestly you shouldn't be making life changing decisions either.

I expressed to Louie the truth about being intimate with Daniel during our break in hopes he would let this idea of living together go, but he still pushed me to move forward with our relationship. What was it about me that he wanted so badly?

I couldn't figure it out, especially since we were treating each other so poorly, yet when things were good, they were really good. If you ever find yourself saying that, just know it is a red flag and it's time to move on. The thoughts running through my head were, "If he is trying then I should too. When we do move in together things will get better." The time came and Louie flew from Los Angeles to Sacramento.

It sounds romantic and a part of it was, but I didn't want to be with him although he insisted. Overnight I was gone and left with him to Los Angeles. No real warning to my mother or younger sister who I was living with, and no idea or real thought with Louie about how we were going to work things out. He had two suitcases filled with my things and I had three.

It was exciting and scary all at the same time. All I had figured out was my new drug dealer in Los Angeles and the possibility of working a job off of Hollywood boulevard. I lived with Louie in his house for a month and a half or what everyone else would call the office. His friends were always over, it never truly felt like home. But I did my best to make it feel like home. I cleaned, cooked and baked all types of flavors of banana bread.

My mornings started at 10 AM, waking up to his blunt smoke. Once we got our day started, we had breakfast together, looked at our social media and gossiped plenty. If Louie had to work, I would spend my afternoons painting or drawing, calling friends or family, just trying to fill my time and not be so lonely. Around 4 PM I'd make my way to the pool with a cocktail. The Hollywood lifestyle for me at this point was pretty relaxed and about meeting new people.

After hanging out at the pool, I'd go back up to Louies apartment to either order in or make dinner. My drinking continued and most days I was drunk by 7 PM. By this time Louie had already smoked at least five blunts, so we were both inebriated by dinner time. Which is when, and why we began bickering and arguing about whatever was convenient.

Louie had been badgering me about my phone because I was always posting to social media. He did have my passwords, so he could easily see what was going on at any given time. He monitored my posting quite often and one day I had enough.

I said to him, "You follow and like other girls' posts, why can't I post like them since that's what you like?"

He didn't take to that too kindly. It was always a constant battle of what I could or couldn't do, say or shouldn't say. But this became my new normal. Some nights he would leave to his friend's house after a fight, and I was always envious that he had an escape. This is when I would turn to cocaine in my lonely hours.

He wasn't always aware of when I was using. When he would leave, I would set out to pick up an eight ball or a gram of cocaine. This scheduled use created a deeper dependence for drugs than I had intended, more than just my regular use, but as a way to fill up myself emotionally.

From picking up, to finishing the bag or even waiting for the dealer, I found temporary fulfillment in being a coke addict. I'd shower to make sure I was fresh and clean, clear my nasal passages and lotion up my body in the mirror. Cocaine users tend not to eat and become very thin, so when I would look at myself in the mirror it would give me another reason to use. I wanted to be rail thin.

I would continue to dress myself after my shower in comfortable clothing so I could lay in bed and do my drugs in peace. The buildup of waiting for a cocaine drop off was just as thrilling as cutting my first lines. When I got the text from my dealer, I would make my way down six flights of stairs and meet them on the corner of Hollywood and Argyle. The exchange of money for drugs was always quick and easy, barely looking one another in the eye. Depending on how much I ordered I'd give him $80 or $300. I would put the drugs into my pocket and tread back up the stairs into the apartment.

Sometimes I'd cross paths with neighbors during my venture which wasn't always ideal. Although I did stop to chat with them trying to remain as normal as possible.

After swift encounters, I continued my way to the apartment which was always worrisome for me for the reason being if Louie caught me out of that apartment, he would be very upset and question me beyond belief. Even if I told him the truth of my previous whereabouts, he wouldn't believe me. Thus, I would become anxious to get back.

Slipping back into the apartment, I made my way into the bedroom to set myself up on his king size bed where I would begin crushing up the white rocks. The biggest lines were always the first for me. Focusing on each little piece of white rock to make it as powdery as possible. I would set myself up at least three long, thick, white lines. Once I had them lined up, I would gaze at the powdered drug as if I was in love and at peace.

I'd take a few deep breaths in as I was rolling up a $20 bill and just like that, one end of the bill in my nose and the other end hovering right above a perfected powdered line. I'd inhale the cocaine into my nose. Nice and slow movement while deeply inhaling every speck of powder I had crushed up. The first line was always my favorite because of the drip in the back of the throat. It was a clean drip, numbing my nose, throat and mind. Soon after my first line came the second, third and so on.

Once I began to feel the high, I put on my make-up and fixed my hair. See, cocaine is an ego enhancing drug. And every time I did it, my ego grew bigger than I could control thus transforming into what I would call my alter ego. While doing my make up, I continued to do more lines and sometimes would suffer from diarrhea. Cocaine was not easy on my body; it was either this or throwing up, yet I still loved the drug.

By the time I was finished with my make-up, Louie would be home. He was always in an indifferent mood even though he just left to get in a lighter one. I would usually be in the mood for make-up sex or some type of fun due to the side effects from the drug. And yes, this was our usual day to day schedule and routine.

It's absurd, but when you have no real responsibility and the only thing of significance in your day is drugs, sex and money, it does not matter how time is spent or what emotions you feel.

This lifestyle became normalized and excused by not only me but Louie as well. We never discussed our addictions; it was as normal as brushing our teeth to see each other high. It was so normal to us that if one of us wasn't some type of high, that's when the other became concerned. The life of a drug addict is a sneaky, toxic, dramatic one, full of deceit and instability.

A few years ago, these were the things, entities and demons whatever you want to call them, that I met when I was on the plant. Now at the time when I did the plant, I had no idea to what degree these words meant, but now because I hadn't learned the lessons prior and lacked integrity with myself and my choices, they came into full bloom in my life. I was completely living in the dark and solely persuade by my demons. This is not the person I was meant to be nor who I wanted to be, but it felt as if it was my only option and what I had to do.

After Louie and I made up we'd usually go out to

whichever club had the biggest scene that night. This was our life; this is how we worked day in and day out. I became a social light in my own eyes.

I grew closer to my darkness and further from my light. This lifestyle became so troubling that there was a week I didn't leave the apartment except to get drugs off of Hollywood Boulevard. No one knew how deep this addiction was, not even me.

The week I spent in the apartment was the first of many benders. I did not know I was in the middle of a bender because I had never experienced one up until this week. The luck I struck of not overdosing or getting a bad batch of coke during this bender was surprising; I didn't die this time. And no this is not where the title of my book came from.

It was now December 2020 and we'd been looking at apartments around the same complex he was already living in. We found a beautiful two-story loft, with two balconies. The ceilings were 16 feet tall with floor to ceiling windows. We could see the Hollywood sign, the W and the Boulevard from our apartment. It was a total dream. We signed a new lease December 20th and moved in the 23rd. I became the main leaseholder and Louie was listed as a roommate. I found a job working at Hospital which was only a ten-minute walk down the boulevard.

It seemed like life had worked itself out in our favor. Louie and I grew closer at this time. We finally had something beautiful and positive to look forward to.

On Christmas Eve, we ate Domino's Pizza on the floor of our empty apartment, we did have some furniture, but nothing was set up. We enjoyed our pizza and wine; he had his weed, I had my hard drugs. This was our home and our first Christmas together.

228

Louie genuinely wanted our new apartment to feel like a home and it did. I was finally able to unpack my bags into my own closet and walk around my own home naked. Life was good. We still celebrated our one-year anniversary on the first of 2021 even though we had separated multiple times in 2020.

The year 2021 was now here, I had my own apartment in Hollywood, a great job and a boyfriend. I couldn't believe the kind of change that came so quickly and effortlessly to me. I wasn't your average drug addict, I was bougie, rich and functioning, at least in my own mind.

The first week of January also came with good news. I applied to become an egg donor with a fertility clinic and had asked for almost double what they usually pay their donors which they agreed too. How my luck had turned I'm not sure, but reassurance like this is what gave me reason that I was doing a good job in life even if I was running on cocaine and no sleep.

The process of donating your eggs involves a lot of hormonal stimulation, which can affect your mental state, yet I paid no mind to this warning.

I focused on work and paid the first month's rent on my own. I truly took pride in my new home; Louie was enjoying it too. He was slow with work and most days when I returned home, he would be smoking a blunt in the living room and playing video games. I hated coming home to a house that smelled this way especially when the laundry and dishes hadn't been done.

He was pretty content with life, yet I was not. I held a lot of resentment towards Louie because of the laziness I saw him to be. Some days I would work 16 hours and would feel completely drained yet still had to come home and clean, do laundry and cook. He always interrupted me because his need for validation remained constant. Louie would want me to love on him and aside from not having the energy, his lack of motivation completely turned me off. I had no attraction to him at this point.

I realized how things changed from me being the victim to now being the aggressor and sole provider. He was trying because of our new sudden dynamic. Louie began to notice how I became distant which inspired him to begin to pull his weight.

Just when I felt like walking away, we pulled ourselves back together even if it meant one of us had to take the lead. Yes, we still argued but we had somewhat of a balance together and started to enjoy one anothers company.

I would begin the process of donating my eggs. This was something I always wanted to do. For a long time, my vagina had always felt impure to me because of the sexual abuse; I wanted something good to happen out of it. Donating my eggs to a couple seemed like the best decision for me, as well as the compensation I'd receive from it.

Louie was very supportive during that time. The hormones I injected into myself daily were to stimulate the growth of my eggs. This made me gain weight, as well as set me off mentally and emotionally (more than I already was). By the middle of February, I finally donated my menstrual cycle's amount for that month, about thirty eggs. The procedure was about fifteen minutes. Again, I had that wonderful feeling of being put out with anesthesia. The donation process was easy, but what I would come to face is the subtle yet significant effects of the hormones.

After what like felt like a year of suffering I was ready to have some fun and now I had the means to do it because of my compensation. I could've bought a car or paid my rent ahead of time, but I decided to do other things with it

Chapter 25

Kats Bag

Do not abandon me, O Lord. Do not
stand at a distance, my God. Come
quickly to help me, O Lord my
savior.
Psalms 38:21-22

Louie's 29th birthday was coming up and I decided to throw him a surprise birthday party. Although we did have problems, things were looking up. I was still recovering from the egg donating process, yet I made sure to make appointments like getting my lips and face done, calling party planners and of course using cocaine.

I was quite a mess, but having money made me feel validated, that I was doing okay in life. I did invest some of my money in bitcoin but, it was only a few days after it had hit my bank account that I already spent thousands.

A friend of mine in Los Angeles, named Sage picked me up just a day after my surgery to take me to get filler and botox. I should've been on bedrest for the week but as they say there is no rest for the wicked. I didn't need filler or botox, but a part of me felt I had to do it.

Even though I didn't have a car at the time, I figured I

could have friends drive me around Los Angeles in exchange for drugs, Sage was the friend. I made an appointment with a high-end doctor and spent over $1000 for the treatment. The moment my addiction saw that I had money, I really began to change physically, emotionally and mentally. It was as if I leveled up in my addiction.

Returning home from the appointment, I ran into a neighbor of mine. This neighbor had one intention of speaking to me this day and it was to hand me a business card. The card was all black with white lettering spelling out The Fun Dealer. With my brand-new face and an ego twice the size of my physical body, I felt honored that he referred me to what seemed like a *classy* drug dealer.

I had never heard of dealers passing out business cards, but here I was enticed by the energy and look of it. I decided to give this business-card-cocaine-dealer a try. I texted the number with a short message, "Can I get a gram? 2300 Hollywood. -Marissa"

The dealer replied instantly and said, "I'll be there at 1pm. $80"

I was beside myself of how efficient and "professional" this dealer was. I was excited to meet whoever they were. I made sure to be on the corner of Hollywood and Argyle right at 1 PM.

When the black SUV pulled up and rolled down the passenger window, I was surprised to see that they were female. We will call her Kat. Kat looked like an older version of myself. I was instantly attracted to her and she to me. Our encounter was quick, but just enough for her to give me her personal phone number. At the time I didn't think much of it other than I had a direct link to my new dealer.

This day was significant for me. I thought I had

reached a new level in my Hollywood fantasy. Between going to the best doctor in Los Angeles to get my face done and then meeting a female cocaine dealer, I had everything I needed. I became everything I thought I wanted to be.

This life seemed so glamorous to me. A few hours had passed and my need for another serving of Kat's supply was greater than any feeling I had felt in my addiction. She definitely had the best cocaine I've ever had. By the best cocaine I mean the most addictive and strongest. By 4 PM I was messaging Kat to get another gram.

Sage was still with me from my appointment earlier and suggested that we drive to go pick it up in downtown Los Angeles. Kat lived in a beautiful apartment building and met us on the corner. Sage and I decided to share the second bag of cocaine. We went back to my apartment in Hollywood and of course Louie was now there, he could sense something was up when we both walked through the door.

He first noticed all the work I had gotten done; my lips were huge, but he especially took notice of my nose. I hadn't gotten any work done on my nose, but it was dusted with cocaine powder.

I had become a stuck up, done up girl he no longer recognized and not just because of the work I had gotten done. My energy and attitude were not me at all. This made Louie insecure which in turn gave me another form of an ego boost.

I victimized myself by thinking, "This is what you wanted me to be, this is who you've said I've always been."

In actuality I did have a choice, but I did not recognize it at this time in my life. Louie was just beginning to feel secure and comfortable in our relationship; I had reached a point where I was over it and ready to be someone else.

Between the egg donation procedure and the work I had done, my body had endured so much. And adding this new supply of cocaine did not help at all.

Louie was very nurturing and loving during this time. I'm not sure if he was scared I was going to leave him or could sense that something was very wrong inside of me. Now that I am sober and look back at that specific time in my life, it is very easy for me to understand how unhealthy my mind was, as well as my body.

The last year of abuse didn't allow me to trust that he was truly there for me. Even though we were living together, I kept my wall up and remained estranged from him. He cuddled me, made me food and picked up the house while I continued in my recovery. Yet this didn't stop me from lying in bed and doing drugs.

His positive attitude shined a light of hope for me, but it was too late. I was already shaping into what I thought I had to be, and he was shaping into the partner I had always wanted.

The problem with this is that I was passed being in a relationship with him when he was just truly beginning. I still had love for him, but I couldn't see him in the same light anymore.

Louies birthday was coming up soon and I was planning something special for him. Although we had our problems, he wasn't a horrible person he just didn't know how to love or be loved, as well as myself.

I planned a casino night surprise party with blackjack, poker, a photo booth and show girls. The cost came out to a little over $9000 which also included the alcohol, food and of course drugs.

I spent the week leading up to his party high on my new supply from Kat and spending money like I wouldn't live to see another day. I hadn't learned this until I reached substance recovery, but when the suicidal person is subconsciously planning their death, they do things like this.

I was unaware of all this. The week leading up to his birthday I didn't get much sleep, I had spent almost $2000 with Kat since I had initially met her. I was her new cash cow.

I was out of the house quite a bit during this time preparing for Louies surprise party, so I talked on the phone, a lot. What I thought I was doing for privacy, but really, I was being deceitful. One person I talked to constantly was, Elliot.

Elliot and Daniel were roommates the year prior and I had gotten to know Elliot well. The first time I met Elliot, we connected over our humor and poor mental health.

I wouldn't so much call it a trauma bond but he and I both felt seen, heard and accepted when we were together. That is what the foundation of our friendship was built on. We could unapologetically be ourselves around one another. We could tell each other the crazy, lame things that we did, why we did it and how we did it. Our honesty with one another was something I hadn't really experienced before.

I wasn't trying to get anything out of Elliot, no sex, no attention, nothing. It was a genuine friendship and still is to this day.

Little did I know that this simple and honest friendship would catapult me into the most transformative, heartbreaking, deathly and lively experience I've ever had. Even more valuable than doing the plant.

One afternoon on a phone call with Elliot, he invited

me to Miami to celebrate his birthday, March 11th through the 15th. Daniel was going to be there, and my feelings hadn't faded for him one bit.

I figured I could go to Miami for the weekend, have fun, get it out of my system maybe even find closure with Daniel and move on with my life. Why did I feel this was a good idea? I don't know, everything sounds like a good idea when you have an abundance of money and drugs.

I was two weeks into what would be a month-long bender. I told Louie that the week after his birthday I was going on a girl's trip to Miami with my two friends from home, Karma and Raquel. Raquel had the streets smarts I was going to need, and Karma was good for drugs. They both knew Daniel so I figured we could all meet up together in Miami.

My plan was coming together, I just had to make sure everything between Louie and I were good so he wouldn't be upset when I left. This is my most obvious example of manipulation.

I booked three round trip tickets to Miami for myself, Raquel and Karma as well as a four-night stay in a five-star beach front hotel. It was only February 30th, two weeks into my bender and I had spent over $20,000. I didn't care.

I had an overwhelming feeling of going out with a bang. I wasn't sure what this feeling was or where it was coming from, but it was present. I was ready to go have fun and get out of my domesticated reality with Louie. So, I sat Louie down and lied to him. I told him it was just a girl's trip to Miami.

I knew, he knew, that there was going to be trouble. Louie had a way of feeling people's energy from the line of work he did, and he especially knew how to read my suspect

236

energy. Not only had my appearance changed right in front of him, but so did my desires, actions and mentality.

Within a matter of two weeks, I wasn't the person he knew. It was as if my veil fully dropped over my eyes and soul. A veil of sheer ego and evil. A veil not of Maya, but of the devil taking form in the shape of me.

Marissa was no longer present, consumed by ego, money, drugs, lust and status. All connection she had with spirit and true freedom were cut. Cut by the lines she cut and the hearts she was about to break; even her own; my own.

Chapter 26

Hollywood Lines

You have had enough in the past of
the evil things that Godless people
enjoy—their immorality and lust,
their feasting and drunkenness and
wild parties, and their terrible
worship of idols.
1 Peter 4:3

The date is now March 3rd, 2021, the day of Louies 29th birthday. He was in good spirits and didn't seem to have a care in the world. His friend Charlie was in on the surprise party and took Louie out to lunch and shopping.

Meanwhile, I was coordinating with the event staff to be at Charlie's apartment at 7 PM. Leann, Charlie's girlfriend at the time, helped me get everything prepared. With a bag of cocaine, and a couple of white claws, she and I were running errands.

I wasn't doing all of this for Louie, it was for my own ego; although I didn't realize this at the time. I ordered Louie two cakes, plenty of alcohol for the party and some decorations.

After we ran errands, Leann and I went back to Charlies Hollywood sky rise apartment. We continued to get ready, do our drugs and drink. Charlie and Louie arrived back about an hour or so after us.

Charlie had boughten Louie a couple of new outfits as a gift, it was incredibly kind and generous of him. I always liked Charlie, he was always humble, kind and big-hearted. I went back to my apartment with Louie were some of our neighbors invited us to hang out.

Louie joined them, and I ended up going back to hang out with Leann, only to do more drugs. I had been gone about two hours, Louie thought I was doing something for him when in actuality I was sharing my new supply of drugs with Leann. Once the drugs were out, I decided to spend time with Louie. To my surprise, he wasn't upset I had been gone.

Louie was clueless about all the time, energy and money I had put towards this. I had my hair done, make up done, and cute outfit on.

It was now 8 PM and I still hadn't done anything for him that day. He was happy, sweet and kind. It was an energy I hadn't seen from him since we first met. I told Louie that his friend Charlie wanted us to come over at 9 PM for drinks.

So, Louie grabbed his weed, and I grabbed my cocaine, and we made our way to the neighborhood liquor store. On our walk, for the first time in our relationship, he felt like a friend. He told me about his day, and we laughed, we were just happy. I don't know how else to describe it, but we were just happy.

When we arrived at the liquor store, I told him to pick out his favorite tequila. Of course, he picked the tall brown bottle of Don Julio 1942.

We walked Sunset Boulevard and made our way to Charlies apartment building. Charlies' apartment was on the top floor, overlooking all of Hollywood and downtown.

I was so excited and felt extremely proud of the surprise he was about to walk into. He exited the elevator first, I pulled out my camera to record him from behind. We rang the doorbell to which Leann answered, she had glitter eyeshadow and a black outfit on. Behind her was a long hallway which led into the living room. It was quiet when Louie and I walked in. He took the lead in front of Leann and I; with both of our phone cameras as he made his way down the hall, he turned to his right and a big group of friends shouted, "Surprise!"

He was so happy and shocked, he began to cry. All his friends, business partners and neighbors were there to embrace him.

Louie was overwhelmed and felt all the love from everyone in that room. His buddies were jumping all over him, dabbing him up while he was at a loss for words. I was right behind him when he turned around and embraced me with the biggest hug.

The party looked amazing, the living room was so grand and had casino games in every corner, the photo booth was right in the center of it all. He was processing every bit of that moment, as was I.

We walked into the kitchen where he poured a shot for us. Everyone raised their glass for a toast and as soon as Charlie put on music, the party started.

Leann and I went to do cocaine while everyone else was gathered in the main room. I told Leann that Kat, our new drug dealer, would be coming by to bring more. Kat had the best supply I ever had, I was hooked on it for weeks prior and had no plans of stopping anytime soon. I had now spent over $4000 with her at this point.

Since Leann and I knew that she was coming we had no problem doing what we called Hollywood lines. A Hollywood line is a long, thick line of cocaine. Instead of a rationed size which most people do when they get a bag, we each took a long, thick line.

To have the party going was an accomplishment to me and snorting a Hollywood line in peace was the reward. See, when you do drugs, the definition of accomplishment and rewards are much different than sober peoples. This party was an accomplishment for me and doing cocaine was my reward.

When Leann and I finally walked out of the room I had cocaine dripping down the back of my throat, my eyes were now wide open, and my nose was dripping snot as well as cocaine dust on the tip of my nose. This lifestyle was not glamorous in reality.

It was obvious to most people what my main objective was that night, and I did not care. I spent so much money on this party, and I was going to enjoy myself the way I wanted to. Louie found me and asked where I had been, I told him I was talking with Leann, to my knowledge he had no idea.

He was clueless about how deep I was in my addiction. And that's okay, my choices were not his responsibility. It was his birthday after all. My high was as good as ever, no bad vibes insight. We took more shots and played blackjack; I surprisingly won multiple times.

I received a text from Kat that she arrived. I immediately sent for her to be let up. When she walked in, she had this energy about her, like she was so touched by the love of the environment that she had to put a thuggish guard up. I didn't care I was just happy as hell my drugs had finally arrived.

The first thing we did when she walked into the party was go to the bathroom and exchange cash for drugs. Then we did them like nobody's business. I was having the time of my life at this point. This night was so fun for everyone. I was so high it was as if I began to sober up, so I drink more. The party flew by with all the dancing, singing, Instagraming, drugs and alcohol. I had only rented out the casino games, show girls and photo booth till 1 AM. It was 12:30am now and the party was not ready to stop.

So, I called a good friend of mine, Bianca. Bianca was the manager of an underground strip club in Los Angeles. This was early 2021 so technically clubs were still following Covid guidelines. There were about 15 guys and girls who wanted to go to the strip club.

We all packed in Ubers and when we arrived, we got a whole section which came out to be $2500. I paid $1300 and Charlie paid the rest. This place was fucking crazy, every girl in that place had fake boobs, fake ass, fake lips and fake hair, but damn did they look good naked and dancing.

We all made our way into the section where there were more strippers than there were of us. Money was being thrown up in the air, it was all over the ground, we partied like rock stars. I don't remember much from that part of the night.

Although from the videos and pictures on my phone, I was dancing with strippers, getting Louie to dance with strippers and smacking their butt like no other. It was a blast; we were in the strip club until 4 AM and I blew about eight grand.

At the time I thought it was worth it, but looking back, I was literally throwing money away. This wouldn't be my last mistake or even my biggest mistake. This was only the beginning for me. This was the night that fueled my ego and

242

entitlement.

When the club closed down, we all left separately in different Uber's. Louie and I made it back to our apartment safely.

The next morning, we talked about the party and had a good laugh together while attempting to cure our hangovers. Our neighbors were all at the pool and invited us to come down to relax and chill. We slowly made our way down there; the sun was shining, and the air was cool. Louie and I were both in sweats lounging by the pool with our friends. A friend brought us some leftover cake from the party, which was the best cure all for my hangover.

Everyone was talking about how much fun they had and all the Instagram posts and whatever else went on throughout the night. Life did not seem real this day. It was like a fantasy and a glamorous one at that. As a 23-year-old, just thinking about the best night of my life while lounging beside my pool in the middle of Hollywood, I was thinking what the hell? Looking back, I took a lot of these moments for granted.

I wasn't who I am now, as I was back then. Above all the fun, there were actual responsibilities I had put off. Louie and I took it real slow that day, up until about 4 PM when I started using cocaine again. The total amount I did the night before was close to three eight balls. The only reason I was able to sleep was because of the sex I had.

My head was stuffed, my nose was clogged, and I could no longer do cocaine up my nose, so I started putting it on my gums.

After our time at the pool, Leann had invited us back over to Charlies for dinner. We ordered Italian food, and how I was able to even eat it, still makes me wonder. I had very low energy and was feeling quite sick. To be honest, even after the party I still felt left out. Not that anyone made me feel that way intentionally, I didn't feel I belonged. I've come to understand that the feeling of not belonging is a biproduct of suicidal thoughts.

I know true friends support you in whatever your dreams are or whoever you are. My problem was, I didn't feel like the people around the table were my true friends because they were Louie's friends. And due to his jealousy in the past, I wasn't allowed to have friends of his, let alone my own. So, I continued to play a part, but in the back of my mind, I was once again thinking about the one friend that kept me inspired, Daniel.

The thing about your inner voice is that it continues to speak to you, no matter how many times you ignore it. We always know what is right or wrong, true or false. It's just a matter of do we actually listen or not.

Soon, I'd be in Miami enjoying life with him. Louie didn't know I was going to Miami to meet up with Daniel and I hadn't planned on telling him.

The week in between Louies birthday party and my trip to Miami were interesting. Louie was falling in love with me all over again while I was planning my escape route. I continued to use Kat's supply night and day, and without my knowing was actually starting to lose my mind.

To my knowledge, through my recovery, I had been in a drug-induced psychosis for two weeks now. I was in a completely different reality. The thing about losing your mind is, you don't know you're losing your mind when you're losing your mind.

Part Four:

The Fall

Chapter 27

Ocean Drive

Don't let the excitement of youth
cause you to forget your Creator.
Honor him in your youth before you
grow old and say, "Life is not
pleasant anymore."
Ecclesiastes 12:1

Louie picked up on the changes happening with me. He heavily questioned my trip to Miami and did everything he could to get a glance at my phone screen. I was constantly pushing him away and begged him to trust me that this was only girl's trip, but he knew better.

It was now March 10th, Karma and Raquel were driving down from Sacramento to meet me at my apartment. Our flight was the next day, so our plan was for them to stay the night and go to the airport together in the morning. I thought that bringing my two party friends to Miami with me would make my plan go smoother, but it would actually be my downfall. The girls arrived at my apartment at 10 PM. Our flight was at noon the next day, Thursday, March 11th.

When the girls arrived, they were both excited and I was happy to see them. It'd been almost two and a half years since I had seen either of them. Karma brought drugs from her supplier in Sacramento, she went on to tell me how good they were, and the best she ever had. I had already been hooked on my supply from Kat that I didn't think it could get any better than that.

How could this not be the best weekend of our lives? I paid for everything and I planned it all. All they had to do was go along for the ride and have fun. I helped them with their bags on our way up to my apartment, Karma was excited, and she couldn't stop talking or asking questions. I thought to myself, "She must be on those drugs she was telling me about."

She continued to express her fears over Miami, it was extremely aggravating to me. I thought to myself, "Then why are you coming?" I was in the stage of my addiction where it was very easy for me to be mean. I figured she had brought the drugs and was going to help me have a weekend away from Louie, so I will just deal with her. Raquel on the other hand was as chill as ever, just ready to have a good time.

When we walked back into the apartment Louie said "Hi" to the girls as they entered, he didn't care to talk with them much or even acknowledge their presence after that.

His energy reminded me of why I wanted to be away from him. I hadn't been truly happy in a long time. All I could think about was the time I would be spending with Daniel. If I had done things in a different way, I wouldn't have invited the girls. I should've had the integrity to tell Louie what I was really doing and only bring myself. It would've saved me about $15,000, although now this makes for a great story.

I realize that I may sound unapologetic. And the purpose of this is because this is exactly how my mindset was during this time. I feel it's important for the reader and for myself to know exactly what type of person I was.

The girls settled in and we all caught up in the living

247

room. They were tired from driving and wanted to rest before traveling the next day. I, however, was eager to try Karma's cocaine. I ended up doing it all night long. It was straight gasoline, which is a term used to describe how powerful and strong the drug is.

I knew right away that it had meth and molly cut into it. And what I would later come to find out, fentanyl. It was similar to Kat's pure cocaine, but it wasn't pure, so I did get higher than usual. The type of high that makes your jaw and muscles twitch uncontrollably.

The only thing that could've stopped the drug-induced psychosis, ego entitled energy I had going forward was myself. This was the first night I remember not entirely recognizing who I was in the mirror.

I didn't think much of it but looking back and with professional help I've come to understand that I was deep into my drug induced psychosis. I was approaching the top of a roller coaster with a steep drop.

It was finally morning and the girls had woken up. Louie was up as well and had gone to the liquor store to get us champagne. That was nice I thought, maybe he was accepting and embracing this moment.

But that all changed when I was sitting on the couch, ordering an Uber to LAX when Elliot texted me that he was going to pick us up from the Miami airport. Louie saw the text and said, "I knew something was going on, go on and have fun."

The girls were confused because at this point, they still didn't know we were going to meet up with Daniel and Elliot. I said to Louie, "I'll see you when I'm back, we can talk then."

He didn't say anything and just went upstairs. Us girls left the apartment and went down to our Uber. The black Escalade pulled up and we piled in with mimosas in one hand and luggage in the other. I was a hot mess all over and ready for what I thought would be the vacation of a lifetime.

We arrived to LAX and checked our bags, Karma's had the drugs in it. We made it through security and ran to our gate because we were running late. Hot mess coming through was written all over us.

The flight was an easy 5 ½ hours, mostly because I was passed out drunk and unfortunately missed my chance to use the bathroom. When we landed, I could've danced on Broadway the way I was moving in my seat. I really had to go. I was so insanely drunk that I didn't even know what time it was.

By the time me, Kylie and Raquel made it off the airplane, I was in desperate need for the lady's room. Once again, we were running through an airport. I couldn't hold it anymore and about 10 feet away from the nearest bathroom I began to pee my pants; down my pant leg, through my shoes and on the Miami airport floor.

I'm sure I got some looks and stares, but I did not care at all. Once I made it to the bathroom stall, I had realized my pants and shoes were covered in my own urine. Luckily, I had a carry-on with extra clothes and shoes inside of it.

When I came out of the stall, Karma and Raquel's face were in amazement, disgust and relief. What an entrance to Miami.

We all went about our time at baggage claim like nothing had happened. Especially myself, I felt good as ever. It was about 8 PM in Miami and Elliot was on his way to pick us up. I made sure to get my phone call with Louie out of the way. You know, letting him know I landed safely, and everything was peaches and cream. He accepted it and was happy to hear from me but, still short with me. Again, I didn't care.

I had completely forgotten or was just way too drunk to even mention to the girls that Elliot was going to pick us up. Karma and Raquel were so confused. They thought he was our Uber driver. They asked me, "Who is this guy?"

I responded, "Elliot! It's his birthday and we're going on a yacht with him on Sunday."

At this point I think they began to realize they were just along for the ride, literally and figuratively. Elliot had a wild, happy and carefree energy. It was his birthday weekend after all.

My energy on the other hand was literally, crazy. I still had cocaine hanging out of my nose and was insanely drunk, but the high of being away from Louie, going to see Daniel and in one of the most sought-after party cities in the country, had me feeling on top of the world.

My girlfriends were adjusting and taking it all in. Meanwhile I was definitely having a main character moment. I don't blame them for just observing. I would've been a little taken back as well. Elliot was also in shock at how wild I was on our car ride from the airport to the hotel. It was quite literally one hell of a ride.

The city looked beautiful at night. All the buildings, bridges and ocean were breathtaking. The air was different, the sky was different, everything about this place was a real fantasy. I had seen movies based in Miami, but the feeling of being there is something to experience.

Raquel, Karma and I were staying in the Brickell district of Miami. We stayed at the Hyatt which was right across from the yacht club and had a perfect view of Miami and the ocean. It was better than I could've ever imagined.

Elliot dropped us off and us girls made our way into the hotel lobby. When we got up to our room, we unpacked, called our families and looked on our phones for the nearest liquor store. We found one only a three-minute walk away... perfect.

We walked together to get tequila, vodka and food. We made a quick trip and hurried back to the hotel to start drinking. Elliot invited us out to Ocean Drive, it was spring break in Miami, and everybody was out.

People from all over the United States and the world were in Miami this weekend, I hadn't realized that. Us girls started getting ready to go out while railing lines in our hotel room.

The feeling and rush of it all consumed me, as I consumed it. Our plan for that night was simple; go see Ocean Drive. My girlfriend from LA let me borrow the most fabulous clothing for this trip. From head to toe, inside and out I went from Hollywood to Miami.

Karma and Raquel were just as excited to see what spring break had in store for us. Elliot came back to pick us up and drove us 25 minutes to our destination. We didn't know what to expect or what we'd see or even what we were doing.

Young adults and college kids were everywhere. It was only 10:30 PM, but because of Covid regulations, bars and clubs closed at midnight. We decided to grab a drink from a bar cart on Ocean Drive and walk around.

It was absolute chaos, they were thousands of people, sirens flashing, people running all up to no good, I felt at home. We hung around Ocean Drive with a few other girls Elliot had also invited. We were only out until about 1 AM that night. We made our way back to the hotel seamlessly and called it a night.

Chapter 28

Polaroid

I know that there is nothing good in me. I am weak and human. I want to do what is good. But I am unable to do it.
Romans 7:18

Waking up in Miami with my two friends brought upon a sense of freedom and happiness I had not felt in years. I was not worried nor walking on eggshells or concerned about anyone's feelings like I had been back in Hollywood. Despite the hangover and come down from cocaine, I truly felt like I was making the right decision for myself by being here. I don't believe I was intentionally trying to hurt anyone. I only wanted to do what I felt was best for me.

The last year of suffering I put myself through caused me to have an overwhelming urge to rebel and be free. Synonymously, I felt lost, yet opening my eyes to the beautiful view outside my window filled my heart with gratitude.

Although I was experiencing psychosis at this point in my journey, the ignorance of bliss which I was experiencing was unmatched to any emotion I had felt in a long time. My reality was the simple fact that I was living in deceit because I lacked integrity while disregarding my own voice for so long.

As good as I was feeling, I'd be facing the consequences of my actions soon.

Elliot texted me just as I was having breakfast in the hotel, that he was on his way to pick Daniel up from the airport. In just a few hours I'd be reunited with my friend who I had longed for. I was happy to be in a place of freedom although regrets of not arriving to this place with integrity broke the hearts of many, including my own.

This is my story. To share my secrets, shameful moments and mistakes has been a journey of its own. When I began writing this book in December of 2021, I felt compelled to finally embrace who I really am. I wanted to take ownership of my mistakes, and accept the accountability necessary for growth, healing and moving forward.

What my true story has turned into is a journey of self-discovery and self-mastery. Although I was lost, confused and consumed by self-sabotage, drama and addiction, I've found transformation through writing, wholesomeness, sobriety and tapping into all five senses again, including the inner voice.

The buildup to this weekend in Miami was not just because of the year I experienced in Hollywood. This was a definite ending that started in the first chapter of this book which is my life. I lacked true healing for so many years and sought out unhealthy ways to cope. This is no excuse for my actions although events such as the ones I have shared in this book really did shape the person I became.

My outer reliance on Daniels' friendship was unhealthy and energy sucking in hindsight, yet he brought an energy surrounded in autonomy that gave me hope for myself. It's not fair the way I treated others yet the moment I knew better I did better. But, in this chapter onward I certainly did not do better.

The humidity from the Miami weather made my straightened hair become curly. I had done my hair back in Hollywood with hopes that it would've lasted me the whole weekend, it didn't even last me the first night. I was determined to look my best though. It'd been almost a year since I had seen Daniel and I wanted to look my best.

My physical appearance was the only good thing I had going for me. Between my own personal trauma and drama which laid across my energy aura like film, I had hopes that my filler, botox and fashionable outfits would represent my energy for me. I had luck with this in Hollywood, but I was a fool to think my true friends, who knew me before this change, wouldn't notice passed the façade.

Raquel and Karma were already suspicious of my behavior. Between my accident in the airport, erratic car ride and my desire to use and drink so early, they were not only concerned, but watching me closely. Would Daniel be suspicious of me to?

I decided to go shopping and get my nails done before any socializing and partying started. I wanted alone time; this was my first experience without Louie badgering me or breathing down my neck. I was finally able to walk out of the door without being questioned by a man. The girls were still getting ready for the day, so I took this opportunity to walk by myself to the Brickell Plaza.

I was taking it all in; I loved Miami, I loved my freedom and most of all I loved this experience. I was on a high I never planned on putting an end to. To be away from my abuser was a feeling I felt was finally, final. I thought this would be the beginning of my new chapter in life.

On my walk alone to the plaza I reflected on how I could do better, how I wanted better and how I was going to make my break for it. The fear I once had for Louie turned into resentment and hate. Although this was unhealthy, I was somewhat empowered. This feeling only grew greater as he continuously sent hateful texts and voicemails. This all reminded me of Jacks behavior.

It became so infuriating that I couldn't put my phone down without him accusing me of something or spewing hate at me. I began to think to myself, "I'll give you something to be mad at."

At this point, I had put up with him, his insecurities, his verbal and emotional abuse for so long, I just did not care anymore. I did not care to comfort him, and I especially did not care to prove myself to him anymore. I was not planning on sleeping with anyone here in Miami. Yet he always called me degrading names and expressed how worthless I was, I felt it was now time to make him eat his words.

The time I spent at the plaza alone, I envisioned a life outside of my shackles. I began to realize how much of a prisoner I was all this time. This freedom was something I was going to hold onto for as long as I could, and I was not going to let anyone take it away.

However, at the plaza, I knew I could afford anything I wanted which made me feel so good. I stuck to window-shopping on my way to the nail salon. I took selfies, danced in public and sang songs aloud. Similar to when I passed the honeysuckles years ago, I was embracing each moment as if this would be my last time in this reality.

In just a few hours I'd be reunited with Daniel, I had no plans of seducing him; I truly just wanted to be embraced by my friend. Though subconsciously maybe that wasn't the case.

I chose a vibrant color for my pedicure and manicure to match the energy of Miami. Within two hours of leaving the hotel, I was already finished with my lone adventure and headed back through the humid weather.

When I arrived at the suite, the girls were drinking vodka and in good spirits listening to music. Our plan was to spend time at South Beach and then hit the bars in that area. Elliot made plans to go to dinner with a girl he flew out, so it would just be us three girls and Daniel this night.

And this was perfect, Elliot and Daniel were great friends, so I would at least have some time alone to catch up with him without distraction. Although, this is foolish to say because we were in a place full of distractions.

I texted Daniel the address to our hotel and told him to be there at 6 PM. This gave me time to get ready and fix what the weather had done to my crazy hair. I should've just gone all natural and not wear any make up, but my ego would not allow that.

Raquel and Karma were unaware that Daniel would be coming out with us, rather that he was even in town. I'm not sure if it was the drugs or a bit of carelessness, but I kept forgetting to tell them things. It was as if I just expected them to go along with everything because I had paid for it. This wasn't fair, but it is the reality of my mentality at this time.

By 5:30 PM I eventually said something to the girls about Daniel, and they were shocked to say the least. See, they didn't particularly like Daniel because of the way they felt he led me on all these years. They didn't even see him as a friend. They never understood that as much as I did love him, he would always be a friend to me. The girls felt otherwise. The shock of Daniel arriving in Miami overpowered them to even ask questions about Louie. I can only imagine their confusion and frustration.

Although they did let it go, I was too busy tidying up

our hotel room and preparing for his arrival to even pay them any mind. With a final touch of Yves Saint Laurent misted in the air, Daniel messaged me that he was downstairs in the hotel lobby. The way everything was working out for me and lining up, I felt that it was a sign of confirmation that I was on the right path.

I was all dolled up and made my way down to get him while Raquel and Karma were cutting up lines of cocaine in the hotel suite. I had never done drugs with Daniel, rather I don't think he even knew I did drugs. Yet, he was about to find out.

I greeted him with a warm smile and a hug, he was looking healthy and handsome as always. Again, I was experiencing psychosis at this point, so I do not remember exact conversation, but I remember all the feelings I had. He seemed confident in himself and happy to be on vacation, who wouldn't be? He embraced me and it was just as sweet as I had hoped for.

When we both walked into the suite the girls were a bit hesitant towards him but, welcomed him anyway. All of us were pretty tipsy at this point and done quite a bit of drugs throughout the day already. Although because of our tolerance, you wouldn't be able to tell.

I showed Daniel our view and we sat on the balcony taking shots and catching up with one another. Across the street, overlooking the ocean, a firework show started in front of us. This moment was perfect. It was exactly how I was feeling on the inside, and to share that moment with him was so special.

After the firework show ended, we came into the hotel room where I unapologetically did a line of cocaine in front of him.

We collectively decided to get an Uber to South Beach Miami where we had plenty of bars to go to. That Uber we took to the beach was a much calmer ride then what we had previously experienced. I was on my best behavior this time because he was around.

Arriving to South Beach was like a scene out of a movie. It was much more packed than Ocean Drive. We were all ready to have some fun and maybe even get into a little bit of trouble. The drugs started to hit me the second we stepped out of the Uber. This is now my third going on fourth week of my bender. My body was at a point where it was ready to shut down. I could feel it coming on, but I was not going to let it stop me. The moment I had been waiting for was finally here.

Raquel, Karma, Daniel and I made our way towards the bars. Raquel and Karma decided to grab a drink, I didn't feel like waiting so I told Daniel to keep walking with me. We walked along the beach and talked some more, I failed to mention anything about Louie. In my mind, Louie was no longer a part of my life; I did not feel it was necessary.

Just as we always did, he and I shared stories of our hopes and dreams and together we took in the scene of it all. We found ourselves a hotel that was serving drinks with plenty of people on our walk. Walking up to the bar, I noticed everyone with giant margarita glasses. They were the size of my head maybe even bigger. Of course, when we finally approached the bar, I ordered a giant margarita. I think he and I shared it; I can't remember because this is around the time I began to black out.

At this point in the night, I'm not sure where Raquel and Karma were. But they had each other and I had Daniel, so again in my mind everyone was safe and happy. Daniel and I grabbed a table just outside of the hotel where we drank our margarita and two beers. A woman came by with a polaroid camera and snaped some photos of us.

Raquel and Karma were trying to get ahold of me which I failed to respond to them. Although I do think they just went about their drinking at another bar on the same block.

Just as the previous night, the bars closed at midnight. We all ordered an Uber back to the Hyatt. Daniel hitched a ride with us because his hotel was just around the corner. When we arrived back to the hotel, Daniel asked me to come back to his place with him.

Without a second thought I said "Yes." The girls seemed a little irritated and concerned, but like I said earlier I was not going to let anyone ruin the high I was on. Daniel and I walked a short ten minutes to his hotel, holding hands along the way walking down a cobblestone path at 1 AM. We finally arrived at his hotel. It wasn't nearly as glamorous as ours, but I was okay with that because I was just happy to be with him.

The second we got into his hotel room, we kissed. Just as we had always done and just as it had always felt. I don't remember every detail of that night, but we did have sex.

The next morning, I woke up at 8 AM, took a shower and ordered breakfast for the girls, myself and Daniel from a restaurant down the street. I was still in my towel when Daniel took a video of me walking out of the bathroom. He asked me if it was okay to post on Instagram and I told him no problem. I didn't care or think much of it, but little did I know Louie was already suspicious and stalking everyone who he had previously suspected I was with.

I did receive a few messages from Louie that morning. But I was in no rush to respond as usual. I mean it was only 8 AM and the time difference between Florida and California was three hours. What was he doing up at 5 AM? I didn't care,

I was wishing he would find something better to do. I had always wished he found something better to do.

Again, I'm speaking unapologetically about this because this is exactly how my mentality was. On our way to my hotel, Daniel and I picked up breakfast for everyone. We had a long day ahead; Elliot had booked a yacht which we were to all go on during the afternoon and early evening.

Arriving back to the Hyatt, the girls were just waking up. We all ate together and before we knew it, it was only an hour before Elliot was going to pick us up to go to the marina.

Daniel left after we ate to get ready, and us girls all sat and talked about the night before. I didn't bother to call Louie this day. Instead, I sent him a text letting him know of our plans and wishing him well. I don't exactly remember his response, but I do remember the energy of it, he was pissed.

At this point, I was unaware that he had begun his hunt for any and all males who were involved in this yacht excursion. And If there's one thing about Instagram, it will tell you exactly what you need to know.

Chapter 29

Best Worst Day

What is it for someone to gain the
whole world, and yet lose or forfeit
their very self?
Luke 9:25

The realization of everything I had done wrong didn't hit me yet. I felt that what happened the night before was okay because I was happy. I could no longer pretend to be in love with Louie, I could no longer control my desires and I especially could not face my reality looking back at me in the mirror. Although, I did do my hair and make up for the day, looking in the mirror, I was not conscious to even look on the inside who I was.

The Polaroids from the night before were placed in my make up bag. Staring at them was the second time I didn't recognize myself. The look in my eyes, my body language were foreign to me. Looking back, the small glimpses I did get of myself were as if I was looking at a stranger. Life at this point truly did not feel real to me. This is a dangerous part of psychosis because I became fearless and not present with reality. The mixture of fearlessness and absence would set the tone for my day without me even realizing it. Like I said, you don't know you're losing your mind when you're losing your mind.

The girls and I took shots of alcohol and railed lines of cocaine while getting ready, it was a morning routine. All the windows in the hotel room were open along with the balcony. The light breeze which entered our room was as if it was familiar with this side of human nature. When the surroundings are so beautiful, peaceful and portrays a way as if it is working for you, the delusion of being a good human overpowers the reality of being a drug addict.

This isn't to shame drug addicts; I know plenty who are recovered that would agree. What we did in our addiction was not the character of the true essence of our spirit.

Elliot texted me that he would be at the Hyatt right at 3 PM to pick us up to go to the marina. The previous night the girls had gotten shrooms from someone at the bar. We collectively thought it was a good idea to take them, once we were out on the ocean. Mind you, we are already high off cocaine.

With a buzz and bikini on, it was now 2:30 PM. Daniel arrived back to our hotel where we'd wait for Elliot. It truly was a dream come true; between the beautiful weather, having my freedom, and just minutes away from spending the afternoon out on the ocean with my two girlfriends and Daniel; I could've died a happy girl this day.

Elliot called for us to come down. All four of us got into his rental car. The marina, where the yacht was docked, was about 20 minutes away. There was truly no place I'd rather be or doing anything other than what I was.

By the time we reached parking, I was already drunk, but in a good mood overall. The cocaine, shrooms and alcohol were secured in my bag; all that we were missing was weed. As we walked from the car to the marina, they were hundreds of people, most of them smoking weed and without a second thought, I asked a group of boys if I could buy some. They had a southern accent and style. I asked, "Hey, you got any of that for sale?"

They replied, "Do you want some za?"

I've never heard this term in my life, yet I replied, "As long as it'll get me high, yeah"

They sold me a gram of weed for $30, "za" is short for exotics. I didn't mind spending money on weed because it was a quick and convenient transaction right before we set sail. Daniel waited for me as I did this, I wonder if my actions up until this point ever made him suspicious of my behavior.

There was a total of 11 of us, Elliot had invited five girls and another guy who he was friends with. We were all here in Miami to celebrate Elliot's birthday, although his actual birthday wasn't until Monday. All 11 of us got on the yacht one by one. It had a beautiful open deck, three stories with custom teak flooring and enough room for all of us to get into trouble. Accompanying us were the captain and his two deckhands.

Daniel and I made our way to the lower front deck, Raquel and Karma followed. As the yacht pulled out of the marina, we all got comfortable taking in the view and the beautiful scenery surrounding us. I pulled out the bag of psychedelic mushrooms and offered them to Karma, Raquel and Daniel. We all took a fair amount with no fear, just pure happiness, and looked out onto the ocean.

Elliot played music through the yacht speakers, when I say everything was perfect, it was more than I could've imagined. Karma took a video for her Instagram, no one was looking or noticed her do it, but she did put Daniel and I cuddled up on her Instagram story. To this day I'm not sure if she intentionally posted us together for Louie to see or not. Louie was already very suspicious and had been waiting for something like this. What is done in the dark always comes to light and this would be the way my wrong doings would be delivered.

Once we sailed out of the marina into the ocean, no one had cell phone service. The shrooms began to hit, the cocaine was coursing through my body and the alcohol was absolutely refreshing. How I managed all of this at once blows my mind and I absolutely do not recommend it.

Once the captain found us a spot to lower the anchor, we were all ready to get in the water. Daniel and I, high on shrooms, swam out from the rest of the group and treaded water. He and I talked and enjoyed the beautiful ocean together. This was better than any moment I could've ever imagined. Daniel said to me, "This is the best day of my life." And in that moment, I realized it was mine too. When I think about this moment, I could've died happy this day.

The rest of our time in the ocean was spent partying on the yacht without a care in the world. Time flew by and before we knew it the sun was setting. I wish I could share more about what happened on the yacht, but once Daniel and I got out of the water, I blacked out.

I came to when we docked back in the marina. I had lost my phone and was a complete mess. Truly, it was the most inebriated I had ever been up until this point. Raquel and Karma weren't much help as they seemed very stressed. Whether it was their own come down or just the anxiety of having to deal with me, I'm not sure what was wrong with them.

Elliot drove us girls back to our hotel and the plan was to meet up at a night club in the next three hours. This all sounded great, but I was completely unaware of what was about to come. I didn't know just hours before what Karma had posted of Daniel and I on her Instagram story, but Louie did. With my phone still missing, all of us headed back to our separate hotels. And with one high peaking while another was coming down it was a cocktail for delusion, confusion and disaster. I was out of it, still living in a façade of a fantasy, I didn't care that my phone was gone.

The moment us girls got back to the hotel; I began getting ready for the night club. I imagined that it would be just as great as my time out in the ocean with Daniel. Raquel and Karma were tired, hungry and didn't want to go out. Karma looked exhausted while Raquel was still drunk from our day. I was going to go out, with or without them. Luckily, Raquel had the idea of writing their phone numbers down on a piece of paper for me so I could call them if I needed to.

By 9:30 PM I was ordering a taxicab for myself at the front desk with no cell phone, just my ID and some cash, alone in Miami. I had no way of contacting Daniel or Elliot; all I knew was that they were at a club off of Ocean Drive where Elliot booked a booth and bottle service. To go out in Miami alone, without a cell phone and more importantly in the mental and physical state I was in, is very dangerous. So many horrible things could've happened to me on my taxi ride.

When I arrived at the club alone, all the people standing outside stared at me as if I were an alien. It must've been my energy. Walking up I was a total mess; I hadn't realized the state of being I was in. I made my way to the front of the line and told security, "I am here for Elliot's booth."

Security responded, "He needs to come down to get you."

I explained how I didn't have my phone and wouldn't be able to tell him I'm here. Security did not accept this answer and turned me away. In survival mode now because I was truly on my own, until I found my friends, I still waited at the front thinking of a way to get in. I was reminded of all the times back in Hollywood California when promoters would get me in. So, I looked for any guy outside who looked like a promoter and to my luck he was standing just to the left of me on the other side of the rope. I told him my situation and how my friends were upstairs in a booth.

He looked at me and said, "I'll walk you in, but you have to let me buy you a drink first."

Of course, I said yes, without a second thought. This small, Middle Eastern man lifted the rope for me and walked me through security and into the nightclub. This club was better than any club I had been to in Hollywood. The lights were better, the music was better, everything was better. My senses were in unison yet, distorted. The club promoter and I walked through a crowd of people dancing to get to the bar. He ordered me a drink and I was amazed by my surroundings; I was not paying attention to him or my drink. He handed me my drink, I took a big sip in front of him and said, "Thank you."

I parted ways with him and now my goal was to find Elliot. I knew they mentioned earlier in the day about being upstairs, so I strutted my way there. When I arrived everyone from the yacht was there, except for Karma and Raquel. When I walked up to Elliot it was as if he saw a ghost, he wasn't expecting me to come. Daniel didn't even acknowledge me. I was oblivious to their energy and simply felt relieved to be around people I knew. Which was a good thing because I began to lose physical control of myself. My thoughts became confused, and my vision was blur. I felt as if I couldn't see, the sound became muffled, and my speech slurred.

I sat with the girls, two of them were very friendly but one seemed as if she hated me. I don't recall the rest of my time at the club because I blacked out harder than I did the night before. By 12:30 AM the lights came on, so we all collectively made our way out of the nightclub. I still hadn't talked to Daniel. His energy with me went from the best day ever to get away from me.

Everyone moved so fast and were going different places in different Uber's. Thankfully the two girls I sat next to at the club had me get in an Uber with them. Their friend who had the bad energy towards me wasn't with them anymore. I asked where she went and they replied, "With Daniel."

Without warning my heart broke. It was as if those words were the crack in a faulty dam and all my emotions just flooded out. The girls I was with had no idea of the now four-week bender I was on, the drug induced psychosis, or how I had feelings for Daniel. Luckily, they were kind, loving and supportive. When we reached our destination, I was sobbing as if someone had died. They didn't know me, didn't know what to do or how to calm me down. I began to have an anxiety attack and had a hard time breathing. They called Elliot to come pick me up and bring me back to my hotel.

The girls walked me down to his car. When I got in, Elliot could visibly see the distress on my face.

He said, "Louie found out from Karma's post and messaged Daniel after we got off the yacht."

Well, this explained a lot. I did not care for Louie's feelings, I hated him. Just as he had always done in my life, he ruined things for me and gotten in the way of my happiness. My only concern at this point was Daniel.

As Elliot drove us across the bridge going 50 mph I opened my door to jump out. Fortunately, my movement was delayed from the roofies the club promoter slipped me. While driving, Elliot was able to pull me back by my bra straps. He said the magic words so I didn't make another attempt, "I'll take you to Daniel right now, as long as you don't do that again."

I didn't intend to be manipulative although my actions proved otherwise. After he said that, I figured I could talk to Daniel and try to work things out. It was now after midnight, March 14th. Elliot dropped me off at Daniels hotel and said, "I'm going to see you in the morning, okay?"

I said, "Okay." I believe Elliot was having me make a promise to make it to the next day. We all need an Elliot in our lives.

Because I was there the night before I knew what room Daniel was is in, but the man at the front desk wouldn't just let me walk by. I said, "I have no phone, my friend is in room 137, I need his help getting back to my hotel."

The man escorted me to Daniel's room and when we arrived, he knocked on the door, "Front desk."

Now, I don't know what I was expecting but this is an image I'll never forget. Daniel opened the door in his boxers looking completely shocked and frightened to see me on the other side. And just behind him on the bed were two bare legs. Again, my heart was broken. I felt like a complete fool, the fantasy and delusion I had lived in turned into a messy reality right before my eyes. The veil of my reality had been lifted in this moment.

I wanted to talk with Daniel about what happened but instead I expressed how I just needed to get back to my hotel. He said he'd walk me there. The cobblestone alleyway we had walked through in joy, we now walked through in darkness and heartbreak. I continued to cry, it felt as if I was dying inside. I hadn't realized how strongly I felt for Daniel all these years until this moment.

When we reached my hotel, the girls came down to get me. Daniel and I went our separate ways, and I felt my world crashing down. I told the girls what happened and how I was feeling. While undressing and moving things around, I found my phone in Karma's things.

Immediately, I saw all the messages from Louie on my phone. He wrote degrading things including how he was going to kill me when I got back. He made accusations that I had slept with both Elliot and Daniel at the same time. Again, I didn't care. I blocked him right away. I called my mom who was in California to tell her how heartbroken I was, how I wanted to die and how I just ruined my life. She thought this was all for Louie.

My sister Harper, who was friends with Louie had been on the phone with him all night. She wasn't happy with me at all, yet again, I didn't care. Although she did say one thing while we were on a three-way call with our mom, "Mom, you need to take this seriously. Marissa isn't okay."

I don't remember the rest of this conversation, somehow, I fell asleep this night. When I woke up at 8 AM, Elliot had texted me, "I am on my way to pick you up."

I still hadn't talked to Raquel or Karma; they were still sleeping when I left to meet up with Elliot. He said we were just going for a drive, which we did. I told him what Louie had texted me and Elliot suggested to come back to the bay area with him and he would then drive me to Sacramento to be with my mom.

Elliot had a solution and so this is what I was going to do. I changed my flight from LAX to San Francisco so I could be on the same flight with Elliot. After we did this, he said, "Now we're going to get breakfast with Daniel, and I am going to enjoy a steak for my birthday."

We arrived at the restaurant where Elliot ordered a steak and Daniel did show up. We talked about what happened and with ease worked things out. I could tell Daniel was upset. Luckily, Elliot mediated our conversation and by the time he was done with his steak, our problem was resolved. Elliot and Daniel took me back to my hotel to get my suitcase because our flight was at 1 PM.

The girls had no idea I changed my flight and was leaving the 14th instead of the 15th. When changing my flight, I ended up canceling theirs. When we all realized this, I sent Raquel $1500 over cash app to buy them both new flights home and another night stay at the hotel. I parted ways with the girls and went with Elliot and Daniel.

We had time to kill before our flights, so we went to the beach to swim and relax. I was done with Miami and Miami was done with me. What I hadn't realized this morning was that I was still heavily under the influence from the night before. Not that this is any surprise, but I didn't have any more drugs and was beginning to have a come down. Without my drugs resulted in my suffering from withdrawals.

By the time we had gotten to the airport, I was feeling it. Yet the messages I was still receiving from Louie through social media made me think, "If you hate me, I'll give you something to really hate."

I specifically remember one message he wrote that said, "You're the talk of Hollywood, you're worthless."

I thought to myself, "I'll give em something to really talk about."

So, before my flight I posted my time in Miami on my Instagram. I didn't care to be the villain anymore; I began to own it. I allowed Louie's imagination to run free. He expressed how coming back to Hollywood would be the end for me, which is why I wasn't going to go.

Daniel flew back to San Diego. Elliot and I flew back to the Bay Area. Our goodbye was short and sweet and couldn't have come soon enough for him. Elliot was a good friend; I began having withdrawals on the plane which he helped me through. As uncomfortable as Elliot was, he physically, emotionally and mentally supported me. When we landed in San Francisco, it was made clear that Louie was now hunting us.

I told myself I wasn't going to let Louie take anything away from me anymore. Even if it meant I had to take my own life to get away from him. I didn't share these feelings with Elliot, but my mind was made up. For a year and a half, I had dimmed my light, comforted an insecure man's delusions and suffered from his emotional, mental and physical abuse. The day I acted on his previous accusations was the day he had been waiting for. I was not ready for war; I was ready to end it, even if that meant taking my own life.

In 24 hours, I went from having the best day of my life to planning on how to end it. I figured I had a good run, that I had endured enough and at least I could hold onto that memory out in the ocean.

Chapter 30

The Morning of March 16th

Focus on me, not the storm.
Matthew 14:22-23

The last 24 hours had been such a mess it was difficult to take account of everything that had gone on. So let's do that now; I had sex with Daniel, Louie found out through Karma's post, Louie messaged and threatened Daniel about us, Daniel had ill feelings towards me. When I found out about this, I tried to jump out of a moving car. Elliot brought me to Daniel. I saw Daniel with another woman and had another breakdown expressing to my family that I wanted to die. Elliot had a solution to bring me back to my mother in Sacramento. I accidentally canceled the flights for Raquel and Karma back to LAX, but refinanced them. Karma became an opposition for Louie. Daniel and I made up over a steak breakfast. I experienced withdrawals on my flight back to the bay area with Elliot, and here we are now, in Oakland.

Am I missing anything? Oh yeah, I did not tell Louie my plan of going with Elliot for the purpose of being delivered to my mother and now Louie was on the hunt for us.

Whew, yeah just telling this is a lot to keep up with, imagine living through it while going through psychosis, suicidal ideation and withdrawals. If it weren't for Elliot taking me out of Miami that day, I would've done something extremely dangerous and irreversible.

So, as much as "Hollywood" and Louie thought I was a whore and an idiot for flying with Elliot, it was for the best. No one had taken an active positive role during this crisis like Elliot did.

When we landed, Elliot ordered us an Uber to his apartment in Oakland hills. He did not seem phased by me. He was laughing, making jokes and doing his best to be a light for me. Even though he too, was now in danger.

Arriving to his apartment, we were both tired. We set our luggage down and he started the shower for me, gave me CBD gummies for my nerves and took my order for McDonald's. Once I was settled, he left to go pick up our dinner. I felt like a damaged bird that just survived an attack from a hawk and Elliot was now my caretaker.

My body without drugs was shutting down, I could feel it. I knew I needed something, anything, within the next twenty-four hours.

For now, I'd just take as many CBD dummies as I could to relax. All my clothes were dirty from the last four days, so I wore a T-shirt and basketball shorts Elliot gave me. I found a spot to lay down on his bed, curled up in a small ball waiting for his arrival with dinner.

I felt as if I never wanted to leave, I was terrified to face my consequences and my true self. I just wanted to be nurtured and told that everything was going to be okay. But that's not how life works when you make a mistake and hurt others.

Elliot arrived back to the apartment with McDonald's

chicken sandwiches, cheeseburgers, fries and soda. He said, "Are you feeling better? Make sure you eat as much as you can."

I replied, "Yes and no, I have the shakes, I'm scared. Thank you for the food and the shower, thank you for taking care of me."

Elliot replied, "You know Marissa, from the day we met, I knew we'd be best friends. I love you; you'll be okay. Just eat your food and get some good sleep. You'll be with your mom tomorrow and everything will begin to sort itself out."

I say with zero confidence, "Okay." I was hesitant to say what I said next, but felt I needed to. "By the way I feel I should go back to Los Angeles tomorrow, I need to face this sooner than later."

With shock on his face Elliot said, "What about going to see your mom? Are you sure it's safe for you?"

I replied, "I have to face Louie, it'll only get worse. He's hunting Daniel and now you, it's not fair. If he is going to be mad at anyone, it should be me. I need to clear everything up."

Elliot replied, "We can handle ourselves; I don't think it's a good idea just yet, but if that's what you want to do, okay."

What Elliot didn't know is that I was in desperate need for cocaine. When he left to get dinner, I was arranging for Kat, my female drug dealer to pick me up from LAX. Reluctantly, Elliot helped me book my flight from San Francisco airport to Los Angeles for the following afternoon, March 16th.

I didn't tell Louie of my plan about coming back to Los Angeles, because I didn't plan on seeing him. Although, I did tell my mother the purpose of me going to Los Angeles was to talk with him and face my consequences. Momma was worried and hesitant, yet supportive. Elliot seemed a little disappointed I wouldn't be going to Sacramento, but he didn't stop me from doing what I wanted.

That night Elliot and I shared his bed, not touching once. I could've slept on the couch, but I was scared of myself and needed some type of comfort. The CBD gummies I took did help me relax just enough so I could fall asleep. My flight was for 1 PM the next day and Kat would be picking me up.

Waking up in the morning Elliot was like a drill sergeant, "Get dressed, I'm taking you for a walk to get coffee and breakfast." It was now 9 AM March 16th.

"Okay, give me ten minutes" I say. This was the first morning in a month that I had not used cocaine.

Back in Miami, Karma and Raquel were preparing for their flight to LAX without me. They would go to my apartment without me to get their car and consequently have to see Louie. At this point, they weren't speaking to me.

Thankfully for myself, I would be landing just as they were leaving. I didn't want to see them either. I put on sweats and brushed my hair to prepare for our walk. Elliot seemed refreshed; oh, how I envied his well-being.

We walked towards a coffee shop about ten minutes away from his apartment. He and I talked about our futures, although I didn't have merely as much to say as he did. I merely engaged in the conversation to not worry my friend.

The lingering feeling, I always had of suicide and suffering was ever-present. The familiar feeling it brought me

276

made me calm, because I knew my suffering would be over soon.

Elliot ordered me an iced coffee and a breakfast sandwich; his order was similar although just with almond milk. We ate our breakfast looking out to a pond across the street. It was serene; I took it in as if this were my last breakfast the way I ate slow and proper.

Elliot and I took what was left of our coffee and walked back to his apartment. I packed up my things and ordered myself an Uber to SFO. I asked Elliot without hesitation, "Do you have any pills I could buy?"

He laughed and said, "Marissa absolutely not, you are not going to commit suicide."

Elliot dropped the conversation right there. His tone was as serious as I had ever heard. It was selfish of me to put my friend in the position I did and then for him to try his best to nurture me only for me to ask him this, must've felt like a slap in the face. He didn't show it but looking back I understand this now. My Uber arrived for pick up and Elliot walked me out. We said our goodbyes, I thanked him and held him tight.

He said to me as I got in the Uber van, "Take care of yourself, okay? Call me tomorrow, okay?"

Elliot always made sure to make me promise him something for the next day, I always said "Okay", but this time I just smiled with my mouth closed and waved goodbye.

My anxiety and excitement to get to LA so I could be with my drug dealer, was as if I had already taken the drug. Kat said she'd be waiting for me and that we could figure everything out from there. A quick fifty-minute flight and I'd be on a sick one, again.

No one knew I was going to see Kat, and I intended on keeping it that way. The flight from SFO to LAX was a blur for me although I do remember ordering a double jack and Coke before takeoff. I was able to sleep on the plane because of that.

Landing in Los Angeles at 2:15pm, the first message to come through on my phone was from Kat, it read, "Here for you, ready for you."

I'm not sure what she meant by that, but I took it as we were going to party. Walking out to the pick-up terminal couldn't have come soon enough. There she was, Kat felt more than just my drug dealer, but my friend, I trusted her.

We made eye contact as I walked towards her in the pick-up line when she held up a bag of cocaine. From that moment, I knew my decision-making skills were long gone. It was certain, I was no longer scared of the consequences. My addiction had never been this out of control, but now it was at the point I'd do anything for drugs.

Chapter 31

Off the Brick

When the enemy can't reach you
directly, he will use people around
you to attack. They're being used
unknowingly. Pray!
Ephesians 6:12

The parallels of my current and past reality were ever-present. Just as I had reached for the door handle to Kats car, it was as if I signed an agreement with her; just as I had done nine years ago moments before I was raped by Jack. The familiar essence which was once a shadow I ran from became so close to me, I did only what I knew how to do; become submissive to the dark energy waiting for me on the other side. Without consciously knowing, I had become the dark energy.

Any lessons of enlightenment were now gone. I barely knew Kat, but to me, she was the only person I needed. Souly because she had the supply I needed and was willing to witness me do it.

Years ago, I opened my heart with the sacred plant. Which sounds great in theory, but what no one prepared me for was that I not only opened my heart to lightness, but darkness as well. When one is unaware of this, the possibilities of the forces around you can completely consume and control your life behind a mask of false enlightenment, if you choose to not follow the path of integrity, integration and balance.

Every Devil hiding behind a charming smile, I welcomed with open arms. Every energy that tapped into my desires or temptation, I welcomed with open arms. This is to say, I had no boundaries, and I was morally and ethically okay with just about anything. My stability and grounding were weak. I was easily persuaded and there was little thought behind my actions. Living a life with no boundaries opened me up to a life of danger, addiction, temptation and persuasion.

A danger I would not recognize until it was far too late. Getting into Kats car I knew something was off, yet I continued to ignore my intuition because in an odd way being off, felt right.

She gave me a big hug and said, "Do as much as you want, or should I say, as much as you need" while holding up a bag cocaine.

She drove out of the airport without a worry while I used my cell phone, driver's license and a hundred-dollar bill to cut up a line of cocaine as long as my iPhone and as thick as my pinky. Nothing else mattered to me, I couldn't hear her or her loud music. I had no thoughts outside of rolling out the perfect bill to inhale drugs into my nostrils.

How badly I craved that drip down the back of my throat, the way it numbed my mind, body and soul. I loved cocaine more than anything. Kat must've noticed my physical adoration for the line I just cut up because she said, "Stick with me and there'll be an endless supply for you."

With that I ingested every speck of white powder. My chest rose, my lungs expanded, and nostrils opened as if I was taking a deep breath. With my eyes closed, I could feel every piece of cocaine flutter inside my body, down my throat and drip into what felt like my heart and stomach.

I laid back in the passenger seat, becoming weightless and strung out. The initial ingestion of the drug shocked me. I felt my heart skipping beats, my vision became blurred and my eyes shuttering. Kat did not notice for she was fighting traffic out of LAX. My hands, chest, head and legs twitched uncontrollably. I hadn't experienced a minor seizure before, but the way I could not control the subtle yet jarring movements my body made, paired with a lousy drool coming out of the side of my mouth, I knew I had a seizure.

This did not scare me. I had mentally crossed the line where I was okay with dying. This lasted less than a minute and I regained what felt like control. Sitting myself up right in the passenger seat, Kat looked over to me and said, "The best shit you'll ever get, huh? I chopped it right off the brick for you."

What she was saying is that she had cut the cocaine I was doing right off of a cocaine brick. I looked down at my shaky hands and said without confidence, "It's definitely nothing like I've had before."

This didn't feel or taste the same as her previous supply. Something was different. She laughed and said we better pick up some liquor before going back to her place. She took me to a liquor store where we bought blunt wraps, Hennessey and soda. Kat had a very intimidating personality. She talked down to any man she came in contact with and had no problem telling them what to do, how to do it or when to do it. I noticed this inside the liquor store, the way she ordered a harmless worker around. Was I like her? I must've been to some degree because she was attracted to me and I to her.

We got back in her car and she took a swig out of the bottle. I copied her movement and took a bigger swig of Hennessy. She said to me, "All of that is for you, you're going to need it."

I didn't question what she meant by that. Kat was aware of Louie and what I had done. She convinced me to pack up all my things and move into her apartment that day. Without questioning her I said okay. We drove to Hollywood, I made sure to text Louie to let him know I was coming to get my things although he didn't respond I knew he saw it.

Kat wanted to come up to the apartment with me and be my bodyguard. I had to talk her out of this because she wanted to bring her gun. I didn't want to hurt Louie anymore in anyway more than I had already done. So, my plan was just to get my things and leave his life. I didn't know how to fix my mistakes, nor did I want to be with him and the only solution I saw fit was to leave him alone.

Kat drove me to my apartment off Hollywood Boulevard. I did not know what to expect or what I would be walking into. She stayed in the car and said, "I'm giving you 15 minutes before I come up there."

This was barely enough time to get up to my apartment, but I agreed, I was submissive to whatever she had planned for me. With just my cell phone, I made my way through the complex. Arriving to my door I could hear footsteps as if someone was pacing through the apartment. I knew he was on the other side and timidly opened the door. The footsteps I heard just moments before stopped and the silence which followed brought a great deal of tension.

Louie was inside, pacing while waiting for my arrival and had frozen the second he heard me open the front door. There he stood about 20 feet away from me down the hall. To me, he looked like the life had been sucked out of him, but it was nothing compared to what I looked like to him.

Louie's jaw dropped when he saw me standing in the doorway. It was as if every ounce of hate and anger he had towards me turned into great concern. The last thing I expected him to say especially with a soft tone to his voice was, "Marissa, what the fuck."

The way he looked at me and how those words came out of his mouth, I'll never forget. Louie saw something dark in me. Louie saw the physical and mental change in me. I was too coward to respond to him.

I went straight to the closet and began packing my things. With angst he followed me in there, "So you're just leaving? You can't talk to me? What happened?"

I looked at him and said, "I'm leaving, I'm sorry it had to happen this way."

I threw everything I could think of into my bags as he continued to speak to me. Not only had I broken his heart, but I was physically damaged and now leaving him. The time limit Kat gave me was the only thing I cared about.

The words coming out of the Louies mouth just pushed me to keep moving and pack faster. I felt terrible, I couldn't look him in the eye. He cried out, "Why can't you talk to me?"

I paused and said, "Because someone is waiting for me and I've already done enough."

This shifted his energy completely, Louie thought I meant Daniel or Elliot. I grabbed my bags and made my way for the front door when he stopped me. I said, "Move, I have to go."

Louie would not budge, that was until my eyes turned dark because with one glare he got out of the way. This did not stop him from following me. He followed me all through the apartment complex and my biggest fear was that Kat would see this and pull a gun on him. I stopped to look at him and said, "If you keep going, they'll hurt you."

He didn't care, he was ready for war. I allowed him to keep following me only because I had told Kat over text to park on the next street over. When we finally came out on Hollywood Boulevard looking like two crazy people, I began running towards Kat. Louie was just about to follow me when his friend called his name out of nowhere. I didn't know what Kat was capable of and I did not want to find out at the extent of him getting hurt.

I reached Kat's car and Louie was out of sight. I was out of breath when I got in her car with my bags. The drama which unfolded in front of me because of my actions was overwhelming and out of control. As dangerous as Louie was, I'm not sure why I felt like Kat was a safer option. She turned on her music as if nothing had happened and scolded me for being an extra five minutes late.

Meanwhile, Louie was blowing up my phone confused on what the hell just happened. I on the other hand had no idea what to say or how to explain myself. Kat and I drove around the city for about three hours. I was getting higher and higher with every drop off and my body was slowing down more and more.

It was now time to go back to her apartment where she said we'd relax, get ready and hang out with her friends. I just wanted a break at this point, but now I was fully under the control of what she had planned for me, which wasn't good.

Arriving back to her apartment there were plenty of

drugs, money and supplies for what she had planned. I was most uncomfortable with the realization that this was now my life. What I didn't consider was how she got ahold of all of this product and who she was working for; I was soon to find out.

Part 5:

The Rise

Chapter 32

The Self Behind the Self

I have heard your prayer; I have
seen your tears; surely, I will heal
you.
2 Kings 20:5

    Kat lived and worked for someone who she called her best friend. At least that's how she referred to him in front of me. This "best friend" was constantly calling and texting her throughout this time. I truly thought for that they were just friends. I guess I was too caught up in everything that was happening in my own life to consider what was happening in hers.

    There was a lot of mystery, but all I knew how to do in this moment with her was more drugs. Her home was every Hollywood girl's fantasy of a dream apartment. I was envious for a moment, but not for long because this was now my home too.

    She made space for me, showed me around her apartment and made sure I was comfortable. Her dining room table had two bricks of cocaine sitting on it along with scales and plastic dime bags. This is what she meant when she said I would be taken care of. I'm not sure if it was the drugs, her or my simple lack of will, but I so easily went along with everything; including her best friend who I'll refer to as Dom, coming over to meet me.

I didn't understand why it was important for him to come over to her apartment at this time. But it was important to her, she said she wanted to get his approval of me, you know, to make sure I was cool enough to be around her. Looking back, she didn't think much for herself either and this was just a soft introduction into what would happen later this evening.

Growing up, my father always warned my sisters and I about drugs and sex trafficking, never did I think that I would find myself in a position like I had. Although in this moment I was still unaware of what exactly was going on.

Kat helped me do my make-up and hair, she planned for us to go to dinner with Dom out to Mastro's in Malibu. She told me how I could really work the men she was going to introduce me too. I was too numb from the cocaine to speak, even at one point passing out while she was doing my eyeliner.

Looking back, in her eyes I was the perfect bait. I was hooked on drugs, just abandoned my apartment and showed her how weak willed I was. I say weak willed because that's what I was, my will, rather any will that I had was broken many years ago. In her eyes, I imagine how a 23-year-old girl who just got back from Miami looking like a hot mess could be so appeasing to the market Kat worked for.

I didn't know this at the moment, but she was preparing me for this night at Mastro's to be looked at as a prospect for her pimp. And this is how they do it. They make you feel special and cared for; they get you hooked on their drugs, they isolate you and then they sell you.

288

My sister Harper kept in contact with me, she kept saying to me over multiple phone calls, "Why do you keep passing out on the phone?"

I didn't realize I was passing out on the phone with her. I told her how I was going out to dinner in Malibu with friends. I can't remember how she felt about that.

While getting ready, Kat deleted photos on my Instagram profile that suited who she was shaping me to be. All 243 photos of friends and family were now gone. She said it was important for me to remain mysterious, like her. In reality she was reaching in every part of my life so I could be bought. And this isn't to say bought by things that she could give me. What I mean is so I could be bought by the men I was soon to meet.

In a lifestyle of drugs, alcohol, darkness and deceit, you don't know you crossed the line until it's too late. I was a good kid growing up, I had a good family, I had such a sweetness and innocence about me. As I'm writing this I'm tearing up because all of that was gone now, it had been gone for a long time.

Here I was March 16, 2021, unknowingly being primed and prepped for another predator, for a pimp. Kat helped me get dressed, she picked out the outfit I wore the night I spent with Daniel in Miami. A quick memory of how sweet, safe and free I felt with him came over me, that was all gone now.

She dressed me up sluttier then previously; she pushed up my boobs, teased my hair, pulled my thong out of my skirt and put oil on my skin. Kat dressed me like a high-end prostitute. I tried to fix a few things, but she scolded me so harshly I sat back down and remained silent. I should've known something was wrong at this point because she was not done up at all. She wore sweats and a hoodie; her hair and make-up weren't fixed either.

I don't know what I was thinking. I really don't remember thinking anything at all. I do remember feeling empty, exploited and addicted. I couldn't stop cutting lines of her cocaine. Every chance I got to do a line, I did. It almost felt like it wasn't doing enough for me at this point.

She had me order a black XL Uber to Malibu. It was about a 45-minute ride and $130 charge. I just did as I was told. I'm sure as a reader it's hard to imagine how I got to this point, I just hope you understand that this moment in my life hadn't just built up from the last weekend or month, but it started when I was 16, and with each traumatizing and devaluing experience I've written about that went unresolved, it's a no-brainer to me how I ended up here March 16th, 2021.

When we arrived to Mastro's there were two African American men waiting for us, Dom and his friend. They greeted me as if they knew they caught a good one. They both escorted Kat and I to a table right next to the ocean, I could stick my hand out and feel the moisture from the sea.

People stared at me, but I stared out onto the ocean. The sun was just setting, and the sky was lit up with orange, purple and blues. I stared into the sun wishing it would just bring me into its light. I gazed at the ocean wishing it would bring those forgiving waters I once experienced. The sunset was beautiful, I looked at the two men sitting across from me and Kat and said, "Can we celebrate my birthday today? I just want to have one last birthday."

They all looked confused but agreed to my request. My birthday wasn't until August, I had no plans of killing myself in this moment, but I think something in me just knew this would be my last sunset in this reality.

The two men made sure to keep me high at the table. They cut me lines and served them to me on a salad plate. Kat ordered me plenty of champagne, the funny thing is no one else drank and no one else did any drugs. Before the main course even came out, I passed out on the table. I woke up to our waiter bringing me a tiramisu cake with a lit candle. Written in cursive on the cake with white icing said, "Happy birthday, Marissa."

It's comical at the parallel of how close I was to death and here I was celebrating my birthday. I wished for no more pain; I was tired of enduring pain. I couldn't stomach the cake. I had too much cocaine inside of my body it felt like acid was running ramped in my veins.

My face began to turn yellow; I only know this because Dom pointed it out. Kat rushed me to the bathroom where I threw up blood and anything else inside of my body. I shook uncontrollably and couldn't help but cry. I was scared, I couldn't see or stand up straight after this. She had to walk me out of the bathroom as I leaned onto her for support. We waited outside until the two men paid the bill. They offered to bring us back to her apartment. They made jokes about how I couldn't handle the lifestyle. I remember thinking before I passed out in the back of their car, "If you only knew how long I've been living this lifestyle."

It was now dark outside, my senses were completely gone. I truly couldn't see or hear a thing. I only knew we were back at her apartment because I could smell the perfume, she sprayed on me earlier lingering in the room. She laid me on the couch, and I could feel the men staring at me. They were examining me as if I were a show dog. I had no idea what was going on, I just knew it wasn't good.

Something inside of me knew I had to leave, but I couldn't move. That was until my sister Harper called me, and by the grace of God I answered, she was pissed at me, but it was as if her voice had the strength of my whole family calling back to me; her voice struck a chord inside of me.

The men said they had some business to take care of, but when they got back, we would go to the clubs and bars off Figueroa. The only thing I knew about Figueroa in Los Angeles is that you could drive down there at any time of day or night and you'll see prostitutes, pimps, and patrons. I've never heard of clubs or bars on that street, only what walked it. They were going to sell me. That was clear to me now. I knew I couldn't trust Kat, and I knew I had to get out of there.

I didn't care if I had to leave everything I had brought behind. All I needed was my phone and my purse. I knew I didn't want to make it obvious that I was escaping so I figured I could just take my ID and phone and hide it in my bra. I knew I only had a window of time to leave before the men came back, so I told Kat that I wanted to get my best dress and heels for the night. I figured playing into this would help my escape.

She said okay and to be back before the men came back. But before I left, she had to make sure I was okay to Uber by myself, which I absolutely wasn't, and she made sure of that. She sat me up, tied a rubber band above my right elbow and injected me with heroin. I had never done heroin in my life; I had never wanted to do heroin in my life. Here I was already clinging on to what life I had left watching helplessly as she stuck a needle into my vein. As I'm writing this, I can't help but see that moment, it was a moment yet again that a piece of my spirit and innocence became broken and impure. It was a moment I knew I had crossed a line and I couldn't go back.

My heart breaks in every chapter of this book and just when I feel that I've healed myself, I recognize I'm still grieving pieces of me I'll never get back.

After she shot me up, I laid back. She told me I had to wait for permission until the two men came back and that this would keep me put. If there was any high from the heroine, I don't remember. All I remember was being scared. I had never wanted my mom or dad so bad, I wanted them to come save me and protect me. I was unable to do anything, I couldn't fight, I was weak.

Her plan worked and when the two men came back, they began touching me. I wish I could describe what they looked like, but I have hardly any recollection. I had been sexual assaulted plenty of times before, but this time with these two men they were just examining me. It was like I was a product or an item. They re-positioned me, took photos of me, telling me what to do. There was no way I could fight back; I didn't have the strength. I knew Kat was in on this, I knew they all had guns and I knew I didn't mind dying. So that's when I said to them, "I think I could make you all a lot of money, I have some better dresses back at my apartment, is it okay if I go and get them?"

I knew I had to get out of there, I was hoping they wouldn't pick up on my lie. They looked at each other and said, "Okay leave your purse."

I left my purse, but I did not leave my ID. I had my driver's license and debit card between my phone and phone case. They let me have my phone because I had to order myself an Uber. The moment I stepped out of that apartment I ran. I don't know how I did it, but I ran.

I went four blocks where I waited for an Uber to come pick me up. The second I got into that car I broke down crying. The realization that I was just a hair close of being sold on the streets of Los Angeles or sex trafficked out of the State hit me like a truck. My self-worth or any lightness and hope I had was gone. The Uber driver dropped me off at my apartment complex, I didn't care if Louie was there or not, I just wanted to be home. Unfortunately, Hollywood never felt like home, no home had felt like home in almost a decade, I was ready to go home though. I didn't understand this feeling at the time but looking back I was ready to leave this earth. I wanted to be in a safe place outside of the hell I'd been living, but I didn't consciously know this at the time.

I walked into my empty apartment on the sixth floor, and it was the first time I had been truly alone in over a month. It was eerily quiet, and the lighting looked as if there was a veil covering everything. Nothing seemed real at this moment, even me. I went to go get undressed when I saw myself in the mirror for the first time in days. I mean a really good look in the mirror.

Funny thing is, I did recognize myself this time. And what I saw were all the times I've been raped, stalked, slapped, punched, choked, threatened, abandoned, manipulated and suffering. I saw my younger self sitting in the back of my mom's car while she did Hardy bread deliveries, I saw my younger self ask my mom about God and His world. I saw my dads' green eyes looking at me and remembering the first time I felt true love. I saw me and my sisters playing in the meadows across from the house we grew up in. I saw the 16-year-old Marissa looking at herself in the mirror right before Jack raped her for four hours. I saw the 16-year-old Marissa who needed her dad, but he was nowhere to be found. I saw all versions of Marissa.

All of this flashed before my eyes so quickly yet so slowly. I could feel the emptiness inside of me. I looked at the vein Kat punctured with heroin, I looked at how my collar bones and chest bones protruded out. My eyes and cheeks were sunken in, my hair and make-up resembled something that wasn't me. This was my first time truly seeing myself since I slipped into a drug-induced psychosis. This was the first time I saw myself in the mirror and felt it was time for me to go home now; I was done with being a victim.

My mind was at ease, I smiled at myself in the mirror as if I was at peace that my suffering was coming to an end. All of a sudden, I could see past myself. My mind, spirit, subconscious and superconscious were all present at once. That's the best way I can describe it. I was looking past myself and into something I still don't understand. Some people call it the self behind the self. And in that moment, I knew it was my time. I knew this day would always come; I knew there was something waiting for me on the other side, and I wasn't scared of what it was either. But what I didn't know is what has led me to write this book.

Chapter 33

The Prayer

The Lord will fight for you; you need
only to be still.
Exodus 14:14

Looking deep into my reflection I witnessed all the lives I've lived. All of the heartbreak I've experienced and devasting trauma I've endured. All the suffering which paled me from the day I became conscious of what a suffering human was. I was tired of suffering, I was tired of being the victim, I was tired of numbing my pain and most of all I was tired of myself. The identity I had unknowingly built for myself through voluntary and involuntary experiences was expiring now.

The day I had always fantasized about was here. The day I envisioned going back home to where I truly belonged was calling me. Tonight, was the night, March 16th, 2021 that I would commit suicide.

I've had plenty of time to think about how I wanted to do it. I knew I wanted to be asleep, I knew I wanted it to be painless, and most of all I knew I wanted to look presentable so when my family saw me for the last time, they'd see peace in me.

I had no way of getting prescription pills so I felt that the 7/11 down the street off Hollywood and Argyle would be the place to get over the counter sleeping pills and alcohol. I dressed in sweats, took off my makeup and pulled my hair back in a low ponytail. I went from looking like a high-end prostitute to a disheveled woman. There was no point in covering up the obvious sickness on my face nor trying to mask who I was anymore. There's not enough make up in the world to conceal what I was at this moment.

I still had cocaine from Kat in my pocket. I figured; the more I could consume of anything the better. I did more lines of cocaine before I left the apartment to embark on my journey of final self-destruction. Nothing could stop me; my mind had been taken over by my desire and lust for death. My body moved without direction from me. I was in motion with the agreement that tonight was my last night.

March 16th, 10pm, I walked to 7/11 from my apartment in Hollywood. The walk was slow, I felt the deepest pit of despair I had ever known. Although I was calm walking into the store, there were plenty of people inside. I must've looked like any another homeless woman from the boulevard because the looks and stares I received when I walked in were jarring.

With my hoodie pulled over my head and head down, I made my way for the medication aisle. I scanned the shelves for something strong. For legal and safety purposes I will not disclose exactly what I bought.

I figured I would need something to wash these pills down with, so I made my way to the back of the store where I picked out three bottles of red wine. I felt this concoction would be perfect for my intentional drug suicide.

Walking up to the counter with my hands and arms

full the cashier gave me a suspicious look but allowed me to pay for my things without a question. A piece of me wanted him to say something that would save me from this trance I was in, I couldn't stop myself. I twisted off the cap of a wine bottle while chugging the bottle of sleep aid then followed it with red wine. The homeless man asking for change outside the 7/11 looked at me with helpless eyes, not for his situation, but for mine.

I could hardly make eye contact with him and knew I needed to make it home with enough time to write my goodbye letters to my family, so I kept walking. Slushing down wine mixed with the first bottle of pills was hard. With every handful of pills, I couldn't believe I was doing it. I cried hysterically on the lifeless walk to my final place of rest.

The walk was slow and depressing, victimhood was all I knew of. I remember with every step, I sobbed loudly hoping someone would hear me and save me or maybe someone would see my pain. But that's the thing, I didn't look any different from anyone else on Hollywood Blvd. It wasn't uncommon to see a man or woman in distress drinking away their pain, walking lifelessly nowhere. 2020 was a hard year especially for the homeless, and those to become homeless. Eventually, the streets were packed with tents and addicts alike, yet lonely and suffering. I was one in 568,000 in Los Angeles, nothing out of the ordinary here. Just another lost angel in a busy city.

By the time I reached the corner where my apartment was, I finished the first bottle of pills and just as I was opening up the second bottle while crossing the street, my neighbor drove by. "Marissa! Are you okay?" she said from her car.

I looked at her with such despair and darkness I think I scared her. The smile on her face turned instantly. I replied, "No... I'm not." Sobbing while barley able to stand because of the shakes in my legs I continued, I didn't want to die here on the boulevard.

The reality of my life at this point was a pit of the deepest and darkest bottom I've known. I knew I'd be walking home to another life soon which is what pushed me to keep walking back up to my apartment. By the time I reached my apartment door, I could feel the effects of the two bottles I had ingested. I began cutting up the rest of the cocaine, while drinking the second bottle of wine and chewing on a handful of antihistamine tablets.

I sobbed out loud. It was as if every pain I had ever experienced filled the room around me. I was hysterical and screamed continuously without restraint. I could feel the drowsiness coming on when I knew I only had minutes before losing consciousness.

I did four lines of cocaine and grabbed my pen and paper. The first letter I wrote was to my mom, then my dad, then each sister. I wrote how much I loved them, yet their love couldn't save me. I confessed my addiction and lack of will. I confessed how I had been raped and stalked through the years. I made a promise to them that I'd always watch over them once I crossed over and that no one was to blame, but myself. I told my little sister Marie how badly I wish I could've been a better big sister. I wrote about the impurity and darkness which consumed my soul and the only way to rid of it was to kill myself.

Then I wrote a letter to my family as a whole; I asked them to heal together and love one another so deeply that no more pain would be felt. I wrote my favorite memories with them that I detailed in chapter one. I wrote these letters so fast it was as if I had rehearsed what my final words were going to be.

The moment I finished writing the last letter my body

began to sway back and forth. I knew my time was ticking and with three of the four pill bottles gone, just one line of cocaine left and half a bottle of wine waiting for me to finish, I made my way up the stairs of my apartment to lay my body at its final rest. I brought the letters, tablets, wine and my phone with me. I crawled into my king-sized bed and played 'The Prayer' by Kid Cudi.

The first time I heard this song I was in the 5th grade and at such a young age I resonated with it deeply. I had always dreamt of the day I'd give my soul and will over to the Lord. I didn't realize I could've done this through baptism or recommitting myself to Him in this life, I felt the only way I could be close to Him was through death.

I laid my head back on the pillow and hummed along to this song with the goodbye letters on my chest, I could feel my breath becoming slower and weaker. My body felt as light as a feather, yet I sunk into my bed heavy as stone. I'm not sure if it was a hallucination or an angel, but I heard from the corner of my room a voice say, "Call your dad."

I always had a deeper love for my father, and I needed to say goodbye or was it that I wanted him to hurt the way I had been hurt by him? I called my father in my last minutes to say I fucked up and can't do this anymore. I sobbed on the phone to him and helplessly he kept repeating, "What do you mean? What's going on?"

I never answered his question, I told him I loved him and hung up the phone. Then I texted my mom and said, "I'll always love you and watch over you."

After sending that text to my mom, it was as if I had come out of this trance I had been in, for just enough time to feel the regret and selfishness of my decision. I felt I was too late, but before I passed out, I texted my friend Sage what I had done and what was happening.

300

The text read, "I took pills, I'm dying, I fucked up."

I'm not sure what her reply was because in that moment I felt the life leave my body. With one last breathe I fell back on my pillow. The last breath I took in this reality was the most peaceful moment I had ever felt. It was more of a gasp, but it put me to rest. My eyes closed, I lost consciousness and that is the last moment I remember on this night.

Meanwhile, Sage was driving 90 miles per hour to my apartment. She called Louie who was out at the bars and told him what was happening. He refused to leave the bar to let her up to the apartment. Sage called 911 right after and told them that I committed suicide. By the time she arrived at my apartment, the EMTs and police were just pulling the gurney out of the ambulance.

Sage along with five EMTS and two police officers made their way up to my apartment where Louie was standing outside. He was too scared to go inside, but thankfully let them in. When they walked in, they found me with just barely a pulse. Immediately the EMTs picked my almost lifeless body up from the bed and carried me down my apartment stairs to where they then placed me on the gurney.

Once in the ambulance they could no longer find a pulse, and this is when the EMTs began preforming lifesaving procedures on me. During the five-minute ride to Hollywood Presbyterian Medical Center my pulse was gone. Yet the EMT performed CPR on me the entire ride to the hospital, until I regained a pulse. A miracle happened not just in the physical reality but in another Godly World, Heaven.

I only know the reality of what happened in the physical reality due to the recollection of Sage, my hospital records, and later speaking to the EMT who performed CPR on me. While all of this was happening, I was dead without a pulse, yet I was alive on the other side.

I had a near death experience which isn't to say I almost died; I did die. I crossed over to the other side. This is a phenomenon that is known amongst others who have experienced this as an NDE.

While EMTs, doctors and nurses were doing everything they could, I was experiencing an NDE. I had left my body and woken up on the other side.

Chapter 34

Death of Me

The same power that rose Christ
from the dead, is living in you.
Romans 8:11

Death, as it is an ending, is also a beginning. The beginning of my death was the most alive I've ever felt. I opened my eyes on the other side. The first thing I took note of was the fresh, crisp air. When I took a deep breath in, it was as if I was breathing for the first time. I could hear animals far and near of all types. The sound of cohabitating animals brought a sense of harmony to me. I looked onward and saw a vast stretch of land that seemed to have gone on forever. I took notice of mountains and valleys, different types of grass, waterfalls and rivers, and the sun gently caressing everything before me.

My surroundings were the most vivid expression of nature and beauty I have ever witnessed. It was as if everything had an inner glow and the essence which shined outward, represented love, purity and harmony. I wasn't sure where I was. I had no sense of time, and I had no recollection of how I got here, but where I went was as real as any other experience I've had. I could hear, see, taste, touch and smell everything around me.

To the left of me were rolling hills covered in foliage, flowers and beautiful trees, some I had never seen until this moment. Everything was lush and alive. The sun which touched my skin was the warmest hug I had ever known. Just passed the rolling hills and the foliage and the flowers and the trees on the highest peak from what I could see, so high the clouds touched the ground, were the most beautifully crafted gates. They were golden gates reflecting the sun back onto me, I stared looking onto them in amazement. I had no outside thoughts other than knowing I was home.

I began my journey towards the gates for I felt they were calling to me. On my walk through the most beautiful land I'd ever touched, feelings that were unfamiliar came over me. I felt safe, I felt truly loved and I felt worthy. But this feeling wasn't overwhelming. It felt like it had belonged to me all along, I was home.

As I made my way through the grass towards the left side of the rolling hills, a path was cleared from the brush, yet covered with many different footsteps. Different sizes and shapes, as if others had walked here before me. Surrounding me were trees and flowers that moved as if they were welcoming me home. I had never felt a sense of peace like I did on this walk alone.

My path continued around a bend and brought me to a cliff which overlooked a beautiful calm sea that seemed to have stretched on for eternity. I looked out onto the sea with tears in my eyes, I was home. A light breeze ran through my hair and down my spine. The message it brought upon me was that I was welcomed. The waves below began to crash against the cliff, as if they were inviting me in. I didn't think to jump towards them, instead I looked for a way I could get down there.

I walked on the edge of the cliff looking for a bridge or steps to get down to the shore, when I heard a familiar, raspy, soft voice call out to me, "Marissa, child, come here."

The voice came from my great grandmother Ira Vivian. She sat under an olive tree on the edge of the cliff and waved for me to join her. GG was just as I had remembered her but with more life and lust in her eyes and smile. I sat down across from her timidly, as if I were in trouble awaiting for my punishment. She looked so effortlessly peaceful with her white hair grazing her shoulders and brown skin specked with gold. She sat on a tree stump and pointed for me to sit on the log across from her.

"I was not expecting you to be the first one here, my dear" GG said to me.

"I was having a hard time, I wanted to come home" I say.

She gave me a soft smile which brought a sense of endearment to me. She had no judgement for how I got here or why, she just welcomed me.

I almost forgot how strong and detailed her hands were. GG handed me split shoots of redbud and willow and said, "These are your materials, split the node of the redbud for sewing strand, I prepared the willow for you, it's dry and ready for basket weaving."

I had never weaved a basket, nor did I have any clue as to why she was instructing me to do so, yet I followed her guise. "I'm not sure what to do with this GG, why are we doing this?" I ask.

Unbothered by my mortal impatience, she says, "You'll see. Be still child, where do you have to be? I am going to teach you how to weave a basket."

GG goes on to say, "Follow the work of my hand, one

strand of redbud at a time to build the structure of the basket, then you'll secure the work with willow"

I began weaving two strands of redbud together. The first coil was difficult as I was following the pattern of her hand work across from me while looking at the strands in my hands. We sat in silence for the first seven coils of basket weaving, my fingers and hands were adjusting to this new movement and style. I wanted to create a strong and elegant basket which required my full attention. GG so effortlessly weaved her basket as her demeanor was peaceful and graceful. This moment with her was surreal; on the edge of a cliff under an olive tree weaving baskets with the sun shining and sea behind us. You would think I'd have so many questions, but it felt natural; I was home.

When the woven redbud began to take shape of a basket, I paused to admire the work I had done thus far and the new skill I had learned so quickly. GG paused as well and said to me,
"You're doing it. The art of basking weaving is much deeper than the depth of your creation. Now, the olive seeds beneath your feet, pluck them off the ground with your toes as you work with your hands."

What a strange request I thought to myself, but I did as I was told. The texture of the ground beneath this olive tree was enriched with a porous surface of soil. I dug my toes into the ground and searched for olive seeds. Still weaving my basket while collecting olive seeds with my toes, I felt aligned and at one with everything around me.

The simultaneous work of my toes and hands connected my mind, body and soul to the bounty of nature around me. This feeling I had longed for on earth, but never felt until this moment here with my GG.

She was whispering and humming as we both focused

on our work together. I couldn't make out what she was saying, but with every completed coil she would look into my eyes as if she were delivering a message to me.

"Child, I want you to think about what you want out of this life, who you are and who you hope to become" she says to me as I picked up my first strand of willow; I did as I was told.

I thought of the things I wanted out of this life, who I felt I was in this present moment and who I hoped to become. I wanted to harbor an unshakable foundation, spirit and strength in this life. I wanted to maintain and build upon my current feelings of safety, love and peace. I had hopes to be pure, innocent, worthy and free from evil and darkness. These are the things I thought about as I weaved my basket.

Time was obsolete here; I don't know how much time had passed when I finished securing my basket with willow and had a collection of olive seeds between my toes and underneath the soles of my feet. GG's basket was big and beautiful, she had used muddled acorn for color in her design and created markings which created a layered effect. Mine was medium sized and had little design other than the continuous pattern I did to complete my basket.

With the enthusiasm of a young girl who was pleased to show her great grandmother what she had accomplished, I held up my basket off my lap towards my GG and said, "I finished GG! I did it!"

She smiled softly with the kindest eyes and said, "Do you want to know the secret of the basket weaver?"

A flush of delight came over me. How often does one share secrets with their great grandparent let alone how often does a great grandparent share secrets with their great grandchild? I ask curiously and joyfully, "There's a secret to the basket weaver?"

"Yes, my dear, the intention of this practice is to weave your prayers, hopes and dreams into reality. The work one does with the mind and body, weaves spirit and soul into your dreams, hopes and prayers. You are secured my dear."

My GG taught me how to pray this day. My GG taught me the foundation of working alongside nature and creativity to become liberated, graceful and faithful. My GG taught me how to be still during the process of transformation.

"What do I do now?" I ask.

"Hold on tight to your basket, clench the seeds beneath your toes and hold your breath" she says.

GG stood up and began walking towards me and said, "When you reach the bottom, release the seeds from your toes."

Her long arms reached for my shoulders and she pushed me with all her might. She pushed me with such force I clenched up as my back toppled over and my feet flung into the air. My GG pushed me off the cliff and into the ocean feet first. There was no time to think, I did as she told me and held my breath, basket and seeds.

I hit the water hard, but the moment I was submerged, I had sunk gently. I didn't resist or become afraid. I trusted the process my GG was guiding me through.

As I was sinking in the ocean at a strong pace, I began to notice whirls of water formations coming off of my body. With each small whirl of water noticeably moving away from my body, I felt intuitively that the darkness, evil, addiction and trauma I had inside of me were being washed away. The feeling of being submerged in water while this spiritual force

308

was at work is a feeling I'll never forget.

My descend down to the bottom purified and replenished my spirit. The ocean went from a baby blue to a dark blue the deeper I got. When I hit the bottom of the ocean, I did as I was told and released the olive seeds from my toes. In that moment, I planted the seeds of my dreams, hopes, prayers and re-rooted my foundation. This expression of cleansing and grounding myself in a spiritual realm was nothing like I had ever experienced, not even on the plant.

The moment the olive seeds were released from my toes and planted in the ground was when the tree began to grow. I saw roots taking over the ocean floor around me. An olive branch wrapped around my legs, torso and up my back when the tree began sprouting up and towards the surface of the ocean. With the support of the roots and limbs of the olive tree, I began swimming to the surface of the ocean. Breaking the surface of the ocean, the tree placed me back on the cliff where my GG was.

"The strength, wisdom and longevity of the olive tree is now a part of you my dear." GG says.

I felt so absolutely forgiven, at peace, reborn, safe and an acceptance I had never once felt before.

"Now, I want you to go back to where you came from and fill up that basket with goodness. Once its full, you share your harvest. Fill it back up and share again. This is the way-the fruit of the spirit." Said GG.

"Go back? What do you mean? I want to stay here with you, I don't want to go back" I say with panic.

"It is not your time; you have plenty of work to do. And now you have a gift within you, and it is your right to share your purpose. If you can heal yourself, you can heal others." GG said to me with conviction.

And with that, the light that shown from every living creature, plant, mountain, and my GG began to fade away. "Thank you, GG. I love you" I said.

"I love you eternally, be free, my child." and as if her reply brought the breath of life back into my physical body, I regained consciousness in the emergency room. The light that hugged me was gone.

I went from seeing the most beautiful, serene landscape touched by a Godly sun, to opening my eyes to hospital florescent lights above me. Sight was my first sense at the time of me becoming conscious. I couldn't believe my eyes. Yes, I had crossed over and had the most enchanting and spiritual experience but waking up in the hospital filled me with disbelief, rage and heartbreak greater than I had felt prior to committing suicide. I felt unworthy of acceptance from the other side, I felt rejected, stuck and abandoned.

Taking my first conscious breath wasn't as euphoric as one might think it would be after a near death experience. The first sound I heard was my nurse saying "Marissa? You're at Hollywood Presbyterian. Can you hear me?"

I let out a desperate cry which moaned from the depths of my belly and filled the room followed by the question, "You mean I'm still fucking alive?!"

My voice echoed and silenced the room. I immediately knew I had failed in my suicide attempt and was reminded of the hell I thought I had escaped from. I was irate, I wanted to die and the fact I didn't, fueled an aggression and darkness in me that was deeper than anything I had previously experienced. My question spooked the nurses and doctors surrounding me.

310

The immediate heaviness of feeling "stuck" came over my body and this was my first reconnection with touch. It wasn't physical, that feeling came from within and engulfed my surroundings. My spirit had felt as if it were jolted back into my body. I felt the intense heavy feeling of what I felt was rejection from the other side, specifically rejection from God. These feelings were the complete opposite of the euphoric sensations I had just experienced.

I couldn't smell due to the amount of cocaine in my nose, but I do remember the drips of the white devil in the back of my throat. March 16th, 2021, I was prepared to leave this earth and escape my pain; but it was not my time. I don't recall a lot of reality in the hospital due to the psychosis I was experiencing although the delusions (audio and visual) felt more present than I. The worst feeling in my 23 years of life at this point was coming to the realization I had failed at suicide and now had lost my mind.

You don't know you're losing your mind when you're losing your mind. All your delusions make sense to you except for the fact that no one around you can understand the reality of your pain and suffering. I overly medicated myself with pills, a blood alcohol level of 0.40, heroin, a heavy amount of cocaine in my body and to my surprise, fentanyl and meth.

The energy in the room went from relief that I had come back, to a dangerous situation with a mentally unstable patient. I was seeing things that weren't there, hearing things that weren't there and crying hysterically because I had visions of men trying to hurt me. I was scared and no one understood what I was experiencing.

I wanted to die, but I was brought back. At the time I didn't recognize the miracle that happened and felt I was being punished now. I had just gone from seeing the gates of the Promise Land to now being strapped down to a hospital bed and experiencing a personal hell on Earth.

Any and all control I had was gone. I had an IV in each arm as the nurses restrained me because of my erratic behavior. As I watched the drip from the bag, I lost consciousness again.

I woke up in the middle of the night on March 17th, 2021. Still experiencing audio and visual hallucinations. I had visions of my father standing across the hospital room looking disappointed and next to him was Louie, spitting towards me. This visual was so real to me. It's how I felt, they both felt about me. I had visions of a man trying to rape me, I kicked and screamed, begging for help when an LAPD officer, social worker and nurse came in.

"Please help me!" I screamed with tears in my eyes. The room turned dark red, and I saw fire. Begging them to help me and let me go as the nurse prepared another syringe for me. The officer said, "Marissa the city of Los Angeles is putting you on a 51-50 hold, you are in no condition to leave and are a danger to yourself."

I passed out again with those words lingering in my mind. Waking up again and felt I had some sense of reality knowing I needed to get ahold of my mother. I asked the social worker, who was keeping watch of me in the room, if I could call my mom and let her know what was happening. She ignored me the first time, but then I began to beg as if my life depended on it.

"Okay you get five minutes" she says.

The nurses unstrapped me, and the social worker walked me to the phone at the nurses' station. My mother had the same phone number my whole childhood up until January of 2021. I dialed the number I had always remembered and kept getting a busy tone. Why isn't my mother answering me?

I told my mom about this months later and she told me she had a feeling I was trying to reach her but couldn't remember her new number.

The social worker laughed at me as I desperately tried to get ahold of my mother and said, "No one cares about you, see, no one is looking for you."

This I believed, I had no self-worth and was hardly stable enough to even comprehend the English language but looking back it is wrong that a social worker said this.

I thought of Marie and dialed her number, she answered me on the second ring and nervously said, "Marissa.... Are you okay?"

The social worker pointed at her watch and said, "60 seconds."

I said to Marie, "I can't talk long, but tell mom I'm alive and at Hollywood Presbyterian. They're going to transfer me somewhere, I'm 5150'd."

And with that she and I got off the phone and I was escorted back to my hospital room. I sat on the bed and they allowed me to be without restraints as I was showing signs of stability. In walked EMTs and they said, "Miss Hardy we're here to transfer you."

"Where am I going?" I ask.

"Exodus, the psych ward" one of the EMTs says.

I had only ever heard horrors of the psych ward. They moved me during the night while the other patients were asleep. I had no idea how long they'd be keeping me, but I was determined to get out as soon as I could.

When we arrived at the psych ward, we entered the side of the building and two large male security guards greeted us. They instructed me to go into the room with them where I was told to undress out of my hospital gown and change into the grey sweats they provided.

I had no belongings with me, even the clothes I was wearing when I committed suicide were gone, I didn't even have underwear or a bra on. I still don't know what happened to my clothes and under garments to this day, I assume they had to be taken off due to the procedures performed on me.

The two guards escorted me to the women's side of the psych ward where I was instructed to sit in a recliner and not get up. The recliner they placed me in faced towards the men side of the room. Men gawked and called out to me. I couldn't sleep a wink; I was terrified that one of them were going to hurt me.

Morning couldn't have come soon enough. They served us breakfast which I tried to opt out of, but they said it was a requirement. I ate a string cheese, everything else looked old or messed with. I heard other patients screaming from padded rooms down the hall, one even saying "I've been here for two weeks, please get me out."

I certainly did not want to be that guy. A doctor walked past me and went straight into his office, I knew I had to be on my best behavior to get out of here. About two hours passed, when he called for me to come in. I reminded myself, "Let him know it's a bad situation and you're not actually crazy."

I don't know why I came up with that, but it worked. He said the magic words, "Call for someone to pick you up this afternoon."

I couldn't think of anyone's number that also lived in

Los Angeles except for Louie's. I called him and with luck he picked up on the first ring, "Hey its Marissa, can you pick me up?"

He paused and said, "Yes give me an hour, okay? Where are you?"

"They transferred me to the psych ward, it's called Exodus." I say.

"Okay we can talk when I see you, I'm glad you're okay." he says.

And within an hour and a half, he was there to get me. The guard walked up to me as I sat in my recliner staring at the wall, "Come with me."

Again, they had me strip down and undress in front of them. They gave me clothes to wear home and with nothing but grey sweats, a white t-shirt and non-slip grip socks, I walked towards the barred doors. When the guard opened the door, there stood Louie.

I had never been so happy to see him in my life. He embraced me so selflessly in that moment my heart was forever changed. The man that I felt had hated me, abused me and manipulated me... loved me more than I loved myself this day. I knew I had to change, and it was this hug that the remembrance of my experience on the other side was brought back to me

Chapter 35

Rock Bottom

The pain you've been feeling can't
compare to the joy that is coming.
Romans 8:18

The date was now March 18th, two days after I had
attempted suicide. Louie was quiet and seemed afraid of what
looked like the responsibility of taking care of me. I'm not
sure how much time I spent in-between the hospital and the
psychiatric ward. Although this was the first time in knowing
Louie that it felt like he saw me as a human, not as his
girlfriend or his property, but as a human being. He treated me
with softness and care; something I desperately needed at this
time.

Our drive back to the apartment was unfamiliar to me,
I hardly recognized the city of Los Angeles. We finally
reached my apartment where he walked me in and got me
settled; asking if I was hungry and in need of anything else to
feel comfortable. His selfless love during this time truly
changed my heart. The fact that the one person who had every
reason to hate me was now loving me unconditionally was a
surprise I wasn't expecting. To this day I wonder how I even
deserved a sliver of it, however, God works through others so

effortlessly.

Louie ordered us food as I stayed put on the couch wrapped in blankets. He told me how he discarded any and all traces of my attempt, except for the suicide letters I wrote. I didn't know what to think of that except for the embarrassment that he had read what I thought to be my last words.

We decided to not speak about what happened in this moment, only what to do next. Louie felt that the safest and best place for me going forward would be drug and alcohol rehabilitation. At this point I still didn't think I had a problem with substances; I had never even considered myself to be an addict or alcoholic in a serious matter such as this. You know, I'd say things lightly about being an alcoholic or a druggie to people I partied with, but I never knew or understood what those words meant coming out of my mouth.

Louie talked about the lightness and possibilities of going to a drug and alcohol rehabilitation. His two best friends were well over five years sober and did it through rehab and Alcoholics Anonymous. I admired the two friends he had spoken about since the day I met them and looked to them as role models for what could be. So, I said yes.

Without Louies recommendation and softness towards the possibilities of sobriety, I don't think I ever would've considered it on my own. I had no idea what rehab entailed, only what kind of people it produced on the other side of it and that was enough for me to go. I strongly believe God gave Louie the strength and compassion this day to guide me into my destiny.

I slept the rest of the day and allowed my body to come back down. My phone had hundreds of texts and missed phone calls; I had written a goodbye letter on my Instagram story which I hadn't remembered until I saw the notifications on my phone. My cry for help might've looked selfish to others and I barred the embarrassment for months after, although it was a real moment for me. People I hadn't talked to in years had reached out asking if I was okay, family members left voicemails in hopes I would respond. All of this was too much for me to handle. My lack of accountability selfishly left hundreds of people worried for days.

Louie kept in contact with my immediate family, while I was recovering. I was too ashamed to face them and answer questions at this time. All they knew was that I was now safe, in my own home and wanting to go to rehab.

All this had shocked my family, no one knew I had a problem let alone did drugs. I was what you would call a highly functioning addict, although any type of addict is unsustainable and has a limit. I had reached my limit and now my rock bottom. Rock bottom will teach you lessons that mountain tops never can.

My mother agreed to picking me up that weekend, March 20th. She wanted to come that day but couldn't get work off. I can't remember any conversation with my father or sisters. This period of time I was still very much in a haze and regaining mental and emotional comprehension.

Louie comforted and nursed me as best he could as if I was a bird with a broken wing and no song. He fed me, helped me shower and spoke in good spirits about my future. I needed that. The thing about a failed suicide attempt and why authorities will 51-50 you are due to the fact that the failed attempt is such a dark and devasting realization that the sick person is 60% more likely to try again in the following 72 hours. I don't know how or why the doctor released me early, but it is extremely unusual and unlikely. Louie kept his eye on me like a hawk.

March 18th-19th I stayed on the couch doing my best to

not think about the horrors of what happened. Although the thought of all my belongings at Kats kept running through my head. Louie agreed to go with me to get my suitcases from her apartment. I told him about her, and he felt it was unsafe for me to do anything alone, let alone this. Kat was angry with me and said that she would pack my bags and leave them outside of her building which I could come for in the afternoon of March 19th.

Louie and I did just that and drove to downtown Los Angeles. When we arrived outside of her building, I noticed her looking down at us from her living room window. The look in her eyes, as she peeked from behind the blinds of her window, was as if she was casting evil and harm onto me, but also scared of me at the same time. I'll never forget that. I was simultaneously the victim and the villain. How long did I bare that identity? It was so blatantly obvious now I couldn't deny the truth of what I had been for so long.

Louie put all my suitcases in the car, and we headed back to the apartment. This was the only time I left the apartment during this time of recovery. I could still smell her perfume on my things which brought back horrible flashes of my reality just a few nights ago.

I went into a panic and was filled with vivid and distinct flash backs. My chest felt heavy, palms sweaty and my breaths became quick and shallow. At this moment, the hardest part for me to accept and come face to face with was the reality that I had put myself in a highly dangerous situation.

Going to rehab felt like the only safe and right place for me to be. Immediately when we got back to my apartment, I began making calls for what rehabilitation centers in Los Angeles county would accept my insurance; about 25% of the centers did. But then it was a matter of finding what centers had available beds.

In arguably, the most saturated city for drug abuse and overdose, I was desperately trying to find an open bed. Something inside of me knew rehab was my only option and I had to find a place. Any and all other options weren't safe for me, I was completely broken and at my rock bottom.

Given the task of finding a rehab and the difficulty of it gave me enough purpose and distraction to get me through this day. I became uneasy around Louie awaiting for my mother's arrival. Not because of anything he did, but because I started to fiend for drugs and alcohol. The 48 hours I had been sober during this time was the longest length of sobriety I have yet to experience in my addiction. I began to realize how I needed it to survive.

This gave me more anxiety; I didn't want to use or drink, but I needed to. Rehab was looking better and better to me. I knew I needed rehab more than drugs or alcohol needed me.

It was now March 20th, although I had called plenty of numbers, I had no luck with finding a rehab. Momma and her sister, my auntie, drove down the California highway to pick me up from Hollywood. They were both so loving and gentle with me I almost felt I hadn't done anything wrong. They had no idea that I was actually planning on going to rehab nor did they truly know how serious the situation was; all they felt was that it was best for me to be under their care at home.

Momma and auntie helped me pack my things for my departure from Los Angeles. I was really sad to leave Louie because he had been so kind the last few days, something I hadn't experienced with him before. Pieces of me wanted to stay and heal with him, but I knew deep down that was not an option. I couldn't heal in the same environment that broke me.

Packing my things once more, I was finally ready to

leave Los Angeles. I didn't know what was next, never mind the duration of my departure. Momma just felt and knew she had to get me out of that place. She and auntie drove me back to Roseville, California (about a 7-hour drive) March 20th.

The drive home brought me peace. I remember stopping for food and ordering $30 worth of McDonalds. My auntie let me know that eating carbs and sugar is a side effect of sobriety. Your body turns to these foods to cope with the loss of an addiction. Essentially trading one addiction for another and attempting to fill a void.

I ate without restraint or care; I was happy to be with momma and auntie. With each mile getting closer to home and further from Los Angeles, I felt my spirits get lighter and more hopeful.

Momma was pretty traumatized from the experience and had arranged for us to pick up a German Sheppard puppy on the way home. This was her way of coping while also giving me comfort in hopes the pup would service as a therapy dog.

When we arrived at the pick-up spot for the dog in Bakersfield, California, the breeder had three puppies for us to choose from; I picked the pup with the darkest colored face and big brown eyes. She and I connected immediately. I named her Shadow, eventually momma renamed her Donatella; not after the fashion designer, but the meaning of the name which translates to Gift of God.

I held Donatella the whole ride home. We still had five hours of driving, but this puppy made it bearable and comfortable. My momma and I both needed this puppy at the time.

We arrived home that night and my only focus was going to bed with Donatella. Before shutting my eyes, I thought to myself, "how am I supposed to go to rehab now that I have a puppy?"

Through the night I cried and shook in my bed at mommas with this eight-week-old puppy resting against my face. Donatella kept me company and from that day forward became the best therapy dog; she was sweet, goofy and loving, not to mention smart and remains this way to this day.

I figured if I wanted to be a good dog momma, I needed to take care of myself first. This may seem like a lackluster reason, yet the sensitive stage I was in, was enough for me. This way of thinking would become a healthy habit I'd integrate into my life. Finding the smallest reasons throughout my day, every day and show gratitude for them, by the way I show up and take care of myself.

Sunday morning March 21st I began calling a list of rehabilitation centers, along with the Los Angeles county department of health to help me find an open bed that would be covered under my insurance.

I spent all day on the phone and internet trying to find a place for me to go. It was exhausting and hopeless. I began to have the conversation with my parents that maybe I could just do an out-patient rehab instead of an in-patient one. They both supported me in whatever I felt was best, except for Louie who urged me to keep trying. In-patient rehab is 24-hour, 7 days a week. Whereas out-patient is more of a 9-5 Monday-Friday commitment. Both are good, but the real magic is being in in-patient.

My list of phone numbers had now all been crossed out except for one which I hardly remember even writing down. I decided this would be the last number I'd call for the day and if nothing happened out of it, I would look for out-patient rehabs tomorrow. The phone rang and brought me to an automated massage where I chose the option to speak with an in-patient counselor.

Miss Barbara answered the phone. "Miracle House, this is Miss Barbara speaking, how can I help you?"

I wanted to laugh at what God was doing by connecting me with the "Miracle House", but I was surprised I had even gotten a real person on the line, so I continued.

"Hi, my name is Marissa, do you have any beds available?"

Miss Barbara replied, "Yes we do, what substances are you struggling with?"

I replied, "I am recovering from a failed suicide attempt, but I have a drug and alcohol problem as well. The LA county health department says my insurance covers expenses at your rehab. When is the soonest I can come?"

This was the first time I admitted to having a problem. Miss Barbara replied, "I am so sorry to hear that hun, you're a survivor now. but I am glad to hear you are ready for recovery. How does tomorrow sound?"

I was in shock because I had lived the last eight years of my life as a victim and now someone, I hadn't known for longer than a minute, referred to me as a survivor.

I responded, "Well I am at my mother's home in northern California, could I come the day after? Tuesday the 22nd?"

Miss Barbara replied, "Sure honey, we'll save you a bed."

Miss Barbara continued to ask me general questions, insurance information and gave me the address to the rehab. I was to be there at 10am, Tuesday morning, March 22nd.

    I went to momma to tell her the good news. Momma was happy for me and proud; I could sense she was a little worried to let me out of her sight, but she supported me going to rehab. I was scheduled to fly back to Los Angeles Monday night and go into the Miracle House Tuesday morning. I explained to Louie what my plans were and he too, was proud of me.

    This was the least bit I could do after all the worry and stress I had put onto others. But I was a survivor now and I was going to uphold what that meant just as I did when I was a victim. I was going to get sober, and I was going to do it by finding reason and purpose in everything I did.

    That night momma took me to my first AA meeting in Roseville, California. There I received my first 'Big Book' and a phone list to call whenever I needed someone from that AA group to talk to. I felt supported in so many ways and had hope that if the 67-year-old women across from me can stay sober for the last 45 years, so can I. It was beautiful to hear everyone's stories and each person shared in vulnerability and honesty. It was as if no one in that room bore shame to their story; this inspired me.

    Monday came and I parted ways with Donatella and momma. I hadn't seen Marie while I was back, I think she wanted to give me space and was shaken up from that phone call in the hospital.

    I felt called and comfortable to wear the grey sweatpants and t-shirt from the psych ward. For some reason this is all I wanted to wear at this time.

    I boarded my flight to LAX by myself. I was anxious to be alone, especially because the last time I was, I tried to kill myself. But I knew this journey was something I had to do and that I wanted to get better. To ease my idle mind, I began reading the Alcoholics Anonymous Big Book on my hour flight.

Louie picked me up from LAX and took me back to my apartment. We cried and embraced one another knowing deep down that this would be our last time together. When I needed support the most, Louie was there to take care of me. Although we had a very toxic relationship, I am so grateful to have had his friendship in the end. Louie, if you're reading this, thank you from the bottom of my heart.

The morning of the 22nd Louie dropped me and my luggage off at The Miracle House in Los Angeles. I was nervous, sad and insecure. I had no idea what this meant or what to expect. The rehab sat on three acres and had two Victorian mansions on the property. Just outside of the gates, to my new reality, I said my goodbyes to Louie and walked into what would be the biggest blessing second to my coming back to life.

Chapter 36

Be Still

The Lord is close to the
brokenhearted and saves those who
are crushed in spirit.
Psalms 34:18

To arrive in a new environment during a period of
time most, including myself, would call rock bottom is not
easy by any means. I wouldn't have stepped across those
gates if I had any other options.

Just as mid-morning came about, I was now walking
towards the Miracle House which sat on the right side of the
property. Outside on the lawn sat twenty women in lawn
chairs all with looks and a curiosity of who I was. With each
step closer to the front door, I could feel their judgment and
questions about me. These thoughts were almost so loud, I
missed the instructor standing in front of all the women before
me. Miss Charlene was in the middle of her "group" talking
about self-worth and what that means. Group is what we call
our group therapy sessions or educational classes on things
like, self-worth, what addiction is, domestic violence and so
much more I'd come to have an understanding and knowledge
of.

Miss Charlene looked stunned that I had just waltzed
in on my own. Most girls show up with a court order or

straight from jail/prison. In fear I would run out from the rehab because I was intimidated by the other girls, Miss Charlene barely greeted me and called out for another counselor to assist me. With a tilt of her head towards the front door and big 'ol yell Miss Charlene said, "We got a fresh one, get her some papers!"

This made me laugh, I knew I was in for a long ride.

Within my walk from the bottom of the Victorian steps, where the residents sat in lawn chairs up to the top of the steps where Miss Charlene stood, I was greeted by another counselor whose voice I recognized. Miss Barbara who I had spoken to on the phone just a few days before, came out of the house with a clip board, papers and a big smile. Both women were strong black women and without hesitation both of their energy was a "buckle up, it's time to do the work" attitude.

"Hi I'm Marissa" I say.

"Pull up a chair and sit here to fill out this paperwork, in the meantime we will be going through your bags. Are you hungry?" Miss Barbara asks.

I sat at a cherry wood table just behind Miss Charlene in the back corner of the patio. Miss Charlene gave me a smile and a wink before she turned around. That always stuck with me, I felt like I had a friend who knew a secret I didn't quite know yet.

"Yes, I could eat. Thank you, Miss Barbara." I say shyly.

"Okay, I'll bring you breakfast. This is Stephanie, she just arrived. Get to know each other." Miss Barbara says.

I look across from me and see Stephanie for the first time. She looked battered and to my surprise pregnant.

327

considering that a pregnant person could also
vondered how she got here, what was her story.
 ..e to judge for I, too, was also sitting at the
 ..able as her on arguably our most vulnerable day in life.

We didn't say a word to each other, only glances, waiting for the other to say something. This made the pages of paperwork at my fingertips look more inviting. I read over the rules, filled out insurance and medical information and then my history with drugs and alcohol. This took me about an hour to do. Miss Barbara brought me a plate with a peanut butter and jelly sandwich, fruit and string cheese, a part of me felt like a kid again.

"Do you drink coffee?" says Miss Barbara.

"Yes, I do" I reply. I had never drank coffee before, but thought it was a good idea to add as much as I could to my already portioned meal.

"Milk?" Miss Barbara says.

I thought "no sugar?" but replied simply with, "Yes please."

I could feel that it was almost time for me to be brought into the house. I made sure to text my family to let them know that I was here, and things were moving along. Everyone was supportive and kind towards me; I think most of them were still wondering how I ended up here.

Another reason for me writing this book is to shed light on how addicts and alcoholics become addicts and alcoholics. It isn't just from one trip to Miami or a life in Hollywood, millions of people do these things without ending up in rehab. If trauma goes unresolved and buried, it'll resolve and bury you.

Miss Cathy finished going through my bags just as Miss Charlene's group was ending.

"We'll wait for the girls to go inside first, before we bring you and Stephanie to your room." Miss Cathy says.

I shook my head in agreeance and sipped on my coffee. The coffee soothed me in a way that I instantly created a bond with it, or some might say an addiction. I knew for certain, this small cup of coffee and milk would be my only indulgence from here on. This still stands true for me to this day; I have plenty to live for now, meaning and purpose, including writing this book. Yet a coffee with milk no sugar is my reason for getting out of bed every morning. It's the small habits, routines and signaling I would learn at the Miracle House that would stick with me.

The girls walked back into the house. I spotted a few who were intimidating, some who looked like we could be friends and others who were just as broken as I. We all had one thing in common, we were here and that was a sisterhood implanted in me before even walking into the house.

Once all the girls were inside Stephanie and I were brought up the great, cherry wood, Victorian stairs to our bedroom on the left side of the house. The room we shared had four empty beds with views of the front and courtyard.

"Okay girls, pick your bed and get settled in." Miss Cathy said as she left the room.

I chose the bed in the corner with a window and Stephanie chose the bed up against a bare wall just behind me. This was still during the time of covid, Stephanie and I were to isolate in this room for 14 days.

I unpacked my bags into my assigned closet and dresser, making sure to leave room for Stephanie. Halfway through unpacking I heard Stephanie snoring in her bed, she was exhausted. I thought it'd be an act of kindness to unpack her things, but she had none.

I thought to myself, "What's her story?"

There wasn't much excitement in our room or conversation. I accepted that this would be my life for the next two weeks and its best to get comfortable, so that's what I did. What I didn't know is how difficult it would be to give up control and stay put. I'd come to truly know the meaning of the bible verse "Be Still", Psalms 46:10.

My first night in rehab I was met with nightmares. Because of my failed suicide attempt and crossing over, I now had nightmares of being stuck in purgatory. For those of you who don't know what purgatory is, it's written in the Bible as the place where people go, who commit suicide. The dream I had was me floating in space with Earth's presences behind me and heaven in front of me. Neither place knew I was there nor could hear me, let alone see me. This nightmare I would have consistently every night for three weeks. I began to have a new fear that I had terribly sinned and that I was now destined to rest in purgatory for the rest of my life. I kept this to myself and woke up just in time for my morning cup of coffee.

Miss Barbara let us know that we would be getting a new roommate this day, March 23rd, 2021. I wasn't intimidated by this news considering I had gotten such luck with Stephanie. As if God was configuring a perfect situation, in walked Kisha.

Kisha looked younger than me but was actually 37 years old. Instantly Kisha, Stephanie and I, clicked. I strongly believe if God wouldn't have put us together during this two-week isolation period, we all would've left. Our friendship, getting to know one another and watching movies like Madea

330

late at night is the reason we all stayed.

In fact, about seven days into our isolation, I had found out that Louie was bringing girls over to my apartment. I was so devastated and frustrated because I had no control. As I was crying on the bathroom floor planning my escape, Stephanie walked in and said, "Marissa, you are the reason I am still here. If you leave, I'll leave, I need you here."

This day, I stayed and found reason to continue in my sobriety for my friend. The thing about getting sober is you have to do it for yourself, but sometimes in moments of weakness there are external factors in what keep you sober, like Stephanie and her unborn child. I agreed to stay, at this point I only had 21 days left in this rehab. Being surrounded by strong women who loved me at my lowest was enough motivation for me to continue. This is the day I realized how important it is to focus on myself because there would be no other time in my life were I could just sit and work on the woman that I am and hope to be. I didn't have to worry about anything else, but myself, as Miss Charlene would say. Once I calmed down, I blocked Louie and decided he would no longer be a part of my new life.

This was my first step in creating a boundary with someone else. One thing I was not prepared for when getting sober was the fact that I would have to end friendships and relationships in order to live in this new reality. See, Louie never did hard drugs, but he was a huge trigger for my addiction. This incident that happened was so triggering that I could actually taste tequila in the back of my throat and feel an itch on the inside of my nose. I was once blind to the triggers and reasons for my addiction and dependence on substances; this was just one. I would come to find that I had many, many more.

During our two-week isolation, we were allowed to go outside of our room one time; and that was for a doctor's appointment to get prescribed medication. Most people who abuse drugs and alcohol have anxiety or depression, so a trip to a psychiatrist was in order for us three girls.

Ironically, the place where we went to get prescribed medication is the same hospital where I was 5150, Exodus. Their Institute is set up where they have in-house and out-house patients. I had gone from being in-housed by them to now being out-housed by them.

However, I had never been on medication before and truly did not want to be on anything. My mind had lingering threads of psychosis and my brain was mush, I didn't trust myself to make any decisions. Going into the hospital again wasn't as scary this time because I had my two friends and a counselor who was certain on all of us going back together.

The doctor prescribed me an antidepressant, Lexapro 15mg and an anti-anxiety medication Buspirone 15mg. She warned me that the side effects for these medications during the first week will throw my hormones off-balance thus settling into a baseline of neutrality, this made me incredibly nervous for what was to come.

After taking these pills for seven days just before being released into the general population of the rehabilitation center, I was more depressed than ever. To the point where I had to sign papers saying I would not kill or harm myself in the rehabilitation center. I still wasn't eating and my only source of happiness was my cup of coffee in the morning, and occasionally Kisha and Stephanie's banter.

Again, it's the little things that made a big difference in my life during this time. Adjusting to the new medication was extremely tough, but by the time my body had regulated to this new baseline of hormonal balance, I felt completely normal. Normal in a sense that I had no fluctuating emotions or extreme thoughts. I was balanced, and I'm glad I did get on

332

the medication during this time. The medication allowed my mind and body to come back down from the extremes I had recently put it through.

All three of us girls were hesitant to join the general population downstairs; we had created such a bond without any drama or fuss that it was intimidating to join twenty girl's downstairs who we heard had plenty of it. So, we all decided to stick together, we knew that we all wanted to be in bunkbeds close to one another and would look after each other's things. Stealing amongst addicts is a character trait that's not uncommon.

I packed up my things and was prepared to be brought downstairs. There were no cell phones allowed or laptops, so I would have to turn in my electronics. Stephanie's mother who she hadn't spoken to in a while because of her addiction ended up dropping off some clothes and toiletries for her. Kisha had two suitcases as she was the fashionable one out of the three of us.

To our luck, there were open beds in the same area of the dorm room. Stephanie and I shared a bunk bed, me on top and she on the lower, while Kisha claimed the top bunk across from us. We all shared a closet area and dressers. It was perfect, we all had each other. Although the second we had unpacked our things, we were swarmed by the other girls. They wanted to know who we were and what kind of energy we were bringing down. The politics inside of a rehab like this is similar to jail or prison, not as intense, but definitely under the same guidelines. They were girls who were associated with gangs that stuck together, girls who did the same drugs that stuck together and then there were people who were lone wolves that were deemed as crazy. As intense as it was at first, I'd become fond of my dormmates.

As ready to meet us as they all were, I kept my distance, sticking close to Kisha and Stephanie, not saying to much or being too cold. I was the youngest in this rehab and surely the most privileged outside of this rehab, this made me an easy target.

I was aware of the dynamics and knew my place. But I was never one to shy away from a challenge and I knew the best way to make the most of this experience was to pave my own way and focus on myself.

From here on out, our bunk beds were to be made at the crack of dawn, followed by a shower and breakfast all before 6:30 AM. Our first group therapy was at 8 AM after breakfast for one hour, the second was at 10am followed by lunch, the third was at 2pm, and the last one of the day was at 7pm just after dinner. In between all of this, we were to do our 12-step work and chores. At first, I wasn't too fond of group therapy, but as time went on, I grew to really enjoy it. This is where I learned all the layers of addiction and alcoholism, the root of my problems, the dynamics of domestic violence and anger, what trauma I had to heal, how to cultivate self-love and worthiness into my life and especially how to stay sober, as well as the 12 steps of Alcoholics Anonymous.

At 23 years old, I thought I knew all there is to know about the world. I had traveled more than most people do in their lifetime, I had experienced things that most people will never get to in their life, yet when it came to simply knowing what self-worth or self-love means I hadn't known the meaning of it at all. I thought I did because of the things I read online or pages I followed on Instagram, but truly doing the work was something I had no experience in.

Day in and day out, I reprogrammed, deprogrammed and built myself up to become healthy, healed and strong. Day in and day out, I learned the value in being still. Day in and day out I began to cherish sobriety, healthy friendships and who I am in this life.

Along with my packed schedule I made sure to make time to run on the treadmill and exercise. I was busy from sunup to sundown and usually in bed by 9 PM after they had passed out our pills. Learning to have a routine and stick to it was another valuable lesson I learned in rehab. I became disciplined and actually looked forward to the next day.

Although, I was still having my purgatory nightmares up until Saturday night April 3rd, 2021. I had woken up out of my sleep just before my nightmare began and felt called to surrender to my higher power, God. I didn't think much of it as I was half asleep, but this was the first night I slept peacefully.

Because we had no cell phones, and every day was the same, I didn't exactly know what the date was, never mind any holiday. I woke up Sunday morning ready for the day ahead feeling a lot lighter. I wrote in my journal about how I am ready to surrender my will to God and how I feel He has given me a second chance to rise again and that I wasn't going to take it for granted or take it lightly. I wrote how I felt I had buried my addictions, bad relationships, bad habits and an old version of myself. I wrote about how from this day forward I am re-dedicating myself to His love and light. I no longer felt like I was living in sin or being punished for my sins.

The day went on as normal, until about 3 PM when Miss Barbara passed out Easter baskets. Today was Easter. It's hard to put into words or even describe the revelation I had when I realized how much God had been right by my side every step of the way. How His love healed me and brought me back home to a place where I felt peace and security. The heaven I was once looking for outside of myself just less than a month ago was now cultivated inside of me. Immediately, I went to go watch an Easter sermon, Pastor Touré Roberts of OneLA, spoke about how sometimes God puts us in the ground to protect us. I related with this because I felt rehab was my grounding. He went on to preach about how what we leave in the grave, stays in the grave. He continued to say how when we rise out of the grave we are forgiven and new. I resonated with all of this.

This was enough confirmation for me to come in agreeance that I would continue to surrender my will to God and work on my relationship with him. The funny thing is, although we have free will, the key to life is surrendering your will back to your higher power. The moment I did this, I became free and made peace with God.

This day I decided instead of spending 30 days in rehab, I was going to do 60 days. I was just getting started and felt that there was more for me to come in touch with. The first two weeks of rehab were filled with isolation, adjusting to medication and the people around me. The third and fourth week were breakthroughs, as I adjusted to my new routine and found God. What I had been looking for the last nine years, during my psychotic break and suicide, I had found finally through being still, surrendering and recommitting myself to a higher power. Not just that, but also doing the work, day in and day out. I continued on at this rehab for a full 60 days, each day was a milestone.

Day 44 is the day I made peace with myself. I had always felt guilty that my first words when I came back to life came from a place of anger backed by me questioning and verbalizing, "I'm still fucking alive?"

The more I came to love my life and cherish each day, this guilt grew larger. That is until on day 44 of sobriety, I was running on the treadmill like I did every day and had just ran my fastest 3 miles. As I was cooling down, I intuitively did a body scan; you know where you take an account of how your body feels. I asked myself questions like, "How's my head feel?" "How are my limbs and lungs working?" "How is my focus and eyesight?" those type of questions.

Every part of me felt better than it had ever felt. And without hesitation or thought, I broke this guilty curse and rejoiced in the truth that, "I'm still fucking alive!"

Not only did I have a pulse and a functioning brain when I really shouldn't have because of my suicide attempt, but I was in the best shape of my life and really living, not for any substance or anyone else but for myself. This day I made peace with myself and I was able to finally forgive myself.

I had no idea what to expect when I went to rehab, and it is by far the greatest accomplishment in my life. Not just because I finished, but because of everything I learned. I accepted Jesus, sobriety and healing into my heart, mind, body and soul.

Closing in on my last 10 days of rehab, I finished my classes and received certificates of completion. I had extra time on my hands. Kisha gifted me with David Goggin's book, Can't Hurt Me.

David became a father figure in my life and guided me into becoming a tough and hard motherfucker to crack. I took every word of his book to heart and knew that if his words could encourage my life, my words can encourage someone else's. I finished David's book in one day, he inspired me beyond belief and gave me focus for when I was to leave rehab.

On my 53rd day, I threw Stephanie a surprise baby shower for her son. I learned the value of friendship and what it means to show up for the people that you love, something I lacked greatly during my addiction.

The last week of me being at the Miracle House, I was scared of what I would encounter outside of the gates. I felt like a newborn deer going back out into the world, but I knew with my new set of skills, friends, and now a purpose in writing my story that I would be okay.

May 22nd, 2021 had finally arrived and it was now my time to depart from the Miracle House. I was to fly back to Sacramento on May 23rd which meant that I would stay in my apartment for one night alone. I hadn't spoken to Louie in almost a month and knew that this would be my first test. As I departed, I said my goodbyes to my friends and counselors. I had a new light shining outward from the inside.

Sage picked me up from rehab and dropped me off at my apartment in Hollywood, I had bangs now and was about 20 pounds lighter than I was two months ago. Walking back into my apartment complex was different this time I felt like Hollywood wasn't who I was anymore.

When Louie saw me for the first time, he seemed irritated and agitated. But his bad energy and negative attitude couldn't take away my light, nothing could take away my newfound light. I had seen clearly how I had worked on myself and how others hadn't. I was ready to go home to my mom and continue my process of healing and growth.

May 23, 2021, I flew home to Sacramento, California. I was planning on staying here for a couple of weeks. I'll never forget the look on Marie's face when she saw me, she couldn't believe how much I changed physically, emotionally and mentally. This made me feel proud because I had finally done something that was inspiring to my younger sister, she no longer had to worry about me.

A childhood friend of mine, Penny, came over to see me. I told Penny that I was going back to Hollywood soon and as if I was looking for approval, she says to me, "Why don't you just spend the summer here? I miss you."

And with that, I canceled my plans to go back to Hollywood and decided to stay at my mom's in Sacramento for the summer. This decision would redirect my life in a way I could've never imagined. My mom was thrilled to hear that I wanted to stay for the summertime. I promised her that I would continue with my rehab online Monday through Friday and contribute to the house. She was so proud of me and happy to have me home. I also reunited with Donatella who was now a large puppy and ready to play. I had all that I needed, and I was ready to take on this new chapter of my life.

Chapter 37

The Good Fight

But the Lord stood with me and
gave me strength.
2 Timothy 4:17

The last seventy days of my life had been the most challenging, rewarding and miraculous. No one had truly known about what happened between my psychosis up until going to rehab. And even then, no one had fully known the transformation that happened for me in rehab, not even myself. I knew I had changed but I didn't know to what extent or how the longevity of this time in life would last inside of me forever.

Getting sober is comparable to being reborn again. I truly had no idea what to expect on this journey and each day I felt better and better. It's not that all my problems were gone, I just knew how to handle them without drugs or alcohol. Jack was still stalking and harassing me even when I was in rehab. I never replied, I just began to rebuild a case on him. I started by going back all the way to 2013 to screenshot all his emails and placing them in a folder. He was my biggest problem and I felt I now had the confidence to face him. This line of action is tedious and a lot of work, but I promise justice will be served in due time.

Along with preparing for this, I repaired my relationship with my father. Starting with forgiving him and realizing that he is just as human as I; for I have made mistakes and so has he. If there's one thing my father has taught me, it's that in this world, we have no place to judge others, our only place is to forgive and accept one another. This doesn't mean to except toxicity and abuse in your life. It means to clear your mind through forgiveness as well as open your heart to the realness of the human experience. My father had been supportive and kind to me during this time. For the first time in years, I felt his heart was gentle with me. We began to rebuild our relationship with one another, and it all started with forgiveness and honesty. Since leaving the hospital up until the present day, my father and I's relationship has been more than I could've imagined. There are days where he is my rock and counsel.

My relationship with my sisters and mother grew stronger; they are an extension of my heart; one that could never be broken. I learned how to take care of and love myself, and in turn I learned how to take care of and love others.

When I was in rehab, I gained an understanding on how the first instance of trauma can build throughout your lifetime. Just as I have written this book beginning with my first traumatizing experience; the terrorizing grooming and rape I faced with Jack, sexual assault from other men, as well as the physical, mental and emotional abuse in relationships. It took me nine years to finally be able to forgive all of these men. It took me realizing and understanding how my heart first became broken and where I lost my will to fight back. Although there has been no justice towards Jack, I've let go of being the victim and I'm ready to finally fight back. I wish I could write about him being prosecuted, but it wasn't until I wrote this book that I finally felt ready to speak my truth and seek justice.

Resilience is a path that is forgiving, but also sacrificial. It takes giving up parts of our selves we may never understand. It's essential to let go of parts of ourselves, in order to become our highest self. Being able to forgive my father and these other men, allowed me to truly heal myself by releasing the burden of their abuse. I was a victim for so long that it became second nature to me.

I learned that if I can't do something for myself, I shouldn't expect others too; similar to as if I can't truly love and accept myself, no one will be able to truly love and accept me.

For so many years I had not truly accepted myself or loved myself and in-turn, I had messy relationships, confusing and abusive relationships, relationships and friendships which were based on ego and lust. Now, I was in a place where I had a standard for myself and goals for the person I wanted to become. I now accepted who I was, I now loved the person who I had become. I did not have the need for any man or friendship to give me reason or purpose in this life like I once did. I was completely honest about who I was for the first time in years and became whole.

Although I was hurt deeply by Daniel, I knew he was hurt by me too. We both reacted in ways in which we both wish we knew better; and with that comes room for growth and forgiveness. Fortunately, we repaired our friendship and to this day we still care for each other as we did before. Only this time, there is growth, boundaries, reciprocity and love.

As you can imagine I began drinking as a young adolescent and this was my first time being sober in eight years. Granted, I was on prescription medication, but I was no longer self-medicating with hard drugs and alcohol. This was my first time learning about my true emotions, my true feelings and who I really was without alcohol, drugs or sex.

Because I had been in rehab for two months, I hadn't had sex; I was able to address the hyper sexuality which was caused by the sexual abuse I endured.

The first three weeks back at home with my mother was an exciting time for me. I was finally out in the world again although I never really left her house.

My outpatient rehab was from 8 AM to 3 PM on Zoom. I still had therapy three times a week and kept in contact with my good friends, Stephanie and Kisha. Life was relatively simple for the first time. I had felt bored for the first time in years, and with that boredom eventually came peace and with that peace eventually became lots of rest.

After years of partying, ups and downs, I finally had peace in my life. And when one finally reaches a place where they can just breathe without guilt, shame or regret, the body rests. When I wasn't running or on my zoom meetings, I was in bed resting. It was the first time I enjoyed being alone and having my own privacy. It was the first time I didn't need to be on social media or had any type of racing thoughts going on. I was truly at peace and I felt that this is a feeling I never wanted to lose again. Sobriety and peace became what felt like a newborn baby to me. I was going to protect it and nurture it for the rest of my life.

In order to protect my sobriety and peace I would have to continue to live a transparent, mindful life. In order to protect my sobriety and peace, I would become vulnerable and powerful in the way I shared my story. In order to protect my sobriety and peace I would create boundaries, continuously forgive myself and others, and stand up for myself. These are all things I promised myself to do but I didn't know how deeply this promise would carry into.

Because I was in such a place of peace and dedication, as well as just ending my relationship officially with Louie, I really was not looking for anything outside of myself. But God had other plans. June 19, 2021 a childhood friend of mine, Nicole, invited me to go dancing. It had been a while since I had any fun, and I knew I could trust Nicole to be sober around me.

She took forever to get ready that night and we were actually running an hour and a half behind, I was a bit frustrated, but I trusted that everything was going to work out just the way it was supposed to. We finally arrived at our destination 2 1/2 hours late, but it was all in Gods timing because just as we were crossing the street to walk into the club right at the intersection of L and 16th Street in downtown Sacramento, two men approached Nicole and I. One of the men was a tall black man with braids and the way Nicole looked at him I knew she would be taking her time in talking with him. I was in a space where I did not want anything to do with a man, so I walked away and gave them space.

I guess I shouldn't have counted the other guy out. He was a handsome olive-skinned man about six feet tall with a big smile and thick brown hair. I went to go stand in line for the club and as I'm waiting, I hear,

"Hi, I'm Carmelo" and their stood this man I just walked away from. It was as if we had already known each other the way he approached me and slightly annoyed me. I wasn't threatened, I just knew I did not want anything with anyone, and I was certainly not looking for it.

"Hi, I'm Marissa" I say.

"Your friend is talking to my friend, when I saw you walk away, I knew you were just too pretty, and I couldn't let you slip away" Carmelo says.

At this point I didn't care about impressing anyone and I wanted him to leave me alone. There was only one thing I

344

thought he wanted, so that's what I gave him.

"Here just take my Instagram" I say.

Carmelo grabbed my phone and said, "Wow your phone is all cracked, you should get that fixed."

I replied, "Yeah, I broke it when I was going crazy in Miami."

I guess he liked that because he laughed and continued to follow himself on my Instagram. Carmelo handed me my phone back and said, "I hope you have a good night, Marissa, it was really great to meet you."

I didn't think much of this encounter, I was more concerned about where Nicole was and if she still wanted to go into the club. By the time I had reached the front of the line, she finally met up with me again and looked as if she had just met the man of her dreams.

"We should go on a double date with those guys" says Nicole.

"Yeah sure" I say with an unimpressed attitude.

Nicole and I went on with our night and had a great time. It felt good to be out in society and not need to be on any type of substance. I was extremely proud of myself and found a sense of trust within I hadn't known before.

As our night came to an end and we were headed back home, I checked out Carmelo's Instagram Page. I didn't remember him being this handsome in person, but I guess I just didn't get a good enough look. I loved his energy and took note of how he was connected to nature, his beautiful green eyes and that he rode a Harley.

Carmelo messaged me and said, "Hi Marissa, I'd like to take you out sometime. When are you free?"

I messaged him that night and said, "Can we go for a Harley ride?"

Carmelo did not reply until the next day. Nonetheless, we picked a day and decided we would go out together. I was aware of how this could disrupt my sobriety, but I was certain that I just wanted to have fun and feel free, a Harley ride seemed like the perfect opportunity.

June 21st, 2021 Carmelo picked me up from Mommas house at 6 PM. Our plan was to ride from Roseville up to Auburn and have dinner, I made sure to dress not only cute, but appropriate for the back of his bike. When he pulled up, it was like seeing a knight on a horse, I tried to not let myself get too excited about his suave.

I stood on the sidewalk as he got off his bike and took off his helmet. He had this confidence about him that I had never experienced before. It wasn't a cocky confidence; it was more that he had known himself and wasn't afraid to be himself. I admired that.

After we greeted each other with a hug, he helped me put on my helmet and gave me some pointers for sitting on the back of his bike. You know, how to swing my hips to the left and right depending on which way we turn, what shoulder to tap for what commands and most importantly to hold on. I already felt safe in his presence and, I trusted him to keep me safe on the back of his bike, but one thing I truly wasn't expecting was how much fun we had. The music we listened to, the way he road and even the way he would reach back to touch my leg was all so sweet.

It was the first time in months I hadn't thought about Louie, Jack or anything that happened before and after Miami.

346

I was truly in the present moment. Carmelo stopped on the side of a country road when we were about halfway to our destination. When we got off the bike to sip on some water, I couldn't help but feel that he and I had met before. The energy between us was so familiar, yet I couldn't quite put my finger on it.

We continued on our ride and finally arrived at an outdoor restaurant in Auburn. I wasn't quite sure what to talk about, so I began talking about the last three months of my life. I told Carmelo everything, it was my first time telling someone outside of rehab in detail everything that I had done and what happened. I described cheating on Louie, I talked about committing suicide and going to the ward, I talked about my experience on the other side and how beneficial rehab has been for me. For the first time, I wasn't scared to share my story, I felt safe in his presence. It felt good to be vulnerable and honest about what was really going on in my life. Carmelo listened so intently it kind of freaked me out. He encouraged me to keep sharing and telling my story. By the end of our two-hour conversation, I could tell he really wanted to take me home. But I didn't want that, and so I said to him, "I just need a really good friend right now."

He said okay and that's what we would continue to be for the next six months. After this first date, I saw Carmelo about two times a week every week during summer. We did everything from going out on his boat, to hanging out at his house and even more Harley rides. The only thing we didn't do was have sex, he was truly my friend.

It felt good to have someone respect me in this way, as well as get to know him as a friend. This was my first time getting to know a guy as a friend before having sex with them. I didn't realize how valuable this time was until months had gone by and we began to fall in love with each other for who we truly were.

Carmelo told me he was in love with me, and my response was, "Congratulations, I'm happy for you."

I truly wasn't looking for a relationship and I knew he wasn't either, so when he said this even though I did love him, I didn't know if I could trust what he meant. So, I decided to wait and see if these were lofty words or intentional ones.

Because Carmelo and I didn't go looking for a relationship and allowed each other to be ourselves, we created a friendship, became vulnerable and transparent with each other and most importantly had no expectations for one another; love just happened naturally.

Carmelo and I kept steady for a year and a half, we eventually did make love and become monogamous. I say make love because it wasn't just sex. We grew in true love together and really became each other's number one supporter. In December of 2021, he encouraged me to start writing "Still Fucking Alive" when he gifted me two journals to hand write the first draft. Carmelo and I celebrated my one year of sobriety together, and he was right by my side when I decided to get off of my prescription medication. This is around the time he encouraged me to shift my mindset from a victim and survivor into a fighter.

The morning of September 3rd, 2022 was my first experience having deep suicidal ideation since my attempt. The thing about a failed suicide attempt is that it's now a feasible option in your mind. And it's very easy to let these thoughts run their course. September 3rd, 2022, the only thing I knew how to do was go about my daily routine. I worked out, went for a walk but all I could do was cry while going through the motions, like I did on March 16th, 2021. I didn't want to kill myself this day, yet my mind did. I came back to this book and read the first four chapters; I read about the time I was raped and thought, "I have always been a victim, I have always been suffering."

It broke my heart that I was in such a beautiful place with beautiful people in my life and I still wanted to die. It became apparent to me that this was an illness I'd have to fight for the rest of my life.

When Carmelo woke up, I told him what I was going through. We talked about the suicidal ideation, my fears, insecurities, abandonment issues and ego. After about three hours of deep conversation, I began to get a grip. He felt it was a good idea to get me out of the house and go to the river.

The drive was quiet, I was suffering mentally but I wasn't alone. Carmelo and I sat on a park bench overlooking the rapids when he asked me to describe what my thoughts and plan were. I shared every sick detail. He listened intentionally and I wasn't entirely sure where the conversation was going.

Carmelo looks at me and says, "Let's swim down the rapids."

It was now 5pm and the damn opened; the water moved fast, and the river rose. Truly my only thought when he said that was, "At least if I die, it'll be easy."

Carmelo and I dressed down to our underwear and headed for the riverbank. The water was ice cold and by the time I put my toes in, he was already in the middle of the river yelling for me to get in. Carmelo is my best friend and to see him in the middle of gushing waters alone scared me, I followed his lead and swam right into his arms. He looked at me as the water began pushing us and shouted, "Keep your feet up, when you break the rapids, swim to the bank. We have about a half mile down to shore."

And with that he went on his back, kicked his feet up

and said, "Let's go!"

I followed him into the running rapids when suddenly I had no control. The water was pulling my body in every direction. I remember looking back to Carmelo right before I went under the water terrified that I wasn't going to come back up. When I re-surfaced eventually, I was faced with giant boulders.

As much as I had felt in my mind that I was a victim and wanted to die this day, my body instinctively fought for its will to survive. It was the first time in my life I felt my will to survive. I felt my will to want to live, I felt myself become a fighter in that moment. The water was pulling me in all sorts of ways quickly and forcefully. There was no time to think, I had to survive, I had to fight.

With each breath as I resurfaced again and again literally fighting for my life down the Lotus American River Rapids, I became stronger. I know what you're thinking I should be tired and winded, but the spirit that came over me was something I had never came in contact with until this moment. I had been a victim and a survivor for so long which was all that I knew to be true of myself, until this day when I became a fighter.

Carmelo and I both made it out of the rapids and swam to the shore on the right side of the river. He was so proud of me and out of breath, we hugged and embraced one another. "You did it! You fucking did it I'm so proud of you!" Carmelo shouted.

One thing to be true between Carmelo and I is that we have both kept our autonomy sacred. We have shown each other how to do things like this and we allow each other to do them on our own. It was just me versus the rapids out there, this experience reminded me of my first plant session. But so much deeper because I had maturity and experience in

350

something to fight for now.

Carmelo and I still had about 100 meters to go. We only had a light swim to finish out our journey; I had confidence, I had fun. By the time we made it to the shoreline and walked out of the water, I felt reborn. I cried again only this time because I realized that I didn't just get a second chance, but I wanted to live, I fought to live, and I've been fighting to live.

I looked up to the sky to give grace to God before stepping out of the water when I noticed on top of the cliff beside us was a 20-foot cross, lit up, shining down on the river. This experience was totally an act from God, a rebirth, and a reminder that I am a fighter and I have been a fighter all along. As sick as I was in the head, I knew deep in my spirit that I would never let myself die in my own hands again; I made a promise to never give up.

The importance of me becoming a fighter has been the most impactful piece of my journey. For so many years, I was labeled as a victim, living in victimhood and what some even called a survivor. But I say screw all of that, I am a fucking fighter; and if you're reading this book, you are too. My definition of a fighter doesn't mean fighting against "the man", big corporations or other people because life is unfair and hard. The fight is between you and the person looking back at you in the mirror.

Every day since recovering from the hospital, I have fought for my life. I understand now that as much as suicidal ideation, trauma, addiction and manic-depressive episodes are a terrible illness, my fighting spirit is stronger. Fighting for my life every day doesn't have to be as extreme as fighting the rapids but simply starting with having to look for the smallest things in every moment so I can remain in gratitude. Fighting for my life means making sure I stick to my routine, journaling, praying, exercising, setting boundaries, having integrity, not giving up, speaking up for myself, taking care of myself in every which way and staying sober. This might seem like a laundry list because every day I have to try. Yet every day I am truly living because I consciously practice this way of life.

What qualities pertaining to your life makes you a fighter? What do you practice daily that reminds you of your fighting spirit?

To be a fighter is to fight for what you really want out of life on Earth while eternity awaits on the other side. To be a fighter is to overcome all trauma, shame, regret, guilt, bad relationships, addictions, and anything else that inhibits you from being your best, most authentic self.

To become a fighter, you become a better lover; the two are a balance. I was so angry and heartbroken for so long that I allowed life's tribulations get the better of me; I didn't know how to fight back, I lost the fight in me. When my mind, spirit, soul and body transformed from being a victim to a survivor and then finally recognizing I am a fighter, my life's story began to make sense. I began to actively release shame, regret and guilt. The ego I once had no long controlled me and the identity I *knowingly* built for myself became rooted in what it means to be a fighter. Through becoming a fighter I've gained compassion and forgiveness for myself, others and my story.

To be able to share my story with you, the reader, I hope you see the good fight in yourself too. Never give up, believe in yourself, forgive yourself, use your voice, have integrity, stay balanced, open your heart to love, trust that your story is being written the way it is meant to be and most importantly have a Carmelo in your corner; one *true* friend is all you need.

What I learned throughout my journey is that we are

all worthy of a good life and to become a fighter isn't easy, but to look in the mirror and see that even through all the years of suffering I was being molded into becoming what I am today, I wouldn't change a thing. I became the woman I was meant to be, and it all started here. I love the life God gave me, I love my family, I love my friends, but most importantly I finally love myself.

I am no victim, I am no survivor, I am a fucking Fighter. And if you've made it to this part of the book, you are too. Look yourself in the mirror, recognize the good fight in your eyes and feel the love in your heart; after everything you've been through, You Are Still Fucking Alive.

ABOUT THE AUTHOR

Marissa Hardy lives in Northern California and has always loved writing but this is her first published nonfiction. Over the last two years, she wrote her story. Marissa is now ready to share her testimony, wisdom and vulnerability with the world. After years of darkness and depression, she's found her voice and purpose. She was a victim turned survivor and through self-discovery became a fighter.

Contact:

Stillfckingalive2022@gmail.com

Resources:

Suicide and Crisis Line: 988

Cyber Bully Hotline: 1(800) 420-1479

Self-Harm Hotline: 1(800) 366-8288

Sexual Assault and Rape Hotline:
1(800) 656-4673

Grief Support: (650) 321-5272

Hope Line Crisis Prevention: 1(877) 235-4525

Substance Abuse and Mental Health Services:
1 (800) 622-HELP (4357)

Eating Disorder Hotline: 1(866) 662-1235

Online Alcoholics Anonymous Meetings:
aa-intergroup.org

In-Person Meetings: AA.org
to find a meeting near you

Domestic Violence Hotline: 1 (800) 799-7233

Mental Health: 1 (866) 903-3787

Made in the USA
Coppell, TX
15 September 2023

21599279R00215